28

The
FASCINATING STORY
of
DOLLS

by
JANET PACTER JOHL

REISSUING JOHL'S "FASCINATING STORY" OF
HER 1941 CLASSIC WITH ADDED MATERIAL.

Century House
WATKINS GLEN, N.Y.

YESTERDAY'S DOLLS

George and Martha Washington
Dolls by Mrs. Emma C. Clear

George Washington wears the low dress shoes of his period and the buckles are of gold. His costume of black velvet is by Miss Helen Siebold Walter of Staunton, Va., who specializes in costuming dolls in replicas after those in the National Museum at Washington, D. C.

The hands are modeled from life. They are the veined hands of age, so perfect that the life lines may be clearly seen.

Martha Washington is costumed in a replica of the gown that she wore at the wedding of Nellie Curtis. The dress is of a lovely dusty rose brocaded-taffeta, with the quaint pattern of a fan and soft, pale, blue flowers. It is lined throughout with rose taffeta.

The waist has staves and is laced in the back. The deep Martha Washington collar is of a rich cream lace, and the sleeves have a flounce of the same lace.

The underwear consists of six garments, including Clear's famous little pair of gold-brocaded corsets. The unmentionables and the chemise have tucks and trim to match. The chemise has half-sleeves, and buttons down the front. One rather plain underskirt, ankle length, and a second skirt, have a deep flounce of embroidery. Last, and most exquisite of all the underwear, is a beautiful rose colored taffeta skirt with a deep hand pleated ruffle and lace trim.

Her wedding band of gold, and her bracelet, adds the final touch to the first, first lady of the land.

This beautiful costume by Mrs. Nelly Upp.

INTRODUCTION

Dr. Freeman and I first met Janet Johl when working on our first Century House book (Cavalcade — Toys). We saw the manuscript of FASCINATING STORY OF DOLLS. She had the folksy touch that encouraged others to become avid collectors. This first book (1941) was soon followed by three others: MORE ABOUT DOLLS (1948), STILL MORE ABOUT DOLLS (1950) and YOUR DOLLS AND MINE (1952). All were limited editions and soon out-of-print. We have arranged with the Estate to reissue her first book as a memorial. Those having the rare $50.00 O.P. will find that while original pagination has been preserved, we have omitted pages 65-72 and 169-177: These were patent papers and are much better covered in our ENCYCLOPEDIA OF AMERICAN DOLLS ($5.50 Century House. 1962). That book also gives more complete and up-to-date coverage of the "latest popular dolls", than the last Johl chapter which has been cut short. Mrs. Johl never made an index beyond the Table of Contents reproduced below. In between those pages, wherever possible, we have added new pictorial material or notes to increase the usefulness of this reissue of her 1941 classic. Other Century House titles include HOW TO MEND AND DRESS OLD DOLLS ($3.00), THE DOLL'S DRESS-MAKER ($3.00) and PAPER DOLLS: A GUIDE FOR COSTUMES ($15.00).

Ruth S. Freeman, Editor

I   DOLLS IN THE CRADLE OF CIVILIZATION 5
      Early Egyptian—Greek—Roman—Asiatic—African

II   MORE EARLY DOLLS 12
      Hopi Katchinas—Tilting Doll—Daruma—Chinese Doctor Doll

III   THE ENIGMA OF CHINA DOLL HEADS 19
      Hard and Soft Paste Porcelain—The Discovery of Kaolin, Dresden, Meissen, Sonneberg—Letters From the English Potteries

IV   CHINA DOLL HEADS 27
      Staffordshire—Chelsea—Worcester—Lowestoft

V   MORE ABOUT CHINA OR PORCELAIN DOLL HEADS 36
      Parian, Lustre, Stone Bisque, Bennington, Victorian Pottery

VI   FRENCH DOLL HEADS 43
      Early Replicas—Jumeau, Père et Fils

VII   ADDITIONAL DATA ON FRENCH AND ENGLISH DOLL HEADS 55
      Limoges—Jumeau—Boltz—Massé—Sevres—World War English Pottery Heads

VIII   AMERICAN WOODEN DOLLS 61
      Ellis, Sanders, Martin, Johnson, Mason & Taylor, Schoenhut

IX   OTHER TYPES OF EARLY DOLL HEADS 81
      Papier Maché, Gutta Percha, Wax, Wax over Composition

X   GERMAN DOLL HEADS 98
      German Monopoly in Doll Industry—Multi-Faced Dolls—Tariff Act—Marking on Doll Heads—Recipes for Doll Making

XI   DOLL BODIES—UNCOMMON DOLL TYPES 110
        Wooden, Wax, Gutta Percha, Kid, Peddler Dolls,
        Mechanical

XII   DOLLS OF UNIQUE INTEREST—REPLICAS 122
        The First American Made China Dolls

XIII   AMERICAN MADE DOLLS 1858-1913 134
        Patent Listings—Godear—Darrow—Dotter—Goldsmith
        Palmer Cox—Billiken—Chase Stockinet—Kewpies

XIV   THE WORLD WAR INFLUENCES THE WORLD OF DOLLS 151
        War Benefit Dolls—English and American Dolls

XV   THE STORY OF THE BYE-LO BABY 161
        A Great American Doll   HOW TO SET A VALUE ON A DOLL

XVI   RAG DOLLS 168
        Walker, Gutsell, Newell, Kruse, Steiff, Poupée en Chiffon

XVII   A FEW OF THE ARTISTS WHO MAKE DOLLS 184
        Powell, Khrabroff, Saroff, Ravca, Bruyère, Heizer, Ackley,
        Jury, Banzhaf, Walbridge, Cochran, Chase, Hall, Keys, Kri-
        ger, Gardiner, Bathe, Zimmerman, Diecks, Baughman, Miller,
        Snyder

XVIII   CRÈCHE AND FASHION DOLLS 205
        The Nativity Scene, Other Religious Dolls, European Fash-
        ion Exponents, The Modern Fashion Doll

XIX   THE MATERIALS FROM WHICH DOLLS ARE MADE 218
        "Sugar and Spice, and Everything Nice
        That's What Little Girls are Made Of."

XX   CHINESE DOLLS 227
        The Wedding Procession—The Eight Immortals—Typical
        Chinese Dolls

XXI   JAPANESE DOLLS 234
        Hina Ningyo—Hina Matsuri—Musho Ningyo—Gosho Ningyo
        and others

XXII   NOSTALGIA 241
        Dolls Commemorating Persons or Events

XXIII   AMERICAN REGIONAL DOLLS—FOREIGN DOLLS 253
        Negro, Indian, Hill Billies, Puppets, Penn.-Dutch, Hawaii,
        Philippines

XXIV   THE EDUCATIONAL VALUE OF THE DOLL 256
        "And Like a Mothering Child With Toys
        Anticipates a Woman's Joys"

XX V   THE LATEST MOST POPULAR DOLLS 270
        Composition Types—Patsy—Dy-Dee—Magic Skin Baby
        Parachute Dolls

Chapter I

DOLLS IN THE CRADLE
OF
CIVILIZATION

Early Egyptian—Greek—Roman —Asiatic—African

Collection Janet P. Johl
Egyptian dolls original-
ly in the Hammer col-
lection.

**Old bone doll of un-
known origin. Egyptian
Ushabti of Carved cedar**

Collection Janet P. Johl

**Early Aztec Figure and Stone,
Pendant like Doll.**

SINCE the dawn of civilization, man has modeled the human figure in effigy. From musty tombs, thick with the dust of the ages, archaeologists have unearthed grotesque little objects, undoubtedly representative members of the image family from which the doll ultimately came. These give the doll the right to be classified as one of the first inventions of the human race.

These first crude little figures, in the form of the human body, were mostly cult objects revealing man's initial attempt to control the unseen by creating something tangible, in which to house the spirits he worshiped. Thus the doll becomes far more than a trivial plaything. Although small in stature, its significance is colossal. It can claim, and, rightly so, a lineage that goes back some 25,000 years to a family tree whose roots began to take hold in the Stone Age, when primitive man made the first image to portray his gods and ward off the forces of evil.

The antiquity of the doll is attested to by students, who have found its ancient story written in the many languages of this earth. The discoveries of numerous dolls in the excavations of ancient Troy have made possible the study of the gradual development of the early presentation of the human form, in loam, in clay, and in stone. In the Iron Age, little figures appeared in metal and bronze.

Ethnologists, through extensive research, have been able to prove that dolls were known to the early Egyptians, for they have been discovered in the sarcophagi buried with little girls. Crude objects, indeed, carved, and occasionally painted, with clay beads strung to represent hair, and bodies, stuffed perhaps with papyrus reeds from the bank of the River Nile. Nevertheless they may be classified as dolls, dolls 3000 years old, home made, and dearly beloved, mute representatives of a people long since passed from sight, but not from the annals of history.

The major premise that the doll was first a fetish, an image for cult purposes, which possessed an occult power, a reaching into the unknown and unseen world which, in some inexplicable manner, united the past and the present, with the future, is usually accepted by most students. Because primitive man evidently gave life and power to his inanimate objects, classic antiquity advanced to the point of giving its sculpture divine life . . . thus the inspiration of the artist of antiquity, was never a dead thing but on the contrary was very alive. For this reason, the Egyptian Ushabti finds its place in the doll world.

Ushabti was the name given to stone, alabaster, wood, clay and glazed faience figures, dedicated to the God Osiris. They were made in the form of the mummy and were left in the tombs, laid along the floor, or in boxes. Sometimes the boxes containing the Ushabti bore the name of the owner, sometimes the figure itself bore the name, and in addition a prayer, from the Book of the Dead, the sixth chapter, in behalf of the owner.

The Egyptians were primarily an agricultural people, who, often, likened the hereafter to a great field cultivated by the dead, where the grain grew to enormous heights. The thoughts of such a future was a delightful anticipation to the peasant class, but the prospect of cultivating crops, even though made in heaven, was of no such interest to the people of the upper classes, or the nobility. It was the Ushabti, the model little slave mummies, who relieved them of such agricultural chores by doing all the manual labor in the hereafter.

The first Ushabti figures were made in the complete mummy form, but later the arms and hands were out, and crossed. Painted on the figures were agricultural tools. Often a basket hung on the back, or the tools were held by the Ushabti, in relief. The demand for these magical mummy-servants was so great that they were actually produced by a factory method in the later dynasties and the result was a deterioration in workmanship, and Ushabti figures that grew smaller and smaller.

These were not, it is true, the dolls of old Egypt, yet they have their place as one type of religious object that paved the way and helped to form the evolutionary story of the doll.

The great museums of the world contain toys of antiquity, many with a marked semblance to the playthings of the present day. Some of the most ancient dolls are said to be in the British Museum at London, England. Taken from the tombs of Egyptian children they date back to the Middle Kingdom, and perhaps even earlier, having been in existence centuries before the birth of Jesus Christ.

An old Egyptian doll made of pottery and wood, of a very early date, may be seen in the Museum of the University of Pennsylvania. Another example, at the Metropolitan Art Museum at New York City, has legs rounded off at the knees. Ivory dolls from Upper Egypt, which have been seen on loan at Metropolitan Museum, show dolls date back to the eleventh and twelfth dynasty.

The common material in Greece during the post classical period was bone or ivory. The Graeco-Parthian doll at the Museum of the University of Pennsylvania has arms attached by wires, slipped into grooves in the upper arms, a narrow high waist, stubby feet and broad hips. Somewhat similar examples have been found in marble and in alabaster. Greek dolls with moveable heads were called Kopal and Vapeac.

Greek dolls, most of which were feminine, served a double purpose, as a plaything and as an offering. The temple precincts have yielded specimens that show that the Greek girls played with their dolls until they married. Then, at twelve or thirteen years, they dedicated the dolls, and the dolls' clothes, to one of the Greek deities, protective of their sex, such as Artemis, or Aphrodite. The poetess Sappho is said to have bestowed her doll, with a beautiful poem, upon the goddess Aphrodite, but the poem, referred to in the Athenaeus is no longer available, for the world has a very limited amount of Sappho's writings.

In the sixth book of the Anthologia Palatine, number 280 is a Greek epigram which Miss Emily Shields of Smith College has been kind enough to translate: "Timareta, the daughter of Timaretus, before her wedding, hath dedicated to thee, Artemis of the lake, her tambourine and her pretty ball and the caul that kept up her hair, and her dolls, too, and their dresses; a virgin's gift as is fit, to a virgin Dian. But, daughter of Leto, hold thy hand over the girl, and purely keep her in purity."*

It is interesting to note that in Greek the same word is used for 'girl' as for 'doll.' Timareta is, of course, a young girl who is following the custom, prior to her marriage.

Records seem to indicate that the Greek boys left their toys to Apollo and Hermes and as jointed dolls have been found in sanctuaries to Apollo it is possible that the boys had dolls too.

That Greek dolls were popular with the children is evidenced by the fact that they were sold in market places, shops and streets, so reasonably that almost every child could possess a little, unglazed, terra cotta figure.

Like the Greek, the Roman children enjoyed dolls. In the Saturnalia at Rome, the giving of dolls to the children was a special feature, and from the records available, dolls were plentiful. Before their marriage, as in Greece, the Roman maidens dedicated their dolls to the Lares and Penates, and later to Venus, the Goddess of Love. At Terracina, a doll set of miniature furniture was found as an offering to Venus of Axur. A very fine example of an ancient doll lies in a white marble sarcophagus, in the center of one of the rooms of the Capitoline Museum in Rome, Italy, beside the daughter of a high Roman potentate. This doll, of weathered oak, rich and dark in tone, has joints at the shoulders and hip limbs, and is able to bend at the elbows and the knees. The body is carefully modeled. As its original owner, a young girl of about fourteen years, died before her marriage, the doll was not left at the shrine of Venus, but, instead, was buried with the maiden.

In the Vatican there are also dolls of ivory, with moveable limbs. Dolls in the Catacombs are of bone and ivory, some with detachable arms and legs. The hair is dressed like a 'nest,' flat across the back, and full across the front.

* Translation from the Loeb edition.

The body of these dolls is long and shapeless. Since the legs and arms are often missing, it may be that the bodies were of cloth, or leather, and have disintegrated with the passing of time.

The children of the Christian martyrs, as well as the Roman children, shared the pleasure of dolls, for in the tombs of the Catacombs at St. Agnes in Rome, where the early Christians lived their lives in secret, dolls have been discovered.

There evidently was no scarcity of dolls in those ancient days. The head of a Roman God, with a body of rags, was found in Egypt. Terra cotta dolls came to light with the excavation of the ruins of Pompeii. At Herculaneum, the figure of a little girl, with a doll tightly clasped in her arms, as if to protect it from the avalanche of lava and ashes which destroyed the city, has been excavated.

In France, and near Vienna, explorers have unearthed figurines called 'Venuses,' although these small stone images are rather too squat and obese to greatly resemble any marble Venus carved in the golden age of sculpture in Greece. Surviving from the Macedonian epoch, they are probably 25,000 years old, and may rather be placed in the fetish class. But they are, nevertheless, connected to the doll, if only by a very distant relationship.

Along the trodden paths of the pages of history, is a Persian doll of the ninth century, from Nishaour. From ancient Babylon is a fragment of alabaster with movable arms. A rag doll of the third century, found at Behnesa, is in the Victoria and Albert Museum of London. It is of coarse linen, stuffed with papyrus.

As far back as one can search in the archives of the past, as far as documentary evidence, legend and myth can carry, there are always dolls. Whether in the tombs of the dead, pictured in plaster, clay or stone, or featured in religious ceremonies that pre-date the great religions now known to man, dolls are found. In India, the so called 'cradle of civilization,' many figures have been found significant examples of ideas about man. Mrs. S. Camille Tenney of New Haven, Conn., who has many unique oriental specimens, with their historical data, has been kind enough to contribute this story of her Tsong-Kha-Pa figure, from the capital of Tibet, Lhassa.

"A few years ago I saw an article about a similar figure brought from Tibet by the famous Russian painter Nicholas Roerich. It had been presented to him by a Lama friend, and in turn, to a New York City artist by Mr. Roerich. The figure stood on a 'what-not' in the corner of the studio. Accidentally, the artist caught his smock against it and pulled the Tibetan figure down. To his surprise, the bottom fell out and the contents within, scattered. A thin stick running from the base to the top of the head had, tied in silk upon it, twelve small rolls of some sort of parchment on which were long lines of unknown script, hand printed. Also a small silk bag, within which was a magnificent ruby. On the bottom of the stick was a sharp needle-like point, which the surprised artist feared might be dangerous. Caution overcame his curiosity. He sent for a rodent to try it on. The rodent died, poisoned."

"After reading this account, I was on the lookout for a similar figure, for my collection of ancient examples. Eventually this came to me in a fine gold-brown figure of the Tsong-Kha-Pa, the Tibetan, fourteenth century Avatar of Gautama the Buddha. He was the founder of the Gelukpa, or Yellow Cap Sect, of Tibet's highest Brotherhood. My small figure bears the seal of Lhassa on the base and it, too, has contents. There is the thin tall stick struck with the tiny parchment rolls, each one of the twelve, rolled in yellow silk. There is also a small yellow silk bag in which are fragments of four of the sacred jewels, i. e., jade, turquoise, carnelian, coral and a beautiful, perfect pearl, the size of a pea. There is, however, no poisoned point. This is one of my choicest figures.''

''There are also several types of the Shri Krshna figures, rare old ones from India. Shri Krshna was the Avatar, or World Teacher, of a period in India antedating the Buddha by several hundreds of years. His spiritual aspect is immortalized in the 'Bhagavad Gita,' the Bible of India. The figures in my collection of Krshna range in age from 500 A. D. (from a cave near Calcutta) to those in marble, brass and wood, of the fourteenth, fifteenth and seventeenth centuries up to modern times.''

''Two of my old Tibetan figures, i.e. the 'Green Tara' representing a primordial cosmic symbol, and a very old Buddha, have rare contents. In the former are the twelve silk enclosed parchments, and twelve tiny yellow silk bags, containing different kinds of earth from several of Tibet's sacred shrines. Also a silk bag with the fragments of the five sacred stones, but with no perfect large one. Within the figure of the Buddha are twelve particularly fine rolls, printed in red, very faded now, of tiny little figures like men. The figure was packed in red earth with literally hundreds of small seed corals.''

The women in Bali, the Dutch East Indies, carry temple dolls as their votive offering. Made of bamboo they have the wide, fan shaped head dress that the Balinese women wear in their ritual dances. A woven bamboo band across the shoulders serves as the scarf which the women wear as a top covering. Earrings are strangely wrought of bamboo.

The Dassivah Festival in India is a nine day celebration at which time the girls dress in their best costumes and solemnly cast their clay dolls, painted and dressed like their elders, into the river to sink or float out into the world. And for three months the little girls of India have no more dolls. This curious custom is said to date back to the ancient custom of putting the dead into the sacred river Ganges. Others claim that the girls offer up their dolls as a propitiatory sacrifice to the goddess who presides over the destiny of the river.

Courtesy R. S. Benjamin
A West African Voodoo Doll

Formerly children were thrown into the waters to oppose the anger of the river god. Later a ruler forbade this practice and figures replaced the live children. Gradually the figures diminished in size until they became small as dolls.

The people in the vicinity of Bengal-Lucknow and Poona dress clay figures and as there are more gods in India than there are people, the dolls serve the children as playthings. In some homes in India, dolls made from clay or wood have a room to themselves, they are so numerous. A strange specimen sent from Lucknow to the Columbian Museum at Chicago, and listed as a 'toy,' is designated as 'posti,' or one addicted to opium. It is made of paper.

Gwalior dancing figures are still made in India and the method, one of the oldest, is fantastic. There is a basic core with a modeled ball type of head. Narrow bands of cloth are bound around the ball head to cover it, and to build up a semblance to flesh. Noses are deftly shaped and the features of the face are painted on.

In Africa there are many weird and primitive dolls. In the Orange Free State the Fingo doll plays an important role with the natives. This fetish is given to the girls when they reach maturity. When the girl becomes a mother, she receives a new doll which she saves until she has another child, and so forth. These dolls are held very sacred and are never willingly given away. A similar custom is said to exist in Basutos.

West African Voodoo dolls are carved out of wood by the natives and represent the wooden voodoo of the jungle. A common term for doll in Africa is 'Mwana Ya Kiti', meaning stool child, and it is a rigidly enforced custom to keep a doll on a stool in the house. In the season of ripe gourds, in Portuguese East Africa, a bisymmetric baby is fashioned whose features are burned in with hot irons, and whose body is filled with small stones.

Mrs. Mary E. Lewis has been kind enough to give the story of African Dolls by John H. Shaw as it appeared in the Club Bulletin of the *National Doll and Toy Collectors Club, Inc.*

"A Masai has but two occupations, one is hunting and the other is carving out these dolls. Their work, if done by civilized people, would be considered good. Done by the supposedly ignorant natives, they are little short of marvelous. A Masai does his carving as he does everything, with skill and thoroughness. Many of their dolls have the actual articles of dress on them; neckbands, the decorative fur loin cloth, the fur leg band, spears, skin shields and other details all in miniature."

In the Lake Nyassa region of Central Africa, tribes use a queer doll symbol when a member of a tribe dies. A rude doll of wood and rags is made in which is hidden a small bark box. The spirit of the dead man is presumedly shut up in the box by the witch doctor. Another crude wooden figure comes from Kalababai in the Dutch West Indies and is made by primitive head hunters. Mrs. Virginia Woodin of Arlington, Va. has two of these dolls in her collection.

Crude stone dolls are still to be found in islands in the Pacific. Mrs. John Hawkes of Boise, Idaho, reports, that she has two primitive clay dolls from the Samoan Islands. She also described carved figures, of wood, which came from Kalababaia, an outlying island of the Dutch East Indies, and a dirt filled doll from Madagascar.

One of the most rare of the primitive dolls available today is the Chola doll from the northern part of Argentina. The people who make the dolls are members of a solitary and somewhat queer tribe. Only when some one in the clan dies, is a doll made in replica of the person. Sometimes, about as often as once in ten years, a lone traveler brings out one of these Chola dolls.

Whether the children of utter savages know how to play with dolls is still a question. The explorers of British Guiana and the Malay Archipelago seem to feel that doll play is not instinctive. They may be right, for even the children living in the depths of our own mountains in the Carolinas do not know what to do with a doll until they are shown.

In his comprehensive book, 'Dolls and Puppets', Max Von Boehn devotes nineteen chapters to the doll, of which eight are given over to these earliest known specimens, under the chapter headings of:

> "1. Prehistoric Idols.
> 2. Ancestor Images.
> 3. Fetishes, Amulets, and Talismans.
> 4. Image Magic.
> 5. Votive Images.
> 6. Funeral and other Images.
> 7. Waxworks and the Mannequin.
> 8. Toy Dolls in Ancient Times."

Courtesy Kimport Dolls

Bisymmetric gourd Baby-African

Also, in his sixteenth chapter, 'Utensils in Doll Form', there is considerable discussion of the doll figure used to emulate the human being in paint boxes, vessels, vases, handles etc., the forerunners of such later utility dolls as hand bells, goblets and nutcrackers.

One could go on ad infinitum, listing the very ancient dolls and those of a primitive nature, still to be found among primitive people. Each type of doll denotes a certain strata in the story of the civilization of man. Civilization? The modern English doll, equipped with gas mask and parachute seems a less civilized effort, perhaps, than prehistoric man's first attempt at plastic modeling from formless clay.

To those interested in dolls, from the children who play with them, love and cherish them, to the collector who prizes them, and the student who enjoys them for the research they afford in educational and ethnological fields, this book is dedicated. Much has been written about the doll, and yet much has been left unsaid. It is extremely doubtful if a complete story can ever be told.

The guiding motive in this book has been to view the subject, the doll, as a record of civilization, and to trace its course from the earliest days to the present. In the hope that this book may prove of interest and of service, it is now humbly offered to the doll minded world.

JANET PAGTER JOHL.

The Chinese Doctor Doll.

MORE EARLY DOLLS

(Hopi Katchinas—Tilting Doll;
Daruma—Chinese Doctor Doll)

COLUMBUS carried grains of corn to Europe after his first trip to the shores of the West Indies, and corn was destined to be one of the great Indian gifts to the white man. It was the Incas who first discovered a wild grass growing high, with thick stems, on which were big kernels. They worked hard to cultivate this grass, toiling patiently for many years, until at last the wild grass grew taller, and the kernels improved in size, and in texture, as well as in flavor. Often the designs on the corn cob were so lovely that the Inca women copied the patterns and wove them into their homespun llama wool, or their fibre baskets.

The North American Indian learned about corn from South America, and the first settlers in Virginia reported that the corn, or maize, stored in great mounds was "finer farre than the richest gold". Perhaps it is not too far fetched then, to suggest that the first truly American dolls were those fashioned either from dried corn cobs or from the corn husks. It is said that the Penobscot Indians, the Senecas and other tribes had such dolls. But even if the corn husk doll fails to win first place among American dolls, it has been authenticated, by the discoveries of the ethnologists that long before the white man thought of attempting to reach the orient by sailing westward from Europe, the Indian tribes dwelling on the American continent, both in the north and in the south, had dolls.

In each grave unearthed in South America, in the region of Paracus, there have been found tiny mannequins, or Huacas, dressed in matching garments and evidently serving as companion pieces to the mummy itself. In many ways the Huacas are very similar to the Ushabti, of Egypt, just as many of the Inca relics resembles the early Egyptian findings. In the Museum of Fine Arts, Boston, Mass. may be seen early Peruvian dolls with faces of woven thread. Folded in the mummy garments of Peruvian children, untold centuries before Christopher Columbus sailed the seas, were little dolls, many of clay, quite gaily dressed. Some of these dolls are now at the Museum of Natural History in New York City. In Mexico there has been found a very old, stiff and hard doll, made from a mixture of mud and cement.

Where the doll stops being a fetish and becomes a doll is a very difficult thing to ascertain.

It is to aboriginal America, and to Japan that the student must turn for the chief source of information. Among some of the Indian tribes, the early relics of artistically painted pots and vases for ceremonial usage, show no trace of actual dolls as playthings. Yet in Bulletin Number 30, Part 1, of the Bureau of American Ethnology, Handbook of American Indians, it is noted that "Dolls were common among the American tribes. They were fashioned from stone, wood, clay, skin, dough, corncobs, plants and rags. Those used as playthings were frequently elaborately dressed by the mother in accordance with tribal customs. Those made of dough were used in a social ceremony among the Iroquois. In the southwest and extreme north, little figures were made for ceremonies."

Among certain of the American Indians, the image of a deity was regarded as sacred and was given to the child as a part of its religious instruction. The Hopi Indians have produced quantities of dolls called, 'Tihus', which represent their Katchinas, supernatural beings impersonated by masked men as the gods, at the annual tribal dances for rain. These Katchinas are the gods of the Hopis.

Some say that they were once a tribe of Indians who were driven from the terrain because the other Indians considered them lazy and shiftless. After their exodus, there was no rainfall for three years. The Chiefs then met and ruled that the Katchinas were not lazy and shiftless but were gods, and a search was made for the exiled tribe. Only one returned, bringing with him a mask, which he explained he received from the Great Spirit, and which made him a message bearer. Each summer from then on, the tribe has held dances to give thanks for the rain, for the crops and the dancers wear masks.

Others hold to a somewhat different legend; that long ago the great gods of the Katchinas came from the West to teach the Hopis how to plant their seeds, and to hunt, to weave their baskets and make their pottery. These gods were strange looking beings with a peculiar manner of walking. At the close of one of the visits, the Hopis were grouped about their fire, and one of the tribe was mimicking the way the gods walked, as if bowlegged. The Hopis laughed and as the

Collection Janet P. Johl

A Mexican Peon. Probable Descendant of the Aztecs.

fire flared up, to their amazement, there was one of the Katchinas whose departure had been delayed. He was furious, and left making dire threats. Shortly after, a terrible wind storm arose wrecking the pueblo and the crops. There was no rain, and desolation and misery fell upon the land of the Hopi Indians. Finally the gods told the Hopis that if they would wear masks and costumes and look and act like those whom they had mocked, the rains would fall again. So ever since the Hopi Indians have faithfully dressed, and danced, like the Katchinas* and their fields have borne abundantly.

The famous Zuni Shalako is a somewhat similar occasion and giant Katchinas perform weird and remarkable dances. The Ye Ba Shai of the Navajos also represents a spirit, and looks like a dancer except for a total lack of facial features. Both are represented to-day in dolls.

To go deeply into Indian ceremonials and the significance of the doll's original purpose in them would take more than one chapter and might even assume the proportions of a book. Suffice to note that the Indian children play with the Katchinas, which serves to give them religious instruction and to teach the legends, and the customs of the tribe. Carved from cotton wood, these dolls represent the four cardinal points, and are painted in six colors, black, red, blue, white, yellow and gray. The more elaborately fashioned, or delicately

carved, dolls are hung upon the walls of Indian houses as a constant reminder of the sacred beings who bring the rain and the abundant crops. There is indeed shown a whole fantastic and fascinating network of symbolism, sacred to the Indian, behind these little dolls. Although the old time Indian would not permit a Katchina doll to leave the village, the modern Indians are not so strict and the dolls are now made for the trade. It is the earlier ones, however, that hold the most interest, often grotesque, but with soft mellow colorings and fine hand carvings.

The Obijway Indians of America, on the northern sea, call their dolls Kitemagissiwin, which means "unlucky". Here the doll represents the child who has passed on, even to being placed in a wooden cradle by the fire. In this way the Indian mother believes that she has helped the little beloved soul to the world beyond. Clay figurines of the Caraja Indians of Brazil may be seen in the Heye Foundation—the Indian Museum in New York City, along with other noteworthy examples of dolls of the Indians.

Eskimo fathers carved small bone or ivory dolls for their children, bearing such a striking resemblance to the art of the Ice Age that some archaeologists suggest that the Arctic people may be direct descendants of the Paleolithic Peoples.

Collection Janet P. Johl
A Hopi Katchina

* Katchina often seen spelled Kachina.

The Eskimo also made a mechanical man doll in deer skin, legs outstretched, arms of whalebone, and drum in the left hand. By pressing the arms, the image beat upon the drum. From Point Barrow, Alaska, comes a little doll of carved walrus tusk, or reindeer horn tips, resembling old ivory, which was the plaything of Eskimo children who lived long before the white man came. In the Hudson Bay region a queer wooden doll, without joints, hung from the belt of the conjurer to ward off evil spirits. Among the East Siberian Korjaks, dolls have been found dressed in the distinctive funeral garments used for the human dead.

From China comes the tilting doll, based on the well known tradition that Buddha cannot fall. This doll is made of thin cardboard, or paper, with two sticks for the body, so correctly balanced that the doll always returns to its original position. Loaded with weighted clay in early days, and later with papier-maché, no matter how this doll is tilted, or tipped, it always rights itself. The tilting toy from South China is called 'ta-pat-to', meaning 'Struck not fall' and is made of stiff paper.

A somewhat similar doll, with a similar religious significance is that of the Japanese Daruma doll which is often known as Oki-Agari-Koboshi, or, 'rising up little priest.' This doll is usually without feet. It is wrapped in a robe that is round at the bottom, and so weighted that it always remains erect. It is painted red with white discs for eyes, and is created in the image of a Buddhist priest, named Daruma, or Bodhidharma, who miraculously crossed the ocean from India, to China in 520 A. D. and founded there a sect known in Japan as "Zen". This likeness doll is made without any feet, because Daruma sat for nine years upon a rock without moving. Association with this doll in Japan seems to be entirely Buddhistic, a symbol of patience and endurance. Sacrificial images from ancient tombs, shown in the original paintings in the Museum of the University of Pennsylvania do not appear

Collection Janet P. Johl

Eskimo Doll, with dark molded face, dressed in natural sealskin with bone ornaments. Also Kiana Indian, of dried Apple, by Mrs. J. Howard Smith.

to have a rounded base. Some believe that this 'ancient doll' represents an earthen idol of great antiquity, known as Jogu.

The most popular toy in Chosen (formerly Korea), is said to be "Ot-tok-i", or "erect standing one". This is a pagan image, with a rounded bottom that is filled with clay. Always standing erect, and representing a woman who sometimes rides a tiger, the Ot-tok-i are also of probable Buddhistic origin. On the other hand they may be a possible survival of an earlier deity once worshiped in Chosen.

Many doll collectors have classified this round bottom, never falling doll as of German origin, but it is, instead, one of the oldest kind of dolls in the Orient. There is a tilting toy known in southern Germany as Putzelmann, and in northern and central Germany, as Putzenmann, a grotesque human-like figure, with the same significance as the 'bogeyman' has in America. Tilting toys found in the United States are chiefly of foreign manufacture, although one doll called "Bouncing Billy" was made in Philadelphia in 1878.

A doll curiosity from China is the figure known as the "Doctor Doll", or the "Ivory Doctor Doll," although this particular doll is found in materials other than ivory. Chinese ladies of antiquity, for reasons of modesty, did not permit a physical examination in times of illness. With a pin, they pointed to the part of the body—on the doctor doll—in which they were experiencing discomfort. Several of these dolls are in the collection of Mrs. Sybil Schwab of Bridgeport, Conn.

At a recent meeting of *The National Doll and Toy Collectors Club Inc.* of New York City (Oct. 26, 1940) Mrs. Greville Bathe of Philadelphia, Penn. read an educational, and interesting, paper on the origin of the *"Chinese Doctor Doll,"* or the *"Medicine Ladies."* In her talk Mrs. Bathe said:

"We are told that Fu Fu was one of the first great legendary doctors of China. It is said of him that when a sick person came to him for treatment, he made a little figure to represent the patient, using a piece of wood for the head and a small bunch of straw for the body and upon this mannikin he blew his breath with prayers for the patient's recovery, if the gods willed. I think in this legend we have the beginning of the doctor doll. Medical history of a reliable kind does not extend beyond about 722 B. C. in China. With the beginning of historic times a very definite school of medical thought began to grow and take form. It was very complicated but it was based briefly on the theory that all illness was caused by the unbalance of the male and female principles which the Chinese believed made up the body. They, therefore, were accustomed to puncture the area of pain in the body with long silver, gold or steel needles with the idea of letting out the bad spirits and letting in the good and thus restoring the body's proper balance. There were definite places on the body where Chinese students were taught to make these punctures and the system was known as acupunctur. Hollow human figures made of ivory were used to teach the students and these had small holes in them at the proper places for the puncture. They were then filled with water and paper was pasted over the holes and the students practiced driving their needles into them to attain skill in locating the proper places, because when they found the right place, the water ran out, of course. Here we find the doctor doll developing in a regular course. Then came the period when high born ladies could not personally see a male physician and so were accustomed to mark on a small figurine the location of their pain and send the figure by a servant to the physician who then prescribed for his unseen patient. It is probable that this form of etiquette grew up with the rise to power of the Manchu dynasty which ruled China so long and with such a rod of iron, from about 1644 until the birth of the Chinese republic. These ladies or doctor dolls almost always represent a nude woman lying on a large leaf, and this rests on an ebony stand or bier."

"Of even greater interest to me are the European doctor dolls or more properly speaking, anatomical figures. They were used throughout Europe from the 16th to even the early 19th century to teach the position of the organs of the human body. It must be remembered that up until 1832 dissection and autopsies were not permitted and in order to teach anatomy to prospective physicians, these figures were freely used and served a great human service. They were made of wood, ivory and other substances and the workmanship was very fine. They were made mostly by French and German craftsmen but a few were also made in England, as well. The finest collection of these figures can be seen in the Wellcome Historical Medical Museum of London. While here in this country, a very remarkable collection of these anatomical dolls is owned by Dr. Arno Luckhardt of the University of Chicago. The Curator of Ethnology at the Peabody Museum in Salem, Mass. informs me that the Museum possesses two very fine specimens of these Oriental Doctor Dolls but they are Japanese and not Chinese at all. Two specimens in the Peabody Museum are made of some sort of papier mache composition and date probably from the late 18th or 19th century .... "

Another unusual doll from China is reported by "*Doli Talk*". It is a rare ink doll carved from a hard ink cake and dating back to the Chien Lung Period. Gold and bright coloring, highlight the glossy black. These dolls are not easily broken but if dropped, like stone, will break but not crumble. They are more like gods and Buddhas, than like dolls, and were given as a symbol rather than as a play object.

According to the zodiacal calendar, the third day of the third month was considered in Japan "the day of the snake," and offerings were dedicated to the gods, to cleanse the people from impurities and evil influences. Dolls in the images of humans, became the scapegoats and were rubbed against the body to free the individual of the impurity. Then the dolls were cast into the nearest stream and carried away with the current. These dolls were always in pairs, a man and a woman. The body consisted of flat folds of stiffened material, sometimes of paper, the heads of wood or composition. The heads were sometimes most crudely cut, but, often, were perfect in detail. Known as sute-bina, or casting dolls, the simple Japanese paper doll of to-day is reminiscent of this belief and custom. Certain forms of carved wooden fetish dolls in Africa, peculiar to regions addicted to magical observances, are very closely akin to the Japanese scapegoat doll, and are held as sacred.

This old time superstition, that the doll serves as a protecting spirit, is seen in Persia where little girls play with dolls made of folded cotton. A similar image is oftimes placed in a newly built temple to bring continued welfare to the building and its occupants. In India, where child marriages prevail, handsomely dressed dolls are presented to the little brides, despite the significant fact that the religious law forbids such representation of the human body. Quite a contradictory thought is found, however in Bagdad where women see in the doll an evil spirit that may bring harm to the child.

Miss Eleanor Bumgardner, of Washington, D. C. has two queer looking dolls, that are very rare, and were the gift of Datu Ombra, the first Moro governor of Jolo of the Sulu head hunting country.

It would be possible to go on and on, for the story of dolls, begun thousands of years ago, is the story of life itself, and is almost as old. Its history is complex, its origin lost in the mists of time. The very word "doll" is significant, as seen in its derivation.

Greek: ei-DOL-on   (Idol)
Old Saxon: dol
English: doll
Old High German: Tocka
Middle High German: Tocke
15th Century German: Docke and Puppe
Norse: Daul
French: Poupée

These definitions are suppositional, and no one really seems to know the actual beginnings of the term "doll". One story is interesting and has to do with the French word—poupée.

That wax effigies, for religious usage, were made in Italy at an early date, is an established fact. It is said that Pursello Grivaldo, an Italian, made wax figures, dressed like famous people, and took them to Paris for a puppet play. Queen Isabella who saw the exhibition thought it would please the King, Charles IV, and the puppets became popular in the French court. The poor mad king took a special liking to one puppet, representing Poppaea, the consort of the infamous Emperor Nero, and kept the figure. Hence the French present the theory that their word for doll—poupée—comes from this incident. Still others hold that the source is from Dorothea, a Christian martyr. Whatever the origin of the word the fact that dolls themselves have existed as far back as man can imagine, makes them worthy subjects for educational pursuits. This brief survey of their extensive, and intensive story, reveals the whole realm of possibilities open to the doll collector . . . the possibility of concentrating on a study of the more exotic races of people, ancient and modern; or of the foreign or domestic dolls because of their age, their type, their size, their composition or costume. Whatever phase of the subject may be perused, the doll collector will find that in the five continents of the world, the doll appears in the same basic form, the cross stick indicating the shoulder line, the vertical stick the back, with a thick end for a head. All dolls, too, serve a common purpose, they show faithfully the customs of a race of people during a certain era, thus furnishing valuable records of the influence of different periods in the "March of Time." From the first crude image back in the Stone Age, right up to the present day, doll history is still in the making. It is a story that leads to many and varied fields, some of which this book will attempt to consider in detail.

If the interests of children were not enough to make the demand real, then the doll-needs of adults would come even more to the fore of our thinking. Year after year the ranks of doll collectors increase till their number is legion. Prices for old dolls soar as in America, where people move extensively, the trunks are being emptied of their precious antiques. Doll collecting is a great hobby, and its amateur aspect is preserved by the fact that its fanciers love the thing they collect. Unlike philatelists and numismatologists, they are less interested in the financial value of their assets than in their individual charm. Some collectors acquire dolls indiscriminately, but others specialize highly.

Chapter III

THE ENIGMA OF
CHINA DOLL HEADS

(Hard and Soft Paste Porcelain—The Discovery of
Kaolin, Dresden, Meissen, Sonneberg—Letters
From The English Potteries)

Courtesy
Mrs. Florence Baughman
A Dresden Porcelain Doll

BECAUSE the origin of doll heads of china, or porcelain, is something of a controversial matter, it has seemed wise to delve rather fully into the subjects, more perhaps than the mere words "china head doll" may indicate. A glimpse into the composition of ceramics, into enamels and glazes, and a knowledge of the difference between hard and soft paste porcelain may serve to aid the collector in the correct classification of china doll heads. About many old and beautiful things, nothing definite can be said. In a measure, doll heads fall into this category, although through suggestion, study, and the process of deduction, much may be gleaned to throw light upon a fascinating, if a mysterious, subject.

Just where do these early doll heads originate? What is a china head? What is a porcelain head? What is a Parian? Was there ever a Bennington? Just what are the differences between Staffordshire and Chelsea, granted that doll heads ever came out of these potteries? What is Dresden? What is Sonneberg? What is Meissen? Were doll heads made at Sevres and Limoges? What about other china or pottery doll heads that puzzle collectors? To ask these questions is so very easy. To give a doll a name is equally easy, but to authenticate each type of doll head, is quite another story.

The following letter, which Mrs. Greville Bathe, a well known collector from Philadelphia, Penn. has been kind enough to share, will certainly prove food for thought. To quote:

"The English potteries themselves disclaim all knowledge of 'pink Staffordshire' as applied to doll heads. Nor will any of the famous English potteries admit they have ever at any time made dolls heads at all. In an effort to run down where the antique English dolls' heads were made, I wrote to every pottery

19

in England, now in existence, and most of them in existence over a hundred years—these included Wedgewood, Copeland, Spode, Boulton, Minton, etc., etc. The answer was a chorus of 'No, we never made dolls heads.' I got in touch with the curator of the big museum at Stoke-on-Trent, the heart of the English potteries for a hundred and fifty years and more. This man is a great authority on the china that has been around him for so long. He said he did not know what 'pink Staffordshire' meant as applied to dolls heads, and he could not find that any dolls heads were ever made in Staffordshire until about the time of the World War when some were made to his knowledge.''

''I myself have come to the conclusion,'' Mrs. Bathe wrote, ''that all the fine china heads of all kinds, were made in Germany and France. I doubt if any of the fine china heads were made in England. Composition, yes; wood, yes; and wax, yes; but china, no.''

Before going into the subject more deeply, here are two excerpts from two letters received from A. K. Sabin, Officer in Charge, Bethnal Green Museum, London E. 2, England, which may prove of interest. To quote:

''April 27, 1939.

''There seems to be no evidence of the making of dolls heads in the prominent English potteries, and indeed the examples we have can be safely attributed to France and Germany. At the same time it would be surprising if the numerous Staffordshire figure potters did not turn their attention to this minor phase of their craft during the second half of the nineteenth century, when the china head was so popular. Of course the potters were legion in number and no record of any kind exists of many of their activities.''

And again, May 31, 1939, from A. K. Sabin:

''The Staffordshire pottery makers who might have done dolls' heads have not been put on record, and none of the numerous small men working at this kind of thing is left. It was an individual craft, not factory work on a large scale, and our books do not give even the names of any of the workers.''

With these three interesting comments, a brief glimpse into the story of china seems fitting.

Early attempts to copy the human face date back to prehistoric man, as has already been noted, and archaeologists have unearthed little images molded in a rough manner, with flat features, eyes created by tiny holes, and a mere pin scratch for a mouth. Undoubtedly the first fire that Adam kindled on clay soil taught him something about earthenware. Ever since, man has employed the art of pottery.

The earliest mention of pottery is the account in the Bible, of the building of Babel, and the oldest known pottery is Egyptian. Unglazed pottery seems to have been the fabric of all nations. At an early date the Phoenicians learned to apply a thin varnish-like lustre to the surface of their pottery. They transmitted the art to the Greeks, but the Greeks do not seem to have cared for it and they confined their ceramic art to unglazed wares, images in clay, or those simply painted and covered with a thin varnish. This art, handed down to the Romans, was lost somewhere in Europe. During the Middle Ages, it is known that England confined herself to making masks, zoômorphic ornaments, pottery vessels, and, says one authority—''*possibly*'' dolls. Until the second half of the seventeenth century there is no serious evidence of works of art in clay.

Photo by Eric Stalhberg,   Collection of Helyn Ewing Fowler.
Northampton, Mass.

A Splendid Group of Old China Head Dolls Worthy of Study

Persia transmitted her knowledge to China, and thence it went to Chosen (Korea) and to Japan. It was either in Persia or in China, some 2000 years ago, that the art of making wares translucent, was discovered. So porcelain was born, and remained an Asiatic secret for quite some time.

The term "*Pottery*" in its widest sense, includes all objects made of clay, molded into shape while in a moist state, and then hardened by fire. Anything entirely opaque or devoid of translucency, is *pottery*. Hard pottery is not easily scratched, is sometimes vitreous, rough and granular, and resists fire. On the other hand, it may be stated that any earthenware material that is baked and glazed is generally termed china.

Porcelain, deriving its name from the Italian word *porcellana*, meaning cowry-shell, is commonly called *China*, because it was first made by the Chinese. It is a certain kind of clay, which is purified and then baked, producing a hard, translucent material. Prior to its introduction into England, the English potters made only earthenwares, wares that were opaque. In popular usage the porcelain, which came from the Far East was called China-ware. When the British began to try to imitate the Chinese products, China ware became the recognized trade name. But it is well to remember that Porcelain and China are two *different* names for the same thing.

An article in *The Christian Science Monitor* in May, 1940, answers the question that usually arises in a discussion of porcelain and chinaware. Although the article has to do mainly with dinnerware, it is of interest to the student of doll heads. To quote in part:

"DID YOU EVER WONDER

What the Difference Is Between Porcelain and Chinaware?

Some excellent authorities declare the terms **porcelain** and **chinaware** to be synonymous. They say that English speaking countries use the term chinaware (which takes its name from its country of origin, China), while other countries use the term porcelain (from the Italian, **porcellana,** meaning a shell, which in turn is from the Latin **porcellus,** diminutive for "hog," the shell being shaped like a pig's back, to designate the same material.)

On the other hand, some dealers in the United States make a definite distinction between the two. In chinaware, they say, the body of the ware is fired at a higher temperature than the glass-like glaze or outer coating, making the body fine-textured and nonporous, not absorbing the glaze. In porcelain, they say, the underbody is fired at a lower temperature than the glaze and is porous when first fired. However, when the glaze is fired at a high temperature, it penetrates and soaks into the porous underbody, making the whole nonporous and glass-like.

However difficult it may be to settle the matter of whether or not porcelain and chinaware are identical, there is no doubt as to the difference between these two substances and the type of dinnerware known as **earthenware.**

Earthenware is relatively heavy and coarse, and is opaque. If the surface glaze is chipped or broken, then grease and other liquids coming in contact with the exposed undersurface will be readily absorbed, discoloring the ware. Bright-colored **peasant pottery** and certain cream-tinted hotel ware are earthenware products.

Porcelain or chinaware is stronger than earthenware, its grain is much finer, and it is highly glazed and thoroughly vitrified. In cross-section, it is hard to tell where the body leaves off and the glaze begins. Even quite heavy pieces of porcelain and chinaware are translucent, not opaque. Holding the ware between your eyes and a bright light you can see the shadow of your fingers through the ware. If porcelain or chinaware is tapped lightly with a pencil it will give a clear, bell-like tone, while the sound given off by earthenware is dull and does not ring.— **W. P. Keasbey."**

It is hard to draw an exact borderline between china and porcelain considering that china is sometimes coarse and sometimes fine. It is well to note that porcelain is thinner, and so more breakable.

Porcelain belongs to two classes, namely that of hard paste, and that of soft paste. This paste is the body, or substance, of the article, and is a mixture of clay and other materials. True porcelain, which is hard paste, is made of natural infusible clay, a union of kaolin and feldspar (petuntze). When broken it appears sparkling, vitreous and finely grained. Specialized branches in hard paste porcelain, include Bisque and Parian. In the latter the English potters excelled.

While *hard* paste, or true porcelain, is hard and smooth to the touch, and often dense, *soft* paste, is soapy and oily to the touch, and sometimes scratches easily with a file or iron. It is made of artificial clays and is apt to be more porous and dull. It is well to note here that all Oriental china is hard paste and that hard-paste porcelain was made at Plymouth, Bristol and Liverpool; soft paste came from Chelsea, Bow, Worcester, and others of the famous localities of the English potters. Staffordshire porcelain was soft paste to which feldspar had been added. The student who is analyzing the china head doll should try to distinguish hard and soft paste porcelain. This is not as easy as it may seem, despite the differences noted.

Glaze, also discovered in some remote period in the annals of time, is a thin covering of glass, as the name itself implies. Enamel colors, on the glaze of hard paste porcelain, do not always fuse, and so they stand up perceptibly from the surface of the glaze. However enamel colors applied over soft paste porcelain melt into it, and become incorporated, so that its presence is neither visible to the eye, nor palpable to the touch. The rims or little rings, on which pieces of hard porcelain rest are left unglazed . . . and the underlying material may be discerned. Wherever there is a clean chip, it is possible to distinguish between hard and soft paste in the finished product, otherwise it is a most difficult task. However all modern china is hard paste. All lustered wares, all 'bone china,' all artificial china, fall into the soft paste class.

For many years the old china of Europe was the soft, mellow kind, made from soft paste porcelains, distinctly creamy and with great translucency. The French applied the word 'Faience,' to all glazed pottery, but not to porcelain. Majolica, a yellow hued bisque, ranks with faience, and the name is applied to the Italian wares. The various attempts of the European potters to produce the true or hard paste porcelain of the Chinese came to naught. The Oriental ware first came into the Continent, overland by way of Western Asia, and it was not until the late 1500's that it came by water, shipped around Africa by the Portuguese who gained great wealth through their control of the trade.

As early as 1470 the Venetians had tried to make this porcelain, and Francesco de Medici struggled with the problem in Florence for some thirty years with no success. Louis XIV of France tried his hand, but always, the secret seemed to elude the most skillful chemists. The story of the young Saxon alchemist, Johann Friedrich Böttger, who labored long for this same purpose, and finally accomplished his aim, in 1790, is comparatively well known. Certainly it marks one of the most important events of his era.

It was at the little royal court at Dresden, Germany, during the reign of the Elector Prince Augustus, II, that a young apothecary's clerk, Böttger, stumbled upon the secret . . . or rather the clay, which alone of all clays would produce hard paste porcelain from kaolin, a white mineral, known in China, and later found in various other parts of the world, America included. Augustus the Strong, had supplied Böttger with a laboratory in which he was experimenting, attempting to convert red and white clays into gold. He was finally forced to face his royal master and confess that it could not be done. He claimed he could, however,

Courtesy of Mrs. John Albright

A very unusual hard paste china head doll

produce a hard white porcelain, equal in fineness to that coming in from the Far East. So Böttger discovered a gold mine although in clay, as he had dreamed he might do.

From 1709, and through another generation, the Saxon ruler and his followers kept the precious secret of their find. They moved from Dresden to a neighboring town, Meissen. Here many figures were modeled that were later copied by the English factories. In fact so many copies eventually appeared that it was indeed difficult to establish their authenticity. If this was true for chinaware, it must also have been true about such minor things as dolls heads, assuming that they were made.

Several factories in France had been making pâte tendre, the soft paste porcelain of chemical composition. Most of these factories belonged to the nobility, the Royal Factory being located at Vincennes. The French court looked with envy upon the wealth of the German Meissen Factory, after the discovery of kaolin, and it was with great joy that the French found the precious white mineral near Saint Yriex, in the Limousin province not far from Limoges. Madame de Pompadour, the favorite of Louis XV, whose son had married the daughter of Augustus III, had the Royal Factory moved to Sevres, and the manufacture of modern china had its beginnings. To-day Sevres is the National China Manufactory of France. Every piece that comes out of the kiln is so carefully examined that if there is the slightest defect, the piece is destroyed. Other factories often sort their china into different grades, the least perfect being sold, without the factory mark, all over France to village fairs, or for disposal at inexpensive prices, but everything coming from Sevres must be perfect. This was true up to the time of the German invasion of France. What the factory is now accomplishing is not known.

At Sevres, both glazed china and bisque were made. The bisque, a dull, unglazed and unpainted earthenware, had a certain whiteness that gave it popularity. The name bisque was derived from biscuit, or bisquit, but any china, or pottery, is in the "bisque" state when first fired, and before being glazed or enameled.

The French bisque is comparable to porcelain and majolica, for where the one is a chaste white, and the other a yellow, French bisque is faintly tinted flesh color. Although this bisque bears the name 'French,' one authority draws attention to the fact that the bisque may have been made in Dresden, and that some of the finest examples of this ware came from countries other than France. The bisque which has a definitely rosy hue is called 'Late bisque," and can refer to any continental, or English bisque. The German porcelain, which was white, had a cold glittering quality which differed from the French. There were no identifying marks during the Böttger period and those that came later, were difficult to determine. Meissen, however, remained the premier porcelain until the Seven Years War, in 1756, when Frederick the Great sacked the place, and took the molds to Berlin. Meissen never again regained its former position in the world of ceramics. The paste thickened, no color could be discerned, and copies were even made from the Sevres originals.

It might be wise to pause here for a brief moment to consider the possibility that the same molds used for the figurine heads might have been used for doll heads. Exactly where can one draw the line between a doll head and a figurine?

Collection Janet P. Johl
A group showing the possibility of other molds having been used for the making of doll heads. Illustrated is a Rouen ware pitcher, a head to hang on the wall, a modern flower vase. It is not easy to discern which are the dolls.

Surely a study of the various statuettes and figurines and of such details as the roses and morning glories of Dresden ware, or of salt glaze, etc. would serve as a guide in the study of doll heads. So called 'Utility' doll heads, used for pin-cushions or as holders, or as decorative wall pieces and the like, might well have come from these molds . . . So far no one has been able to prove this point, but it does seem worthy of consideration.

Mrs. Izole Dorgan reports that she has seen a few—but very few—doll heads which she believes are Meissen. One, circa 1810, had a most peculiar neck with three holes in it.

The hair was lavender hue and the delicately covered bust phalanged out. Here is an instance where it is quite possible that a head was obtained from the mold of a figurine. Another doll head which Mrs. Dorgan reports is identical to the Meissen but is of pure white, with rectified bust and proper holes, and with the Royal Berlin mark inside. Still another which Mrs. Dorgan calls Berlin pottery, a very early type, is marked, and on the Nymphenburg style with almost Chinese eyes . . . "It seemed rather an ornament than a toy." The paste of the Royal Berlin is thicker and not as interesting as the original Meissen. Asked about Sonneberg, Mrs. Dorgan had this to say "They were a slender, aristocratic type, with an odd pinkish hue that is different from the tinted flesh color of Dresden. Sonneberg must have made different qualities judging from the figures available for study in the museums. Some were quite the common sort, much like the present reproductions . . . the pinkish ones were as good as the Dresdens but more substantial looking. The good ones were Biedermeier type. They made tons of cheap heads. A careful study of Sonnenberg paste, coloring, modeling would help identify the doll head. Hunch, experience, and a knowledge of paste all enter into the picture.''

Royal Berlin Doll Head. Similar to Meissen

But the ordinary collector knows how hard it is to find such rare dolls as these lovely old German ones. White porcelain doll heads, of this era, are believed by many to be entirely of German origin, forerunners of the pasty white china doll with hair in tight curls, which was popular in 1850 and was exported in a number of sizes to America. Heads of Austrian origin were of a heavy rich paste, of 'ash, or, rose pink.'

All this may seem far removed from the world of dolls but in reality, it is not, for a great part of the controversial matter on the subject of the china doll heads, leads back to Germany, either because the head is classed as Dresden, or because the collector sees the Dresden influence in a head classified as English.

The influence of Dresden is seen in the extensive use of molded patterns, flowers, ornaments and gilt reliefs raised from the flat ground of the dead white porcelain. There was a diversity about Dresden. The factories made decorative accessories, as well as table ware, figures and busts, with a local individuality and distinctive European or continental character. The use of enamel colors on the hard paste porcelain gives the collector the opportunity to test a china doll head and note whether the colors fuse into the glaze. There is often some underglazing in Dresden, in lovely soft colors, in blue and in shades of yellow varying from straw to lemon. Later a Sevres influence appeared in the use of painted decorations and the manner of gilting. A doll offered for sale, recently, was listed as follows: ''Dresden. Blonde hair arranged in a double cluster of curls in front, surmounted by a gold and rose bow of ribbon, upswept at the sides, and arranged in puffs at the back. Gold ear rings. Around her neck, forming a square neckline, is a frill of rose and gold deeply fluted, and perfect, of porcelain. Below, the shoulders are painted in soft blue in design of a dress.''

Chapter IV

CHINA DOLL
HEADS

*(Staffordshire—Chelsea
Worcester—Lowestoft)*

Courtesy of Mrs. Cyrus Beachy
A china doll head with a swivel neck.

O F all the English Potters, those of Staffordshire probably hold the most interest for the doll collector because so many of the old china heads, given English origin, erroneously or not, are termed 'Staffordshire.'

Staffordshire china originated in a district known as The Potteries as early as 1700. The Potteries is a name applied to a district of North Staffordshire, the principal seat of china and earthenware in England. It includes Burslem, Hanley, Longton, Fenton, Stoke-on-Trent and Tunstall, amalgamated in 1910 under the name Stoke-on-Trent as one municipal borough. Some of the famous names connected with the industry include Enoch Wood, A. Stevenson, Ralph Stevenson, R. J. Ridgway and many others.

The story of the Staffordshire Potteries begins with Enoch Wood, the 'Father of the Pottery,' who made all kinds of tableware. The Wood family and their imitators also produced interesting porcelain figures copied from the French, and during the nineteenth century miscellaneous 'image toys' and 'chimney ornaments,' were in popular favor.

In a discussion of dolls, it is impossible to go into the matter of china in minute detail, but this much should certainly be noted. The characteristics of Staffordshire are its fine cream color. Of most interest to Americans is the printed blue ware which, of course, does not enter the doll world. Spots often developed in the Staffordshire, which sometimes could be cleaned off with

27

bread, or, when deep seated, with warm soap, water and a soft brush. It was the cheaper type of the pottery, the cream colored ware, that created a world market, held for a long time despite continental rivals. Mrs. Emma C. Clear mentions "a china head with one little dark speck in the finish of the chin, a defect often in English china and Staffordshires." Mrs. A. Raymond Reeves reported a doll which she termed "Staffordshire," with a mark at the bottom of the shoulder, 1086#9. The texture and coloring, Mrs. Reeves says, are different from any of the other china heads in her collection.

Wedgwood classified his products as "the ornamental" and "the useful." Of his ornamental products there were twenty classes. Class 10 included heads of "Illustrious Moderns." In 1787 there were some 230 heads listed in the catalogue, selling for a shilling each, and they probably belonged to the medallion portraiture class. He also lists in Class II, "Busts, small statues, boys and animals." "But it seems that these busts were made of black basaltes, and only occasionally in red, white and cane colored terra cotta."

There is little that is poetic in the Staffordshire figures, found in humble homes as chimney piece ornaments. And yet it is this unpoetic something that may serve as a clue to the doll enigma, for often, the early china doll heads, were found serving exactly that purpose, as ornamental chimney pieces. These figures were usually of the creamy white ware and the use of gold was meagre. But there were hundreds of patterns used, and it might be well to study some of the faces of the ladies and the little boys as a means to classify, if possible, the doll head, through a resemblance in features, and in texture. Most of the examples of English china in the translucent wares are of soft paste, easily identified, as 'bone paste porcelain.'

Again to quote Mrs. Emma C. Clear, who has handled dolls for a great number of years, and has experimented with the making and firing of china and porcelain. "The head that we have called Staffordshire has a coarse body and the glaze wears easily. The color on most of them is faded and dull. The ones that we call Chelsea, are of a harder and whiter china, generally not worn and the cheeks are brilliant. The Chelsea is often lumpy, sometimes has flakes of a sharp, black flinty substance. Perhaps they are both misnamed, but there are two different materials, obviously of different clays. The models are similar, the age probably the same. There is another head of this period, with more cameo like features, better workmanship, with a dull, flesh tint all over, that is not the bright pink of the 'pink lustre' which is pink under the glaze of the 'Chelsea 'type. They, too, are generally called, 'Staffordshire,' but they bear no relation to the pottery like heads of the first order." "You see no one really knows if Staffordshire and Chelsea are not really German heads. Then they are wrongly named, just as I have thought all along." It might be well to re-read this statement for it contains a considerable amount of meaty material. Leaving the problem still unsolved, true, but giving a great deal of 'food for thought."

Lewis Wiggin of Northampton, Mass., reports a "Staffordshire doll head with lovely coloring. On the very top of her head is a black crown a little smaller than a fifty cent piece. This doll has parian hands and feet, the shoes, green with gold trimming.'' Mrs. Catherine Richards Howard tells of a ''brown haired 'Staffordshire,' her curls piled high all over her head, and down around her shoulders in overlapping rows; a curled fringe across the forehead, with a black lustre band above.'' Mrs. Howard also reports a similar doll, with honey blonde hair, as ''Staffordshire, 1860.'' A similar black haired china doll had impressed on the back of the shoulders ''Pat. Dec. 7, 1880.''

Evidently these dolls were of the same type. However Mrs. Howard writes: ''The one patented was a rather crude copy of the other two, the hair was not so good and the shoulders were more shallow. Of course, most molds were in use over a period of ten years and some longer, or the mold might have been passed, through a change of hands, from one factory to another. I wonder if this could have been an American copy of an English mold? This is pure supposition but it does seem that the American potters never did get the results that the foreigners did. Perhaps the materials were not the same.''

There seems to be no record anywhere of a patent for this particular doll head, dated 1880, unless some one of the factories simply put the date impression into a doll head, which seems highly improbable. The United States law requiring the marking of imported articles was not passed until 1890, so there was no existent law which made it necessary to date a doll 1880. The question raised by Mrs. Howard is an intensively interesting one, worthy of additional study.

Mrs. Earle E. Andrews, of Winchester, Mass., reports a brown haired china doll now in her collection. Mrs. Clear writes that there are not many of the brown haired china head dolls, in comparison to the black and blonde types but that about one brown haired china head appears in every two hundred. One with a funny pug, sticking straight out, and a long neck, is quite unique. Mrs. Andrews also has in her collection a china head doll, with carefully pencilled curls, and brown eyes which is said to have been brought from England over 100 years ago. This doll is now named 'Sophia Smith' although she originally bore the name of 'Mary.' However because of intermarriage into the family of Sophia Smith, the founder of Smith College, her name was changed. Although she is very old, the texture and coloring of her face have remained exquisite.

Mrs. Estella Graham of Long Beach, Cal., writes of a china head doll, circa 1880, that has gray eyes. Most of the china head dolls have either brown or blue eyes, painted on. Some few have the inserted glass eyes, but gray eyes are not at all usual. Mrs. Graham also has a china head doll, about sixty years old, with a slightly open mouth and four china teeth, inserted and not painted. There are no numbers, nor any other markings on the head or shoulders of this doll. It is said that a similar doll is in a museum in Chicago. This is surely rare in a china head doll of this era.

The transitory period in china making in England was from 1750-1800, and the English potters, encountering difficulties in making artificial porcelain, were seeking to overcome their troubles. As early as 1749, Thomas Fry of the Bow Pottery took out a patent to use bone ash with a little glass. Joseph Wedgwood, the most celebrated of all English potters, directed his earliest efforts toward refining his wares, and took out a patent in 1763 for a beautiful porcelain, cream colored, which became known as "Queen's Ware." He was assisted by his most famous artist, John Flaxman, who modeled very characteristic designs of tinted bodies, and small cameo reliefs. But were any doll heads made? To date there seems to be no definite answer to the question. Only one small detail that may interest the collector, and that is, what has already been suggested, that the flesh tinting in the composition differed from the pasty white of Chelsea.

During this transitory period in the Potteries of England, shortly after 1765 to be exact, kaolin was found in Cornwall, along with feldspar, and hard paste porcelain became a commercial possibility for England. However the potters continued to experiment with the bone porcelain, and found that by adding ash to the soft paste a distinctively white finish was obtained. The porcelain was then glazed so that it might lose some of its absorbent character and porosity, and thus be of more service.

Yet some collectors refer to certain old china heads as "pink Chelsea", truly a puzzle to mystify and confuse. Mrs. Greville Bathe remarks, "Personally I think that so called 'pink Chelsea,' and so called 'pink Staffordshire,' (in doll heads) are the same thing." From Mrs. Catherine Richards Howard comes another suggestion. "As to distinguishing between Staffordshire and Chelsea, after all, Chelsea was only one of the many Staffordshire groups. The ones I identify as 'Chelsea' are usually of pink porcelain with a decidedly peach tint and they look more like real people than the other dolls do. Also I have noticed that their eye-balls are molded, rounded, as a real eye should be, not just a flat painted surface".

Another report comes of dolls with wooden jointed arms and legs, and heads of porcelain of the finest quality, with a pinkish hue that looks like the enamel of a Chelsea snuff box, and, which, because they were called 'Chelsea' by a well known collector, have carried the name ever since for no particular authenticated reason.

Who really knows? When is a discrepancy not a discrepancy?

The origin of the famous Chelsea factory is a matter of conjecture. It is likely enough that the secret of its porcelain was brought over to England by a foreign workman. But whoever the alchemist, it seems more plausible that he came from France rather than from Germany, although some feel that the Chelsea styles were inspired by Meissen. It would seem, however, that in the case of Chelsea the French influence may be seen in all the Chelsea periods. The lovely colored grounds of Sevres were imitated and Oriental patterns, after the Dutch, were also copied in the china ware. Although its beginnings were vague, Chelsea enjoyed a great popularity from 1750 to 1765.

It is certainly the most original of the English porcelains, an artificial porcelain, or pâte tendre, largely composed of glassy grit and coated with a soft glaze that contained lead.

In periods, Chelsea is as follows:

1745-50

(1) Creamy paste, resembling the French St. Cloud. Satiny, translucent, resembling opaque white glass, waxy to touch, pinhole flaws, fine granular texture.

1750 to 1765

(2) Thick porcelain, sandy paste, rich glaze, thinner, very translucent, soft, mellow creamy tone.

(3) Bright spots on which moons appear, thinner, similar to (2).

(4) Sandy, no moons, whiter pure translucent.

The body of Chelsea is uneven. Held to the light the unmistakable Chelsea spots appear. The early china from Bow was similar in quality to the Chelsea, transparent where the ware was thin, opaque where it was thick. However the Bow figures show a slightly yellowish tinge, with a glaze not as thin as Chelsea. Many objects were made of porcelain, at Chelsea. In a list, made from a study of an old sales catalogue, fortunately preserved, there was not found *one* actual mention of doll heads. Old catalogues did mention "diverting conceits". What were these "conceits"? Could they have been doll heads? If so, why were they not worthy of mention? The potteries consistently refuse to acknowledge the fact that they ever made any doll heads. Individual potters, as has already been suggested, may have been responsible for the doll heads that *seem* to have come out of this locality.

Chelsea Toys is a name often given the articles of Chelsea ware, but these are not toys in the present use of the word. Here is a list of " 'articles Made and Contour', . . . 'trays-sugar bowls-inkstands-jardineres-milk jugs-table garnitures' (could these be dolls?) 'candlesticks-pot pourri jars-snuff boxes-thimbles-perfume and pomatum pots-needle cases-sauce boats-basons-ewers-small flower jars-jewel caskets-portrait medaillons-busts-groups-and figures of biscuit porcelain, modeled by eminent sculptors' ''. Again no mention of doll heads.

In the *Victoria Albert Museum* at *London* there is a patchbox of Chelsea, in the form of a lady's head, the mold of which might have served to make doll heads. *Ethol M. Watson*, of Cornwallville, N. Y. has this to say on the subject of Chelsea doll heads. "What I call Chelsea has the moon spots of old Chelsea, regardless of whether pink or white. Two old heads I have seen were marked with a tiny red anchor, and small figures, one reading 40 and the other 50. Both these heads were alike as to coloring, and very beautiful in detail with long, slender necks and glazing. The faces had the same long human look. I have seen a pink china but I would say this is not Chelsea, but Staffordshire."

How can one be sure?

In 1770 the Chelsea factory was sold to William Duesbury, proprietor of the Derby factory in existence since 1750, but whose porcelain figures in Chelsea styles were of comparatively little merit. After the Chelsea works closed, this ware became known as Chelsea-Darby. This changing of hands does not help to solve the problem of the china doll heads, unfortunately.

To quote Mrs. Catherine Richards Howard again, because of her interest and study of old china, as well as dolls, "It is rather difficult to say just why I feel that some dolls are 'this or that'. The museums will not admit anything, neither will the factories. But isn't it true that many of the factories are no longer operating? I think through the study of china one can come to recognize certain characteristics of the English potters arts. I cannot believe that the Germans made as delicately featured dolls as the English and French did. Maybe I am wrong."

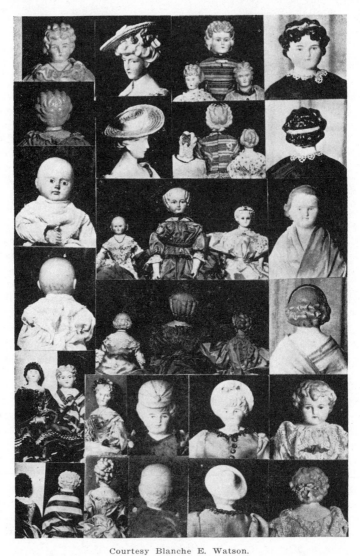

Courtesy Blanche E. Watson.

A Composite Picture of some of the interesting doll heads in the collection

Worcester was only in its infancy as far as china was concerned when Chelsea and the other chinas had already achieved name and fame. The Worcester Porcelain Company was formed in 1751, for the manufacture of chinaware, and turned its attention first to blue and white, imitating the Chinese in form and color. Later it diverged into the brilliant colorings of Japanese ware. Worcester made no figures or groups, and no mention of doll heads can be found. However the undecorated Worcester porcelain was sold, and amateur and professional artists did the decorating. The earliest mark on this china was a script 'W'. Mrs. Dora Walker of Rutland, Vt. reports a doll that may have been made in Worcester, for a script "W" is inside the head, plain to be seen. The head is a heavy white paste, the expression of the face not different from that of other dark haired, blue eyed china head dolls. But the script "W" is interesting. Mrs. Walker writes. "I have only a very few doll heads that carry a mark. Tucked down in the clothes inside this doll was an odd bit of paper with writing on it in French." Mrs. Walker also reports a similar head,

very large, with a " " inside the head.

No. 24
Medaille   Medaille

Epingles
Doubles
I cr. choix
A L'Exposition Universelle

J R
Paris   1855
Depose
Paper found inside Doll Head
Courtesy Mrs. Dora Walker

Lowestoft came to America in large quantities and has a most baffling history. Some china collectors believe it to be Oriental porcelain, decorated in England, at the town of that name. Others believe that the decoration as well as the porcelain came from China. All agree that as early as 1756, and up until 1762, soft paste pottery was made in Lowestoft in imitation of Delft ware, in blue and white. The porcelain called Lowestoft is of a fine pearly tint ,the usual color of Chinese porcelain. The glaze is thick and characteristically rose tint, the usual color of Chinese porcelain. The end of the manufacture of Lowestoft, or at least its decoration is quite as mysterious as the rest of its history. It ceased between 1803-1804, for a number of reasons one of which was the competition of the Staffordshire potters. There are no traces of a factory left, and no fragments of the china have ever been dug up.

Ethol M. Watson reports what she believes is a "Queen Anne" doll head that is Lowestoft. This is what she has to say about it.

"I compared the quality, its deep tone, color and composition with a Lowestoft tea pot, covered sugar bowl and helmet creamer in rose sprig pattern that I have. And it is the same. The paste is not white at all. And inside, the head is very unlike any I have seen. The coloring is of a pink, in streaks, and inside is that unmistakable Lowestoft look. I can only say (with no definite word to go on) that one knows Lowestoft by instinct. I am unable to get any

A group of "Chelsea" Doll Heads. Boy Head in Profile, Pink lustre glow on faint
    tinge light tan. Note hair arrangement on Lady Dolls. Collection Helyn
    Ewing Fowler. Eric Stahlberg photographer.
Doll in chair has script "W" on head.
        Courtesy Mrs. Dora Walker.
Doll Standing. A brown haired china doll. Collection Mrs. Earle E. Andrews
    Group of small china dolls—flesh hued and white. Collection Janet P. Johl.

reliable word as yet about the history of this head, only that it is definitely more than 100 years old, and was handed down from a great grandmother.''

In the face of letters from varied sources it would seem that these conclusions, on unusual dolls, by serious collectors, are more than supposition, and yet who can really say?

On Feb. 15, 1940, Mrs. E. C. Hultman, President of the China Students Club, Boston, Mass., answered an inquiry as to the place of origin of the old china doll heads. To quote in part:

"I have asked Mrs. Bertram Little, an authority in many ceramic fields, and she tells me she has no information on the subject. I will bring your letter before the next meeting of the China Students Club and am sure that if there are any members who can assist you they will gladly do so.

I am sorry I have no information on the subject, but like you am inclined to think that most dolls were of continental origin.'' . . . Very truly yours,

Elizabeth B. Hultman.''

Nothing further was heard from this source. Mrs. Izole Dorgan has suggested that if 75% of the dolls were credited to the continent . . . and most of them given German origin . . . no great error would be made regarding doll history.

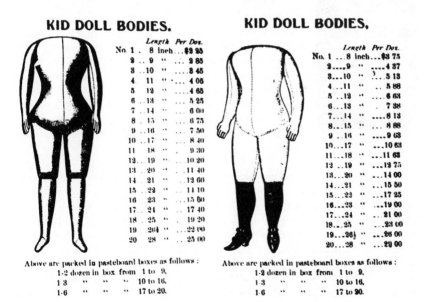

KID DOLL BODIES.

	Length	Per Doz.
No. 1 .	8 inch	$2 95
2 ..	9 "	2 85
3 ..	10 "	3 45
4 .	11 "	4 05
5 .	12 "	4 65
6 ..	13 "	5 25
7 ..	14 "	6 00
8 .	15 "	6 75
9 ..	16 "	7 50
10 ..	17 "	8 40
11 .	18 "	9 30
12 ..	19 "	10 20
13 .	20 "	11 40
14 .	21 "	12 60
15 .	22 "	14 10
16	23 "	15 60
17..	24 "	17 40
18 ..	25 "	19 20
19	26½ "	22 00
20	28 "	25 00

Above are packed in pasteboard boxes as follows:
1-2 dozen in box from 1 to 9,
1-3 " " " 10 to 16,
1-6 " " " 17 to 20.

KID DOLL BODIES,

	Length	Per Doz.
No. 1 ..	8 inch	$3 75
2....	9 "	4 37
3...10	"	5 13
4 ..11	"	5 88
5 . 12	"	6 63
6...13	"	7 38
7...14	"	8 13
8...15	"	8 88
9 ..16	"	9 63
10...17	"	10 63
11...18	"	11 63
12 ..19	"	12 75
13...20	"	14 00
14...21	"	15 50
15...22	"	17 25
16...23	"	19 00
17...24	"	21 00
18...25	"	23 00
19...26½	"	26 00
20...28	"	29 00

Above are packed in pasteboard boxes as follows:
1-2 dozen in box from 1 to 9,
1-3 " " " 10 to 16,
1-6 " " " 17 to 20.

Illustration from catalog of 1902, shown through courtesy of Ted Brait
Braitling kid doll bodies, however, are believed to date some years prior

Chapter V

MORE ABOUT CHINA OR PORCELAIN DOLL HEADS

(Parian, Lustre, Stone Bisque, Bennington,
Victorian Pottery)

Courtesy Elma Fuller

"Bennington Doll".

IN 1846 William Taylor Copeland, of England, invented a ware which because of its likeness to the fine textured whiteness of the marble found on the Isle of Paros, Greece, was termed Parian.

It is believed that doll heads made of Parian appeared about 1855 and perhaps one of the best ways to date a Parian head doll is by studying the style of hair dress, both of the period and the doll. Parian itself may be defined as a special kind of hard clear paste, a bisque that is unglazed, and very often hand painted. Stone bisque is often mistaken for Parian, but although a pure white, it is never so finely grained. A great many of the dolls, wearing bonnets and hats, are not Parian, but are stone bisque. Parians have exceptionally fine, delicate features.

The city of Dresden, Germany, which was engaged in true porcelain making as early as 1709, turned out some lovely Parian pieces. In dolls, the heads were often decorated with wreaths of miniature glazed flowers, or with a gold lustre hair ornament or a band of black satin, shiny ribbon, a comb or a gilt net snood. Cameo perfect features graced many of the French Parians, with flowers caught in the hair, and charming hats with gay colorful plumes. Many of the Parian heads have glass eyes, usually blue, and a deep study of doll head types, brings this conclusive fact: That dolls of Parian, bisque china and papier maché came from the same molds. Miss Elma Fuller of Bristol, Vermont, reports a Parian doll in her collection with glass eyes and earrings. She has the same doll in china without glass eyes. Many of the Parians, circa 1850-1860 had strings of beads molded into the neck, and beautiful fluting, sometimes in lustre, and high necked guimpes simulated a dress of fine material.

Mrs. Emma C. Clear has this to say of Parian: "No particular manufacturer has any exclusive right to the name. It is a common name for the marble-white, unglazed porcelain. Some is very finely ground and has a satiny feeling. Some is much coarser and there are between grades. I do not know just where one can draw the line, or who would be entitled to draw one."

Mrs. Catherine Richards Howard writes:

"Some people call a great deal of late, 'chalky junk,' Parian. I do not. But the lovely smooth early Parian is very beautiful, I think. It seems to me that the Dresdens always have some porcelain about them. A frill about the shoulders, a corsage, or a wreath or bows in the hair. I am even inclined to think one of the type of the waterfall coiffure, and porcelain collar and tie, is Dresden, because of the decoration on the porcelain part, and the exquisite texture of the Parian. There were some extremely attractive Parians in the early seventies, attractive as to high hair arrangements. But the Parian is much rougher. The ones from 1850-1860 are the finest, I believe."

Several advertisements mention this type of doll, giving interesting descriptions, as for example "A doll with black hair caught in a gold snood, and a porcelain scarf, in lustre, wound around her head." . . . and . . . "A brown haired Parian with hair arranged in curls above the forehead and two black bands across the top, and another black band holding together a low cluster of curls at the nape of the neck. Pierced ears with ear rings, and lovely sloping shoulders." Still another . . . 'A blonde Parian, replica of Countess Dagmar, with clustered curls at the forehead, upswept at the side, arranged in puffs divided by two braids at the back. Simple high necked blouse molded into the chest."

A most important means of dating any doll is the study of the costuming of a given period. Very often it is the only possible way to estimate an approximate date. As the Parian dolls often have decorative touches in lustre, a brief glimpse into the question of lustre may be advisable.

Before the pottery received its final firing, a metallic solution was applied to whatever part was to have the lustre finish. Exactly who discovered lustre is unknown, as the authorities do not agree as to the name. That it was an ancient art is acknowledged by all. Lustre finish is found in gold, silver, copper, purple, violet and pink. The pink lustre was manufactured in great quantities from 1810 to 1830. It is a thin coating of deep rose, irridescent, over which gold is applied. The depth of color depends upon the amount of gold coating and the lighting effect that results, comes from the firing in a special kind of kiln.

Mrs. Emma C. Clear writes "I have seen no lustre heads with any markings that I recall. I have four here now, two quite brilliant pink, doll like faces, two of the pioneer type, with more of a flesh color, long sloping shoulders, and cameo-like features. All four are exquisite. I wish I could definitely date and place them."

"On the Parians again, the exquisite heads with flowers and lustre plumes and ribbons. I have never seen an elaborate model yet that I have not also seen plain without any of the flowers or fancy work. They were cast plain. The other work built on in the moist but firm clay stage before fusing. I have done a little experimenting in that kind of work, enough to know that it can be done and easily, with the proper tools. I believe they had tools like miniature cookie cutters for the petals and leaves. They put the little flowers together as one would wax flowers. I had to cut mine with a pen knife, so it was too slow. If I ever have the time, I will work it out.''

It is interesting to note, while on the subject of Parian, that the coarse white bisque which was made at Bennington, Vt., is not Parian. Its very coarseness of texture makes it a poor facsimile for finely grained marble. The question of the existence of authenticated Bennington dolls is a controversial one. A letter to John Spargo, President and Director of the *Bennington Historical Museum* asking for information on the possibility of doll heads, brought this reply.

''No doll heads were ever made here at any time. To the Doll Society (I don't recall its exact title) I wrote a very full and explicit statement in the hope of killing once and for all a legend that was deliberately started by a very dishonest person just for commercial gain.''

The 'Doll Society' to whom Mr. Spargo wrote was, undoubtedly *The Doll Collectors of America, Inc.* In *"American Made Dolls and Figurines,"* the booklet recently published by this club, there is this information on the subject of Bennington Dolls, which Mr. Spargo contributed. ''It is our belief that no doll heads were ever made here. It is certain that no evidence that any were made here is known to exist anywhere.'' . . . ''I have talked with old potters who worked at the potteries here, no one of whom ever mentioned dolls as being produced. Over a period of years I have examined tens of thousands of fragments from the old refuse heaps of the potteries, along the river bank, and pieces plowed up on the land where waste used to be cast. From the fragments I have learned much about the types of ware, designs used, articles made and so forth. Never as much as a fragment of a doll's head. We have numerous bills for goods sold to the potteries, reams of correspondence about the business orders, invoices and so on. But never one mention of doll heads. And in all the pieces preserved in potter's families, embracing personal things like toy whistles made for whimsies, not for commerce, never a doll's head has been offered as even being presumed to be Bennington. In short, there is absolutely no evidence that such articles were made. I am convinced that they were never made here.''

''Heads have been brought to us here at the Historical Museum with plausible stories of attribution. In each case, all there was of truth was that the 'old lady,' who had once owned it, claimed that it was brought to her from Bennington, or something like that. It was a dead 'give away' that in each case the date when the purchase in Bennington was made, estimated by the alleged age of the lady at the time, came long after the United States pottery had ceased to make anything.''

However, native Vermonters are not all in full agreement with this statement, even though John Spargo is an outstanding authority on the subject of Bennington pottery, and other early American pottery. One such doll has even been reported to be in New Jersey, a bluish white specimen, 'lovely and old looking.' Miss Ariel Bissell Cutler of Petersborough, N. H., well known doll collector-lecturer comments:

''So far as I personally know there were not any Parian dolls at Bennington, Vt., but I have been told that a lady, recently moved to Claremont, from

Bennington, has a Parian doll, made there. I have never had it proved to me that the doll was made there, nor have I personally seen it, nor do I believe all I hear, until I prove it to myself. A great many times workmen, in all manner of articles, stayed overtime and made, for some special reason, things on their own hook, and it just might be possible that dolls were among those items, but of course unless one runs onto a family which has brought one down along the family tree, it is next to impossible to prove anything. I cannot help but feel that it may have been possible for there to have been Parian Bennington dolls now and then. I will make another attempt this year to contact the lady in Claremont and see what her story is, and the doll, if she has it.''

Mrs. Catherine Richards Howard thinks the chalky Parian of 1890-1910 might resemble the Bennington. Mrs. Izole M. Dorgan says, cryptically, ''I am betting on Spargo.''

Mrs. Clear reports an 'old Bennington, belonging to a lady in Bristol, Vt., the largest and best she has ever seen,'' and then she adds ''The thing that makes me think these dolls were handed down is because we get so many of them, family dolls called 'Bennington Parian.' Was there any other Bennington? And what about Victorian bisque? That is supposed to be a sort of coarse bisque similar to Bennington but I took it for granted that it was made in England.''

Mrs. William Harvey of Cortland, N. Y. might be able to answer Mrs. Clear's question for she writes, ''The Queen Victoria doll I have is said to represent the Queen Mother and was put out at the time of Queen Victoria's coronation in 1838.''

''Virginia''. A Parian Aristocrat

Mrs. Blanche E. Watson, of Geneva, Ill., describes Virginia, one of her Parian dolls as ''from Philadelphia, about 1870, a blue blooded aristocrat modeled in Parian. She is the loveliest doll I have ever seen.'' As Mrs. Watson has some extremely beautiful dolls, this particular doll must be of exceptional design and artistic workmanship.

Bertha Smith of Jamaica, N. Y. writes of an Alexandra doll which she has seen ''A china head of fine quality which took a high glaze, big ears, red cheeks, blue eyes and hair a glossy black in a rolled back hair dress, slightly resembling the Floradora pompadour. . . . ''I am told that all Alexandras were made in Europe. The first were English, then French, then German. England loves blondes. Germany also is blonde minded. France likes brown eyed blondes, and also loves brunettes. I surmise that Alexandra was honored with a doll, as a bride, as the English were very fond of her. As Alexandra wore a wig for years, the doll seems to hook up with her youth. . . . I am sorry I cannot give you dates, potteries, etc. but no one knows the answers.''

Mrs. Harvey has two heads that are said to represent the Queen, one brunette, the other blonde, with elaborate necklace embossed in the mold.

"*Doll Talk*" mentions a pair of marriage dolls representing Queen Victoria and her consort, Albert, in wedding costume, the Queen doll being about ten inches high. The Magazine *Antiques* carried an advertisement from England of two dolls for sale, Queen Victoria and her Royal Consort, Albert.

A very rare doll with a wooden body, pegged, and a shapely waist is in the collection of Mrs. William Harvey of Cortland, N. Y. The doll has a solid china head, which has a hole in the base into which a wooden peg in the center of the shoulder line fits. Hands and feet are of china, with orange colored slippers, and one foot, regrettably is broken. The doll is between seven and eight inches in height and the arms are considerably longer proportionately than the legs. The china legs are white but the rest of the china is flesh hued. The eyes are blue, the cheeks are rosy and the hair, in boyish arrangement, is black, with ears showing.

Two other interesting dolls also in Mrs. Harvey's collection are worthy of consideration. One is termed the Victoria doll, and has the waterfall hair arrangement. This particular specimen has a triangular inset of gold on the top of the head. Mrs. Frederic Ripley also reports a doll with this type of hair arrangement.

The other doll has a Mona Lisa expression, on an elongated face of pinkish hue, and dark brown hair, with four corkscrew curls on each side of the head. Inside this doll head is an unusual marking, in blue, not unsimilar to the Russian double eagle found on Russian stamps. The initials are K P M. The J. D. Kestner firm of Waltershausen, Germany had a king's crown for their trade mark, with streamers pendant, and this was generally colored blue, and bore the initials J. D. K. Whether there is any relationship between the two it is difficult to say.

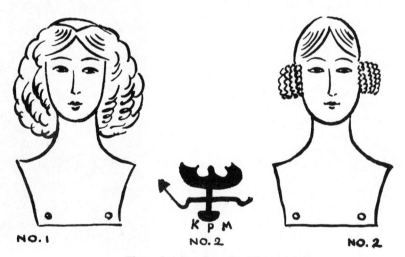

NO. 1   NO. 2   NO. 2

These sketches show the 'Victoria' doll with waterfall coiffeur, and the 'Mona Lisa' type with an unusual marking within the head.

Courtesy of Mrs. William Harvey.

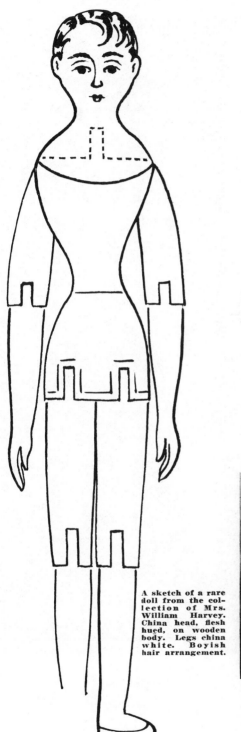

A sketch of a rare doll from the collection of Mrs. William Harvey. China head, flesh hued, on wooden body. Legs china white. Boyish hair arrangement.

The question of Bennington and Victorian dolls remains unsolved, and so it must be left for the time being, as must the study of Parian, but before leaving the subject completely, mention must be made of a rare and very unique American pottery doll head owned by Mrs. Elsie Nadelman of New York City, which evidently came from the Pennsylvania Pie Plate People, Lower Penn. in the Shenandoah Valley. This pottery head is yellow and red and very crude. It is marked on the back "Bertha, 1822." No one seems to know anything more about it.

Janet Ehnes of Detroit, Mich., reports a brown pottery doll head, not older than 1890, that is most unusual. In the *Museum of Modern Art* in New York City there is a wooden polychrome doll made by an unknown craftsman of the early days, and found near Ephrata, Penn.

Courtesy Mrs. Elsie Nadelman
American Pottery Head, marked "Bertha, 1822". Very crude.

Circa 1880

1. Toinette, a Dresden Doll.   Collection Mrs. Cyrus Beachy
2. Group showing Parians.   Collection Mrs. Florence Wadsworth
3. A Parian Head.   Courtesy Mrs. Velvalee Dickinson
4. Mme. Le Bou.   Collection Mrs. Cyrus Beachy

Chapter VI

Courtesy of Helen Siebold Walter

**Antique French Doll. Wooden Body, Hands, Feet.
Bisque. Empire Period.**

FRENCH DOLL HEADS

(Early Replicas—Jumeau, Pere et Fils)

That dolls were made in France to represent well known personages, or characters, is a fact which George Herzog, of White Plains, N. Y. believes to be true. Mr. Herzog has spent his entire life in the field of dolls, undergoing his apprenticeship with his father, as a boy in Hungary, where he learned a great deal about continental dolls. "For years", he explained, "The French made dolls of rags, of painted silk, of wax and carved wood, and perhaps of other materials. These dolls resembled the nobles of France. Personages like Napoleon, the Louis, Mme. La Pompadour, Mme. DuBarry, and others, appeared in the very likeness, fashionably dressed in the costumes of their period. These dolls were very popular. Their heads were not made of porcelain, but from a similar, ivory colored material, harder than porcelain, called piro . . . an earthernware burned like porcelain, which was first found in southern France, and was yellowish in color.''

Mrs. Izole Dorgan reported a remarkable group of very rare, historical French dolls of carved wood, originally owned by the Princess Lambelle, and played with by Marie Antoinette and adults of the gay French court in 1776. These dolls represent men and women of the court and are not toys for children. Mrs. Dorgan writes ''They are Marie Antoinette, Louis XVI, Princess Lambelle, a gentleman of the court, the tallest man of the Royal Family, not identified, Duc de Provence, Louis XVIII with double curls, Duc d'Artois, with one curl, Louis X, Duc de Barton, Chevalier d'Eon. At the *Exposition des Costumes Anciens*, held in Paris at the *Musée des Arts Décoratifs*, in October 1909, beautiful examples of Louis XVI dolls, well preserved, were shown. Eight ladies and seven gentlemen in complete costumes of elaborate brocades and laces, with high heeled shoes, high coiffeurs and tiny jewels, were displayed. The dolls seem to have been very like the ones which Mrs. Dorgan now has, and even may be the same. But likeness dolls were in demand before the days of Napoleon, and the baby doll, and the little boy and girl dolls came into popular favor during the childhood of the little King of Rome.

Throughout the eighteenth century, especially during the vital 'rococo period', the *joie de vivre* was assuredly manifested in dolls, and, particularly, in portrait dolls. Artists turned to porcelain, and, by 1800, the china factories were attempting to outdo one another in the exquisiteness of their products. Technically, the English porcelain was more creditable, but not artistically. Through royal patronage and a lack of endowment, the English were the losers. It was the Continental potters who were the real masters in porcelain making. Models of china heads appeared, with faces like cameos, with china curls painted on little round heads, in comely waves. Many a lovely china head, and china arms graced a plain body of wood. Finely grained Parian heads took the place of the china as time rolled on, and, according to George Herzog, ivory white heads, called 'pirodon', were plentiful. Many of these heads bore very definite resemblance to certain individuals . . . It was the socially correct thing to have ones portrait done in porcelain, and to give oneself, as a doll, or doll head, to a friend, or a lover. Many collectors have dolls which bear a marked resemblance to the Empress Eugenie, or to Louise of Austria . . . many merely seem like the ladies of a given period, possibly some, now unknown, Duchess or Countess.

Mrs. John T. Hawkes, of Boise, Idaho, has a 'glass French doll resembling the Empress Eugenie, with black hair, pink cheeks and blue eyes.' The head dress, it must be repeated, is a fine indication of the age and era of a doll, the arrangement often being of more importance than the hair color.

The great majority of the well known brunette and blonde china doll heads, unattached, or attached to bodies, found their way onto old merchant ships, and so sailed across the sea from the old world, to the shores of the new world . . . America. These were all lady dolls in every sense of the word, some even boasting double chins, and many having glass blue eyes, set into the china.

During this period, and earlier, the porcelain makers of France thought it beneath their dignity, as artists, to spend their time painting doll heads, and France was obliged to neglect the doll industry, comparatively speaking. In 1844 at the Industrial Exposition in France, two persons came to the fore in the manufacture of the doll in France, namely Messieurs Belton and Jumeau, who were established on Rue Salle-au-Comte. Their dolls were very well known and very well made, and as a result they enjoyed a profitable business, a part of which was designed for exportation.

These lovely French dolls were bringing fame to M. Jumeau, for they preserved good taste and a cachet of elegance, but because the china doll head industry was thriving prosperously in Bavaria, Austria and Prussia, and had developed extensively in Coburg, Sonneberg, and Nürnberg in Germany, the French manufacturers soon found that they were not able to meet the competition and were more or less, obliged to obtain their doll heads from Germany. Although well made, the German heads, at this time, were not always beautiful. The back of the head was hollowed out, supposedly because the particular type of porcelain used paid a higher customs duty, and the weight, therefore, had to be reduced as much as possible. Postpaid the heads cost ten centimes a piece, while those made in France cost as high as forty centimes. This may seem incredible, but in reality it was not, for the lack of experience which the French laymen had regarding the doll industry, brought the cost of manufacture up until it far exceeded the German.

About 1862 M. Jumeau decided to free the French industry from its bondage. He wanted to make a doll with an exceptionally pretty face, knowing the French love of beauty. So he set to work to create something that would be truly distinctive. He modeled a certain type of head, had it reproduced in bisque by an artist skilled in porcelain ware, and then had the head colored by another gifted artist. The result was lovely, a joyous looking doll, with rosy hued cheeks, sparkling eyes and a flesh tinted complexion, a doll which was destined to mark the true beginning of '*la poupeé de luxe*', and brought about, ultimately, a decided improvement in the porcelain and pasteboard heads which came from Germany. Subsequently the German makers adopted this doll head for their own model.

In choosing bisque, M. Jumeau was wise, for bisque shrinks uniformly and bisque heads are never deformed. When speaking

Courtesy Jennie L. Abbott
Louise Jumeau

Courtesy Mrs. Izole Dorgan
**A Very rare group of French Dolls from the Court of
Marie Antoinette and Louis XVIth.**

of bisque the collector refers to the paste that has an all over flesh tint and not to the white, with pink cheeks and red lips. A bisque head, it is said, can be exposed to the rays of the sun and will not change. When tapped, it rings like a bell.

In his first models, M. Jumeau made the head and bust of his dolls in one piece. Later the head was separated from the bust and his son thought of an improvement which gave the head movement, up and down, round and round, simulating a life like motion. To this lovely doll head was added an improved body and clothes, fashioned à la mode, in styles all the world knows as "exclusively French". These dolls were very different from the German, both in the texture and in the painting. Jumeau used the whitish type of bisque before he made the turn head type. When ordinary bisque ages it darkens and uniformly becomes more pink. There are a number of textures to be found in bisque doll heads, and the two early French doll makers seem to be at opposite ends in fineness of texture, with Germany in the middle. Bisque may be either white, Parian, or colored. There is blonde bisque and deep flesh bisque. The color may even be ground in. The Jumeau dolls have a lovely soft, flesh hue that is decidedly more beautiful for doll usage than the white bisque.

For the September, 1940, program of *The Doll Collectors of America, Inc.* Miss Jennie L. Abbott, the historian of the club, prepared a paper '*Jumeau Dolls*'. Through the courtesy of Miss Abbott and Mrs. Earl E. Andrews, the President of the Club, this paper is given herein, a most illuminating and interesting story of the Jumeau Doll.

JUMEAU DOLLS
By JENNIE L. ABBOTT

"The Jumeau family of Paris, the best known and most distinguished of French doll makers, first came into prominence in 1844. (Singleton) By 1862 they had created a doll that was truly French, a fine lady doll, graceful in form, well portioned, with a biscuit porcelain head having a beautiful face colored by a skillful artist, and dressed in correct reproductions of the latest French fashions. At first the heads and busts were made in one piece, later the eldest son of the family invented a movable head, by means of which the head could be turned in any direction, up, down, backwards or forwards, or at an angle, imitating in a lifelike manner every human motion or pose. The eyes of these dolls were very beautiful with the sparkle of real eyes. The dolls came in fourteen sizes, the largest being about 39 inches."

"The first of the movable heads were applied to bisque busts which were fastened to a kid body. Later in the '70s the son used this type of head on a composition body which was shaped like a child's body rather than the wasp waisted torsos of the previous era. The manufacture of these is described in the following translation from "Playthings; their history and manufacture" (Lea Jouets:— Historie-Fabrication), by Leo Claretie, a book published in Paris about 1895."

"Come to Montreuil, beyond the fortifications. Stop before a grilling which separates the street from a pretty court planted with green groves, surrounded with workshops with large glass windows. It is the Jumeau factory, manufactury of baby-dolls, as the sign says. We go to make a tour of it, and to witness the very strange genesis of the modern doll.

"There is first the 'crochetterie' (Hook-makers shop). A boy twists some copper wires with the aid of a most ingenious apparatus and makes hooks of them which will be the joints, knee-caps, collar-bones, in this extraordinary anatomy of the composition doll-baby. Some large wheels, gigantic screws, presses, shears are used in this work of twisting from which comes hooks, rings, spiral springs, props of the artificial machine that is going to imitate the human appearance.

"Besides, they mold bodies of every size in heavy matrices of steel, the outer sides of which can be taken apart. The bust is formed from a single piece and is without seams. The workwomen stuff the hollows with old paper moistened in the paste, in a way to secure an even thickness on the inner surface. When they open the matrix they unfasten it from an object in relief, which is a bust artistically curved, with a most excellent outline and graceful curves, the gray color of old paper that has been moistened and dried. There are piles of sacks full of them emptied helter-skelter. They are ruins, long lines of greenish busts, headless, with holes for the insertion of arms and legs which they lack.

"The limbs are molded in other matrices, from which they come in the same dirty green color, but with the fine slender form of objects of art. The hollow grooves of the molds are of a perfect design and very exact anatomy. The hands are stamped apart in a very complicated machine, from which they emerge the color of flaxmeal, but prettily made, chubby, plump and childish with the wrinkles of infancy. It is now a question of assembling these scattered parts.

"This is what they are busy at in the adjacent workshops. Work women are very busy gluing hollow balls in the places of the humerus and neck of the femur. From these balls protrude the hooks which we have just seen made and which serve as clavicles or tendons. In the interior of the bust has been glued a crosspiece of wood to which are hooked the copper tendons of all the members. A workman draws from a pile two legs which are the same length; for sets of them are made in all sizes. He inserts with a tool the thigh bone into the groin, stands the creature up to be sure that it does not limp and that its legs have the same dimensions. Then he sends it to rejoin the heap of dolls which already have their beautiful legs and are waiting for their arms. Here is a concrete representation of the myths of Prometheus, Pygmalion, Eden, of the Last Judgment, when the busts are looking for their respective legs. Each extremity of the limb is provided with its ball and hook, and as in the teachings of Eleates, the arms come to be joined to the shoulders, the hands to the wrists, the legs to the body: at the end of the workshop are piled the finished beings, which lack only heads. This lack is not sufficient to distinguish them from human beings.

"Push on the door; you are in the shoemaker's. There each doll, whatever her size, finds footgear for her feet. The vamps are cut out with a cutting machine of beautiful reddish-brown leather, then glued on the first sole which another covers, some stitchings with a machine imitates the sewed shoe. They are decorated with rosettes, ribbons, cockades, imitation buttons, and there come from the hands of the workwomen tiny ladies' boots, pumps, dance slippers of red and white satin, various modes and pictures of which adorn a panel of the wall and give varieties and sizes: there are some large enough for a child of six years.

"We shall pass through the blacksmith's shop where the tools are made, where machines are repaired, where slabs of copper are cut up, where lead is melted. It is the cave of Vulcan near the workshop of Prometheus. Here on the ground at the foot of the scissors machine, is a series of triangular shaped cuttings; they are supports for the ball of lead to which are attached in the head the eyes which close themselves when the doll is laid down so that she may sleep. A very bright hall is opened finally; it is the workshop of the hairdresser who makes curls. The dolls have magnificent wigs. You may have observed it. They are sometimes made of hair; these are then real wigs which are expensive. Others are made of Thibet (hair of the Thibetan goat.)

"Bales of Thibet are brought in small bundles. Small locks of this are rolled on wooden curling pins surrounded with paper and boiled, then dried in a closet heated by gaslight. When the curling pins come out of them the hair is at once curly and cannot be uncurled.

"They pass then to the stitchers who sew them in rows put close together on the skull caps of cloth with curls in front and plaits behind. That makes lovely wigs which are nailed on the skulls of the dolls whose occiputs are of cork, to aid this somewhat brutal method of fixing the hair on the head.

"Another door, open it: it is dazzling, a vast symphony in rose, which gives to the whole shop a delightful tinge of lilac in which the blouses of the women resemble great clusters of white lilacs. The whole wall is studded with little pegs and supports, fastened on their points are a whole army of rosy baby-dolls which are drying. It is the dressing in color of the dirty, soiled moldings. They are daubed with a beautiful salmon shade, they are painted, brightened up, gone over again with several successive coats until this tint of rosy flesh which distinguishes them is attained. They are stuck on the ends of sticks like Nisus and Euryale before the camp of Rutulus and wait until they are dry for pumicing. A bay window opens on the laboratory where big drums of varnish repose near buckets filled with fine glazed color like a sauce for shrimps.

"What objects, what equipment, accessories, inductions, operations, displays, people laboriously busy, and different shops, all for an unfortunate doll! Here a big machine is used to stamp only hands. All day long the piston goes in and out, and, at each blow, there falls a hand, a little veined hand, with nerves, joints, phalanges glistening with oil from the machines and of an ugly brown color. The little hands fill the baskets, dry on the ends of tiny sticks stuck on shelves, one would believe that he was passing through a horrible place of corporal punishment where hundreds of dwarfs might have passed under the grand executioner's ax.

"More pleasant is the sight of a linen room where some designs of dresses adorn the walls, among patterns in zinc and boxes of sewing machines. There are some embroidered chemisettes, dresses, hats with feathers. It is a very small meeting place for all the arts of women. Other workwomen are busy dressing these little ladies, combing their wigs, dividing the curls on their foreheads, drawing on their stockings, clasping the belts, fitting the necks and shoulders, stitching on the jewels, and assuring the new Galatea of her seal of a Parisian woman which is her mark of origin.

"In spite of so many operations, notice that our doll still has no head. Her neck is open with a gaping hole which lets the eye plunge into the intimate and black depths of her bust through which cords and wires pass.

"The making of the heads approaches an art. It is no longer the time when M. Leon de Laborde fretted and fumed against the ugly faces of papier mache. It seems that his protestations have been heard: they have ceased to be acceptable.

"We enter first the shops of sculpture and molding where artists sculpture in plaster faces of all sizes and expressions, and even small statues, exquisite groups of outline and finesse to which they consecrate spare moments, and which patrons give as gifts to influential men, as the state gives Sevres vases.

"Jumeau house,' writes M. Pean gayly, 'has succeeded not only in making its heads, but dressing them and decorating them in its factories.'

"Formerly, the manufacturer of dolls had recourse to specialists: he had only to put together the different parts going into the making of the doll and to look for markets for the sale of his work; today all that has changed; many do well in this way yet, but it is to the injury of the future of their house, for in order to do well and to succeed in selling much, it will be necessary to unite the whole factory.

"The model heads are molded and the print of these molds is taken with the help of a paste porcelain clay of a wonderful purity, filtered, strained, washed: The strainer in the last operation resembles a silk tissue. It is made to run through some taps into a mold which it fills. The walls retain a certain thickness which will be that of porcelain. The rest is emptied at the end of a few minutes into a trough.

"When this casting is finished, the heads come out of the molds, and are placed in the round trays of earth called Gazettes which are piled near with the tackles: these piles present the aspect of great trunks of shining trees. After baking, these white masks have the lightness, transparency and the fineness of grain of the most valuable porcelain.

"They pass then to the cutting out, which consists of making holes for the eyes which were left blank as in ordinary busts. Artificial eyes, the making of which we are going to be shown, are inserted into these holes.

"One enters a dark room, all hung with dark material, as at the photographers. Here and there blue flames shine and whistle loudly. They are the blowpipes. Each of the workwomen has her own; one notices only figures bent over and strangely lighted up by the jets of flame. Here is one of them who is beginning her eye; let us watch her make it. She delicately holds in each hand a frail stem of enamel, the two ends of which she plunges into the fire of her blast apparatus. With an agile movement of her fingers which recalls the Japanese busy eating rice with chopsticks she turns the stem which melts, spreads out, widens, and becomes round under the skillful direction of the other stick. With astonishing skill and agility, she plunges her work into the fire, draws it back, presents it again to the flame as she has need of a substance softer or more resistant. The ball is made round, is lengthened at the two corners, like an almond: there is the white eye. Then she picks up another stick of colored enamel, which she handles with sureness, which melts and sticks to the center of the pupil. There is the finished eye; it is a little miracle. The cornea is of bluish which resembles reality. The iris appears in the depths of the pupil through watery transparency which gives the illusion of a real eye.

"All these eyes are carried in baskets to the gluing shops. It is a question there of joining and sticking the corneas to the eyes. This operation allows quite numerous varieties and processes which differ with the price of the article for sale. There are set eyes, movable eyes, lifelike eyes, automatic eyes and some others, just as in the faces of people. The set eye is quite simply stuck to the inside against the wide open eyelids, and no longer moves. Other eyes are secured by systems of copper mounted on pivots and controlled by a stick that comes out at the bottom of the nape of the neck and which can be managed 'from outside' by a concealed button. The eye obeys the hand and makes the four movements permitted it by nature; it is raised toward the sky, it is lowered modestly or turns in a groove to the right—to the left. The eye with the reciprocating motion stays open when the doll is on her feet; closes as soon as the doll lies down, drawn by a counterbalance. Shall I say that these movements of the eye in the most general way are horrible to see, because they are atrociously imitated in spite of the most recent progress, the process most ordinarily used, consists of painting the upper part of the eyeball in flesh color; when the eye turns and is lowered the pupil disappears under the cheek and the visible part of the eye is then the tinted surface imitating the eyelid. This imitation was once made by a coat of color, which crumbled and gave the appearance of a scaly eye. Today, the painting is baked into the enamel and is unalterable. The effect is not much more successful and I reproach these dolls for having less the appearance of moving the eyelid than of turning the eye. They all caricature their ability, even the most perfect, I mean the dolls with the baked eye.

"These heads thus finished are covered with the freshest colors of youth, painted, daubed with rose; there are in the painting shop, workwomen who make eyelashes all their life, others eyebrows, others lips, others cheekbones. A certain practice and some sureness of hand is necessary, especially for the eyelashes, which are equal and parallel strokes. It appears that eyelashes are not so good when the workwoman is nervous, has a nervous headache, or has gone out the night before. How everything is linked together!

"What still remains? It is necessary to put the doll's head on her shoulders, supply her with a cork skull, to fasten the wig with little nails, dress her in a skirt, give her socks, shoes that will not come off, even to sleep. She no longer lacks anything except speech. Here is the shop where it is given her. They fix in her stomach a little whistle, one of the most ingenious types, with springs, a box for air, valves, a little apparatus for words. There is on a wall a pasteboard to which is sewn all the pieces which enter into the making of a whistle: one would say a swarm of locusts.

"Before going out one passes through the stores and shops where are piled up the gross material or half finished busts, arms, legs, eyes: it is a horror. One does not know in what obscure corner of the catacombs one finds oneself, or if it is not an annex of the ancient charnel house of the Innocents. The innocents are here well named, for one would believe he saw an ossuary of newly born children, greenish busts with holes for shoulders and groins, long lines of legs which seem moldy heaps of hands grown still, piles of amputated arms, in an offensive odor of dry glue and old rancid paper.

"In a corner of the yard, there are thrown in a heap the old plaster molds in which they have cast heads and which they can no longer use; it is an accumulation of white debris where still appears in the mold the design of the lines of the face, broken noses, eyes put out, cheeks shamefully scratched. These molds have given birth to heads which are now no one knows where,—in the closet for valuables, in the box for sweepings, or on the knees of a little girl who slaps her doll with blows of the fist to punish her.

"The mold is broken to pieces, the head is cracked, the factory smokes and works to make others: and one would believe he is seeing on a small scale the work of nature herself. She pushes toward the light, recruits ceaselessly renewed who are ignorant of their origin, their destiny who yield their places to others and are thrown into the rubbish holes where they find again the old whims and the old molds. It is sad, the manufacture of dolls with its feverish and tireless activities which is scarcely sufficient to cover the holes which the little demolishers make, a gloomy image of life which is restless agitation to repair the destruction of time and men. From the shop of the molding to the yard of waste, it seems one passes from the cradle to the grave."

Miss Abbott further comments that the Jumeau doll in her collection has no speaking voice, but that there are marks on each of the shoes and on the back of the head in French. The doll was supposedly brought to the United States in 1870 by a returning tourist. It had been made for home consumption, and bought in a shop in Paris. Another Jumeau in Miss Abbott's collection shows the wire arrangement inside as described in her article. There is a Jumeau doll, in facial expression like Miss Abbott's doll, but with two strings protruding from the waist which, when pulled, emit the voice sound, from an opening in the body. The head seems identical. The body is labeled 'Bebè Vrai Modele, Fabrication Jumeau', and the head is marked 'France-Paris'. The markings on Jumeau heads are readily discerned. Some read 'Deposé Tête Jumeau', some simply 'Tête Jumeau.' The expression on the faces of all these dolls is very French, and the eyes are exceptionally beautiful.

Mrs. Ruffin A. Smith of Birmingham, Alabama reports a Jumeau which came to U. S. A. in 1863 with a small trunk loaded with finery and a letter which read "Dear June—I am sending you this little doll from the Rue Salle au Compte. She was made by M. Jumeau a famous maker of dolls and dressed by girls who sew all day on clothes. She will arrive at Christmas so you must name her 'DECEMBRE'.

Decembre went through the firing lines of the Federal army, carried by her little mother on the day of the great battle of Lookout Mountain, during the war between the States. She also survived her own funeral performed by some pickaninnies. She was dug up, soiled but sound."

Mrs. Cyrus Beachy, of Wichita, Kansas reports that she has a glazed china head on china shoulders which is very like the early Jumeau. She suggests this theory . . . "It may be possible that the first Jumeau worked with the German doll makers. The clay in the early blonde bisque heads is definitely different in composition and workmanship from the pink bisque later known to be made in France." Mrs. Emma C. Clear states that she has seen "the moving Jumeau neck on Parians, and blond bisques, with hair ornaments typical of Dresden.

This was a Jumeau patent." She adds, "A ball jointed china head on china shoulders, I have never seen." Mrs. Greville Bathe comments, "I do not think the Jumeau heads were ever painted in Germany. These are French bisque heads of the 50's, and always, I think, had hair wigs." To quote 'L. C. S.' a staff member of the American Embassy at Paris (1939) "The ordinary china doll in biscuit, or dull china, was made in France in the early sixties, by one Gautier at Charenton near Paris. This factory was taken over by Mauger who moved it to Montreuil, near Charenton. The Jumeaus soon bought him out and the real doll industry was born in France. By 1914 the Jumeau works had been turned into a stock company, most of the stock being German owned. The Director was a German who fled to Switzerland and the factory was put under sequester as alien property." The *Gazette des Beaux Arts* says this, in an article printed September 7, 1914: "Before 1900 many French houses were unable to compete with Germany and so were absorbed by the *Jumeau Bebe* company which became a monopoly. One Ger-

Courtesy of Mrs. John L. Albright

Possible Jumeau Head on Automaton Doll

man house was even merged with them. They were the only dolls made entirely in France. The eyes were made of enamel and constructed with an iris, like in a real eye. The other companies depended on Germany for porcelain heads and glass eyes. The French doll makers lived poorly, from hand to mouth because the Germans could undersell them. The dolls, with natural heads in porcelain, were for the little girls who wished to dress them, comb their hair, wash their faces and care for them as if they were real children. After 1900 the German houses continued to increase and absorb all the trade. At Sonneberg, many houses were devoted to making dolls just to sell in France. They produced dolls carefully and the factories were better equipped and could produce cheap and expensive articles at the same time. The German workmanship was not imitated by others. After the war, there was more initiative in France."

Prior to the World War it is safe to conclude that La Societé Française des Bébès Jumeaux was the largest toy concern in France. In the French Patent books and the French catalogues studied there is no mention, nor any patents listed for Limoges, 1827-1880, other than the mention found and described under Doll Heads, of the firm of Dareval, at Limoges. For Jumeau, père, there were also no patent listings in these sources under the name 'dolls', although there were patents for other articles, such as the wheels of railway trains (1858), under the name Jumeau, address Saint Martin-en-Bierre. However on February 5, 1885, there is a patent noted, undoubtedly, for Jumeau, fils . . . 'pour des perfectionne à la construction des poupées et bébèes.' Another appeared March 21, 1887 for perfecting the movements of the eyes in doll heads.

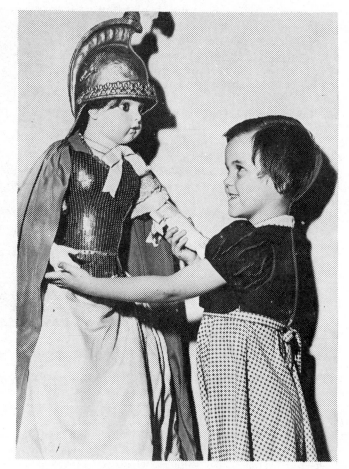

The City Museum of San Diego,
Courtesy. Goodwill Industries, and Olin Gillespie.

**This picture, which appeared in a San Diego, California newspaper,
Oct. 1, 1939, shows little Mary Lou Ferris inspecting Califia, a Jumeau
doll representing the seal of the State of California.**

It is known that both the Jumeau were active in the doll world and several
times mention has been made by doll collectors, that each Jumeau was granted
a patent. At the present time, it has not been possible to obtain further information from France, direct, to verify this statement. The sources available
here do not seem to have any notation of a patent for Jumeau, père. The
'jointed' doll is credited to Jumeau, fils. It seems safe to conclude that the
elder Jumeau made the jointed flexible heads, moving on bisque shoulders.
And that the full jointed bodies, with wires in the kid arms and legs that permitted life like positions, were by the younger Jumeau, and appeared a generation later.

"Mrs. Earle E. Andrews holding a French doll from her collection. Circa 1870-1880.
Fine all white kid body and hands, dressed in white taffeta trimmed
with red, and high red button boots and garters."

The City Museum of San Diego, Cal. has a most beautiful early Jumeau, called 'The Seal of San Diego.' This doll has the jointed head on bisque shoulders and is dressed in a coat of mail. A Parisian masterpiece, it was brought to San Diego in 1866 by Mrs. Phoebe Hearst and given to the Doll Fair being sponsored that year by the Rev. Henry E. Restarich, local Episcopalian rector who later became Bishop of Honolulu. The little girl who won the coveted prize, over fifty years ago, was Ella Juanita Levet, in whose memory the doll was presented to the children of the Fine Arts Gallery in Balboa Park.

One thing is paramount. And that is, that to Monsieur Jumeau must go most of the credit, for he stood first to preserve that 'cachet of elegance' that has always marked things '*made in France*', and it is to be hoped, will do so once again.

Antiques for December 1938 reports a fortune telling doll wearing billowy petticoats, each composed of individual sheets of paper with a printed prophecy. Another doll of this type, owned by Mrs. Everitt Morgan, of Marion, Ohio was also reported. "On the multi partite petticoat of heavy pink and green paper is written a maxim, or little fortune, in French which translates as follows 'Do not please yourself so often. Reflect before speaking. You will speak more to the point. Think with your heart as well as with your head.' This doll was bought in France and seems to have been popular during the mid-Victorian days in France. The doll is 12 inches, svelte of figure, is dressed in silk and lace and has a bisque head."

Toys and Novelties reports a French Doll of the 17th century now in the Newark Museum: "She wears a gold cloth dress trimmed with gold lace and pale pink roses in front. She has the now-fashionable wasp waist. Her head, hands, feet and body are of wood and she is nicely jointed. Her underwear is hand-made and of linen, and there are tiny buttonhole scallops on the ruffle of her petticoat —it must have taken weeks to make. All her clothes are beautifully hand-stitched. Her dress and petticoat are lined with paper, which is now crumbling but intact in spots. She wears white silk stockings with a blue cross-stitch design at the tops. She has red hair, restored (not the original wig). Her cheeks are delicately rouged and her eyebrows arched. There are holes punched for the nostrils, and her ears are pierced for earings. She wears gold slippers."

Mrs. Emil A. Riemenschneider of Milwaukee, Wis. tells of a wooden French Provincial doll in her collection, hand painted and very crude which was picked up in an out of the way place in Paris. The face is almost square.

THE LADY DOLL AND HER DRESSING:—From the standpoint of sheer artistry, the golden age of the doll was from 1860 to 1890. Here was no utilitarian object used to carry fashions for adults, no chubby lump of rubber for the squeezing of babies, but a true 'lady' doll conveying something of the magic of a fairy godmother to the fortunate child who possessed it. These grand dames were seldom treated as babies to be fed, fondled, or spanked as their little mothers willed. Rather they were dressed and undressed in imitation of the role which the little girl would enact as a grown up.

Chapter VII

ADDITIONAL DATA ON FRENCH AND ENGLISH DOLL HEADS

(Limoges - Jumeau - Boltz - Masse ́- Sevres
World War English Pottery Heads)

Courtesy Toys Novelties Magazine
(Newark N. J. Museum)

"French Doll Circa 1870. Does not have the Jumeau mark on the back of the head. Wears a green and black striped silk gown. In the traveling bag are toilet articles that match the gown. The wardrobe includes hats, blue and cotton dress, a dressing gown, under-wear, fans, combs, hair pins, watches, jewelry and gold coins."

TWO efforts show the beginning of the French renaissance in dolls. In August, 1914, Mmé. la Baronne de Laumont designed some dolls and a few months later *L'Association des Petits Fabricants* urged the porcelain makers to fashion bisque doll heads immediately. Six months later Damerval and Laffranchy were in operation. Limoges and Boulogne-sur-Mer followed. Perhaps the doll was made in the city of Limoges, and obtained the name from the locality, rather than from the more important china factory. But a doll marked Limoges does exist, on the head of which is the mark "Fabrication Française Limoges." On the shoulders of this model is the name 'Cherie 1.' Mrs. Emma C. Clear reports that she has seen other dolls marked Limoges; that they date about 1880-1890. Mrs. Izole Dorgan dates Limoges dolls 1890-1910. What factory made these dolls is the question. Mrs. Clear writes that she has seen both the shoulder and the jointed heads, but never a doll with the original wig, or with any mark save that of the potter.

The Jumeau doll head seems to be more like the finest of the German bisques, but the Limoges is different, being quite coarse. A query to the present representative of Limoges china in New York City, brought this reply "I beg to inform you that the Ancienne Fabrique Royale Limoges, France, of which I am a representative, never manufactured doll heads and I really do not know who did these heads . . . "

Before the war, nearly all dolls heads and enameled eyes used were purchased by the French from Germany. Since 1914, they have been made in France at Limoges, Boulogne-sur-Mer and in the suburbs of Paris. The French doll factories were situated near cities, where living was expensive. The German doll factories, located in remote districts, were able to keep their costs of operation low, and to employ peasant, instead of city labor. Therefore the French industry remained small and limited, except for the luxury class of toys due to the French lack of capital, and lack of ability to meet keen foreign competition. But, regardless, the French did make doll heads, not only of wax but of wood, porcelain china, bisque, parian and papier maché. Mrs. William Bender, of New York City, reports a most interesting doll, with a mark on the inside of the shoulders reading "Patent Boltz-Massé." This doll is known to have an elaborate trade mark, of a palette and mall stick, although Mrs. Bender does not mention that the trade mark is on her specimen. The Boltz-Massé doll, put out by a French firm, was also made in papier maché models, from the same mold as the one used for Parian heads. Mrs. Bender's doll has brown hair with a black comb, blue eyes and a lovely expressive face. She came originally from a little town in New Hampshire, circa 1850-1860. Records up to 1897, and from 1901-1914 give nothing whatsoever on the Boltz-Massé doll. Mrs. Dorgan reports that the texture of this doll is finer than the Jumeau.

Collection Janet P. Johl

NTI HANCOCK GIRL World War Doll. Supposedly American attempt at bisque. Marking on head "NTI Hancock Girl."

French Doll. Circa 1914-1918. Marked "Fabrication Française Limoges. Cherie I."

French made Doll. Pre World War Period.

The French used cork to put the hair wigs on the doll head. The porcelain head was hollowed out and the hole at the top served as the place into which the cork was fitted, and to which the wig was glued. Often the French doll head had a bend in the neck, and the back of the head, instead of the top, was hollowed out to receive the cork covering. The head being open all the way to the neck made it possible for the insertion, at the base of the neck, of the mechanism which, attached to the bust, permitted the head to move in all directions.

In commenting on the French dolls, Mrs. Catherine Richards Howard says: "Undoubtedly they made very beautiful doll heads. Is it not more than probable that the factories which made exquisite figurines may have devoted at least a part of their time to equally lovely doll heads? I have one that SEEMS to be Sevres; the hair dress is distinctive, the features definitely French. Hand modeled, it has glaze and texture altogether different from any other I have ever seen."

This is a most interesting suggestion and yet a paragraph from a memorandum on 'Porcelain Dolls Heads in France' prepared by L. C. S., a staff member of the Embassy of the United States in Paris, upsets the apple cart. To quote:

"No dolls were ever made at Sevres. They made figurines groups, and boxes, umbrella handles in both glazed china and biscuit. The Sevres biscuits are famous the world over and are enormously expensive . . . far too much to be used for dolls heads. In 1915 there was a movement to make artistic dolls heads in France and the project was submitted to Sevres. They made casts of some of their famous busts and these were sent to two factories, both of which are now out of existence. Some heads were made from the Sevres models and models from artists. The daughter of a Cabinet Minister centralized the work, the idea being to help artists not called to the colors. The dolls were dressed by the greatest Parisian dressmakers and were sent, with other artistic treasures, in a ship all over the world as propaganda. This was the first time that glazed porcelain doll heads were made at Sevres."

Mrs. Izole Dorgan reports an article about dolls in the *Gazette des Beaux Arts*. "Although the article spoke of *en biscuit*, and not doll heads," Mrs. Dorgan comments, "It seems safe to believe that the reference was to doll heads. Mention was made of models created by a certain Madame Noufflard and it was suggested that Sevres adopt her sculptures of dolls to their financial advantage. BUT not a word that Sevres had ever contemplated making any doll heads."

However, this article appears but a month after the outbreak of the World War so it is very possible that the information obtained by L. C. S. of the Embassy Office may be taken as fact. As to Sevres Doll Heads, prior to that period, it would seem that only one conclusion may be drawn . . . There were NONE.

This French Propaganda use of the doll during the World War had its counterpart in England. Even the Museums and the Potters will admit that much during the war period, dolls were made at the Potteries for purely patriotic reasons. Unfortunately not many of these dolls are available for study.

Mrs. S. Camille Tenney of New Haven, Conn., has a doll marked "NTI BOY ENGLISH" which she purchased in Wylie's China Shop in 1916, in New Haven. This head came from the English potters, from Wedgwood, and was designed for the express purpose of raising money for the English soldiers fund . . . there were about four or five of these china head dolls in the shop at that time, and they were quite expensive. The doll is fourteen inches high, with a typical little English face, large lips painted on a soft cream bisque, small blue eyes set in the bisque and red brown hair. The body is of rough plaster. In fact the doll is quite crude, the head fitting into a cheap type of body of paper pulp, or some such material. However it is quite unlike any of the earlier dolls made in Germany, of bisque or china, with a much softer coloring. It has the NTI mark similar to the "NTI Hancock Girl" of supposed American origin. Here are excerpts from letters from the English firms, themselves.

From the Chad Valley Works, Harborne, Birmingham. "During the World War Period the earthenware people in the Potteries in England made the pot heads with a certain degree of success but when the war was over they dropped them for some reason or other. They are an independent race of people and the pot head trade went back to Germany."

From W. J. Marshall's Toy Shop, London. "It is not correct to say that the dolls heads were never made in The Potteries; During the latter part of the last war, dolls heads were made by one of the leading Pottery firms at Stokes, but although there were a lot put out on the market, they were not altogether a success."

From Merrythought, LTD., Merrythought Works, Dale End, Iron Bridge. "In the first place it can be considered that no practical manufacture of dolls was taking place in England prior to 1914. China heads were certainly not English prior to 1914 . . . these were Continental. Pot or china heads were definitely made at Staffordshire during the War and also here at Iron Bridge and Broseley, district of Shropshire, possibly in one or two other parts of England. They were not up to the quality, finish or design of the pre-continental supplies but they improved, and by 1920 were really quite good. Within two years after the War, continental supplies became available again and for some years following pot heads practically ceased to be made in England and supplies reverted to coming from Germany again."

Notice the use of the words 'continental'—'reverted,—and "again."

A letter to Joseph Wedgwood & Sons Inc., at their New York City address, brought this reply:

"Replying to your recent letter we are sorry that our Factory no longer makes doll heads and we feel quite sure that none of these are available. Since we do not know of any firm making dolls' heads we would suggest that you write to the Pottery Gazette and Glass Trade Review, Stoke-on-Trent, North Staffordshire, England, who will perhaps be able to throw some light on the matter." Signed Hensleigh C. Wedgwood, Vice Pres.

From the *Pottery Gazette and Glass Trade Review* came this answer to the same old inquiry:

"In reply to your letter of the 25th inst. we very much regret that we have no information available on the subject of dolls heads. So far as we know very few were made in the Staffordshire Potteries before the Great War and never in commercial quantities. During the War several firms did commence making them but afterwards the trade all went back to Central Europe. We believe that some of the higher grade potters have made one or two specimens from time to time but we have no record of them."

The research was becoming repetitious but there were still a few more sources that might uncover something more definite on the pre-war making of china dolls heads.

A letter to Tiffany & Co., of New York City, brought this result:

"We are able to help only a little in the matter of the china dolls' heads. We have learned by inquiry that during the World War, 25 years ago, when the German manufacture was interrupted, it was taken up by some English Potteries simply to provide work for some who needed it and could make these articles successfully. We have learned that these

TRADE MARK
Trade mark on Mrs. Tenney's World War
Wedgwood Doll

are now being made in earthenware, but not in fine china, by the New Chelsea Porcelain Co., Stoke On Trent, England. We never had any of the heads here and cannot recall even seeing them."

Notice "When the German Manufacture of these heads was interrupted."

Plummer, Ltd. received the next inquiry and this was their answer: "We wish to say that the dolls to which we presume you refer were made by disabled soldiers during the World War and we sold them for charitable return. We have no more left but if you will write to Meakin and Ridgway, the agents for the dolls at the time, they probably could give you all the information you desire."

From Meakin & Ridgway came another lead: "We believe that the 'Chelsea' china heads were supplied by the New Chelsea Porcelain Co. Ltd. Stoke-on-Trent, England, but of course we are not quite sure. Nor do we know if the dolls used by the Potteries in 1915 for charitable purposes are still available."

A last letter of hopeful requests for information went forth to the New Chelsea Porcelain Co. Ltd. Here is what they replied:

"We are sorry to say that we are not manufacturers of Dolls Heads. We do not make an earthenware body and have never at any time, made these items. It is just possible that the 'Chelsea' heads were made by the original Chelsea works which was in London, not Staffordshire, but since this firm is out of existence we do not think any such articles have been made in this country. Several continental firms, Czecho Slovakian and Japanese, have definitely made this line."

That the Japanese made interesting china heads is easily proven by study of a doll which could readily pass for German, if it were not for the marking 'Japan.' The high blonde head dress and the swivel neck make a very interesting china head, a very well executed "steal" from the continent.

So, here we are, back where we began, except that now it is an established fact that the Potteries *did* make doll heads during the World War period. Prior to that time, the mystery shrouding English china head dolls still persists.

"Doll collectors seem to have made up a nomenclature that is not in conformity with china designations," says Mrs. Izole Dorgan. "The Chelsea, Staffordshire doll, etc., is disowned in England but runs rampant here. There is no reason to believe that individual potters did not make up odd things for their families BUT, if the English Museums do not vouch for them, they cannot be given much weight."

It would all seem to lead back to the conclusion made by Mrs. Greville Bathe that "all fine old china heads came from Germany and France."

The collectors themselves certainly have confessed to a certain degree of ignorance about the origin of these dolls heads as manifested by comments made. To quote: "I think it is very hard to get the truth about old dolls. So many people insist they are so and so, and you know absolutely they are not."

Yes, but do you know what they *ARE*?

Another collector remarks, with determination: "I do not have any dolls less than 50 years old, and I never take one that is marked Germany."

An interesting comment but not a very illuminating one for dolls did not have to be marked prior to 1890, for entrance into this country.

Many seem to take it for granted that a doll is a Staffordshire or a Chelsea, with no real study or analysis. This same may be said of the French, Parian and Dresdens . . . and others. The true student of the doll wants something more accurate than instinct. Hands trained to know old china by touch, are of help, but they cannot be taken as authoritative evidence, without additional study. This much can be said. In all the many books and magazines, the catalogues, lists and pamphlets which have been read on this intriguing subject, NOT ONCE has there been found a mention of English china doll heads, earlier than those of the World War Period in England, (circa 1914-1918).

Here then is indeed a subject worthy of further research, and study. Perhaps some day a chemically minded doll enthusiast will analyze the various porcelains and chinas and give the world the real answers. Until then the matter must rest.

Chapter VIII

AMERICAN WOODEN DOLLS

*(Ellis, Sanders, Martin, Johnson,
Mason & Taylor, Shoenhut)*

Courtesy Maude Eunice Willand
Photo by Charles C. Willand

Joel Ellis Doll. Chair dates from 1805, said to have been obtained from a descendant of John Quincy Adams. Collection Maude Eunice Willand.

It has already been noted that the oldest dolls were often rough unpainted wood and that at a very early date they were manufactured at Sonneberg, Germany. England made some disproportionate dolls of wood that are equally interesting. Queen Anne's Doll House, preserved in the Victoria and Albert Museum in London, has wooden jointed dolls, with real hair. The faces are painted with flesh colored enamel, as are the hands and feet. It has been reported that there is an English Pre-Anne, 'Annie', in a collection in New York City. A Queen Anne doll, circa 1740, eighteen inches tall was recently exhibited by Mrs. Velvalee Dickinson in New York City. Very often these dolls have hands of bamboo. Records also tell of a sturdy oaken doll, said to have been purchased in Boston, Mass. in December, 1773 which had been brought originally from England, to the colonies. Miss Eleanor Bumgardner of Washington, D. C. has one of the rare Queen Anne dolls.

Courtesy J. Gerry and Mrs. Imogene Anderson
The one and only 'Letitia Penn.'

One writer of Americana believes that crude objects resembling dolls were the first types to reach these shores. However *American Made Dolls & Figurines* notes that the late Dr. Walter Hough, Head Curator of Anthropology at the Smithsonian Institution, had this to say in regard to the first doll to come to these shores from Europe, in '*The Story of Dolls Tells the Story of Mankind*'. To quote:

"The first doll that ever came to America was given to a little Virginia Indian girl in 1607 by someone belonging to the expedition of Sir Walter Raleigh, commanded by the redoubtable Captain John Smith. It is fortunate that John White, the artist of the expedition, recorded this event in one of his pictures, giving us some inkling of the joy of the dusky little maid over her Elizabethan doll with its stiff ruff. The quaint old book which describes the Indians of Virginia in 1607 says of the little girls: 'They are greatlye Dilighted with pupetts and babes which wear broughte oute of England' ''.

A copy of the original painting is in the *Smithsonian Institution* at Washington, D. C.

A doll often called the oldest doll in America was originally in the collection of Mrs. Izole Dorgan of New York City. Mrs. Dorgan obtained the doll after she, and Mrs. Imogene Anderson had read about it in an old book on dolls. Mrs. Dorgan promised to pass the doll on to Mrs. Anderson if she ever parted with it, and now it is in the Imogene Anderson collection of Early American Dolls at Greenwich, Conn. Known as 'Letitia Penn' this doll was brought from England in 1699 by William Penn for a friend of his little daughter. Letitia Penn is twenty inches high, and wears a full court dress of the period, made of striped brocade and velvet. The full skirt is stretched by crinoline. It has been said that this doll once belonged to Dr. Mahlon-Kirk of Maryland who lived on a grant of land given by Queen Anne.

These few early dolls, brought from Europe to the more wealthy members of the American colony in Virginia, do not really represent the early colonial dolls, which were not dressed in elegant European fashions but were very plain and often crude. Many of them were, of necessity, home made, whittled from pine or maple wood in the long, cold winter evenings. An object as homely as the commonplace potato masher was converted into a doll with candlewick arms, and no legs. Many of these dolls were pegged, so that the joints moved, enabling arms and legs to assume more natural, if stiff positions. Sometimes they were quite flat, carved from just one piece, as in the case of the 'Gingerbread Doll'.

In the "Subject matter Index of Patents for Inventions Issued by the U. S. Patent Office from 1790 to 1873, inclusive, V. I. Washington Government Printing Office, 1874," there is found on Page 445 the name of J. A. H. Ellis of Springfield, Vermont, applying for a patent of a, 'Doll-Joint', May 20, 1873, Patent #139,130. There is also reference to Joel A. H. Ellis in *"The History of the Town of Springfield, Vermont"* by C. H. Hubbard and Justus Dartt, Boston, Geo. H. Walker Co., 1895, page 132.

In 1856, at the age of 26 years, Joel Addison Hartley Ellis of Springfield, Vermont, formed a partnership with D. H. Smith, Hamlim Whitmore, H. H. Mason and Albert Brown to engage in the manufacture of a patent farm basket, in the brick shop standing just above the lower bridge. This venture proved unsuccessful and the firm went into the making of children's cabs. These sold slowly and the cost of manufacture was greater than had been anticipated. But these first toy carts, offered to the market, led to the formation of a new company, in 1858, with a capital of about $1000. In five years the business outgrew the brick workshop, and violin and guitar cases, the first ever made in the United

States, were added to the line. One hundred and twenty-five hands were employed and the sales soon grew to $100,000 a year. In 1869 a great flood swept away factory, stock, and machinery. Undefeated, still another company was formed, with J. A. H. Ellis as treasurer. It was known as the Vermont Novelty Works. On Feb. 21, 1873 Mr. Ellis filed application for a patent for doll joints.

UNITED STATES PATENT OFFICE.

JOEL A. H. ELLIS, OF SPRINGFIELD, VERMONT, ASSIGNOR TO THE "CO-OPERATIVE MANUFACTURING COMPANY," OF SAME PLACE.

IMPROVEMENT IN DOLL-JOINTS.

Specification forming part of Letters Patent No. **139,130**, dated May 20, 1873; application filed February 21, 1873.

To all whom it may concern:

Be it known that I, JOEL A. H. ELLIS, of Springfield, in the county of Windsor and State of Vermont, have invented new Improved Doll-Joints, of which the following is a specification:

This invention relates to the manufacture of dolls, and to the class of dolls which are usually made of wood, with joints for the legs and arms; and it consists in the manner of forming the joints and securing the requisite friction thereto.

In the accompanying drawing, Figure 1 represents a doll-body with the joints constructed according to my invention. Fig. 2 is a leg detached, giving a front view of the joint. Fig. 3 represents the mode of connecting the arms with the shoulders. Fig. 4 is an end view of the arm-pivot.

Similar letters of reference indicate corresponding parts.

In the manufacture of dolls it is important to secure sufficient friction at the joints of the limbs and body in any desired position, so that the doll may stand erect or in an inclined position, or be supported on its head by the arms.

This friction I obtain by means of a slot, A, and tenon B, fastened together by the pivot-pin C. The tenon B is divided by a saw-kerf, D. The double tenon is designed to fit the slot a little full, and the double tenon be sprung together slightly, when the tenon enters the slot, thus producing the requisite friction, and preventing any bind or looseness by the shrinking and swelling of the wood at any time. E is the soulder-piece, which is cut or slit at right angles, as seen in Fig. 4, and fitted into a round socket, G, having a groove, F, to receive a pin, so that the arm will be securely held, while it will freely revolve. The socket is a little smaller at the back end, so that the shoulder-piece is compressed, as represented, which secures at this point the required degree of friction. The arm is attached to the shoulder-piece in the manner already described.

The tendency of the two parts of the tenon to spread when compressed in the slot is constant, and compensates for wear, and affords the necessary friction.

Having thus described my invention, I claim as new and desire to secure by Letters Patent—

A doll-joint constructed and formed substantially as shown and described—that is, with the slot A and tenon B, the latter having the saw-kerf D, as set forth.

JOEL A. H. ELLIS.

Witnesses:
ALBERT BROWN,
ADIN H. WHITMORE.

The heads and bodies of the Joel Ellis dolls were of green rock maple, hard wood steamed until softened, the heads compressed in a hydraulic press and the bodies turned on a lathe. Mrs. Izole Dorgan, who has seen and handled many of these dolls, feels that the Ellis patent was not practical as a doll.

The upper part or top end of the arm 6, fitting into the socket of the shoulder s, is held in position by means of an elastic or spiral spring passing transversely through the top of the trunk r from shoulder to shoulder, and thus uniting the ball-tops of the arms, and holding the same firmly in the shoulder-sockets, so that the arms may be operated in any position.

The hip-joint is formed by first turning the upper end of the leg or thigh ball-shaped; then cut and remove one half of the globular part, so that it leaves a flat face to fit into a circular recess in the lower part of the body, having an internal circular flat surface to receive the corresponding flat surface of the ball-joint. The leg is secured to the body by means of a screw, n, or otherwise, that will allow the limb to move freely backward and forward.

The elbow and knee joints 1 2 3 4 are formed of half-sections of a ball or globe, one half of which forms a part of the upper section, d, or the limb, and the other half of said ball constitutes a part of the lower section, d¹, of the arm or leg, so arranged that the two flat faces of the sections of the ball-joints are secured together by rivets, or otherwise, passing through the several joints of the doll, and operating in separate concave alternate recesses opposite to each of the revolving half-globes, to hold the same in position when operating upon the rivets V.

The neck and waist of the doll may be jointed in a similar manner to the limbs, if thought best.

Fig. 2 shows the manner of uniting the arms by the application of an india-rubber or spiral spring, H¹, secured to the shank S and hook-shank H, which form a part of the disks b b, let into the top of the arms, as shown in dotted lines at b, also shown at b, Fig. 1.

Having described the individual parts of my improved invention, I will next state what I believe to be its novel properties, to wit: First constructing the joints in the form of a globe or ball; then dividing said globes into half-sections and fitting the same to corresponding sections in the other parts of the limb or body, so as to form a joint closely resembling the contour of the human joints.

What I claim as new, and desire to protect by Letters Patent of the United States, is—

A doll having its jointed portions formed with half-sections of a globe or ball pivoted together, and having concave recesses formed opposite said half-sections, all constructed and arranged in the manner and for the purpose set forth.

In testimony whereof I hereunto subscribe my name in the presence of two witnesses.

FRANK D. MARTIN.

Witnesses:
J. W. HASTINGS,
SAML W. PORTER.

UNITED STATES PATENT OFFICE.

HENRY H. MASON AND LUKE W. TAYLOR, OF SPRINGFIELD, VERMONT.

CONSTRUCTION OF DOLLS.

Specification forming part of Letters Patent No. 242,210, dated May 31, 1881.
Application filed January 5, 1881. (No model.)

To all whom it may concern:

Be it known that we, HENRY H. MASON and LUKE W. TAYLOR, of Springfield, in the county of Windsor and State of Vermont, have invented a new and useful Improvement in the Construction of Dolls; and I do hereby declare that the following is a full, clear, and exact description of the same, reference being had to the accompanying drawings, making part of this specification.

This invention is in the nature of an improvement in the construction of dolls; and the invention consists in a composition head for a doll provided with a device of wood or other suitable material, which forms the neck of the doll and fixes the head to the body and permits the head to revolve.

In the accompanying sheet of drawings, Figure 1 represents a section through the head and shoulders of a doll constructed with our improvements; Fig. 2, a cross-section of our doll through the line x x, Fig. 1, and Fig. 3 a detail view of our device for connecting the head and body together.

Having thus described our invention, what we claim as new, and desire to secure by Letters Patent, is—

1. A device for uniting the head of a doll to the body thereof, constructed with a flange, which forms the neck of the doll, and a bearing for the head on the body and a groove, in combination with a pin, whereby the head is fixed to the body and permitted to turn thereon, substantially as and for the purpose described.

2. In a device for uniting the head of a doll to its body, an opening, e, for the admission of air to dry the interior of the head, substantially as described.

3. In a device for uniting the head of a doll to its body, a head, b, groove a. flange B, groove d, and opening e, substantially as and for the purpose described.

HENRY H. MASON.
LUKE W. TAYLOR.

Witnesses:
JEROME W. PIERCE,
J. W. HASTINGS.

Another famous American doll, a wooden doll called 'The tops of all American dolls, with the finest body ever put on a doll' is "The Schoenhut All Wood Perfection Doll."

In 1872 the A. Schoenhut Co. was established by Albert Schoenhut. At first this company made only toys and toy pianos. Then on July 3, 1909, application for a patent for a 'jointed figure' was filed. In 1911 the doll appeared, with patented steel spring hinges and swivel joints. An entire doll of wood, with no rubber to wear out the joints, and no rubber cord used in the jointing.

George W. Schoenhut of Schoenhut Incorporated, Philadelphia, Penn., was kind enough to give the story behind this doll, and here it is, quoted from his letter.

"The Schoenhut All Wood Art doll for which you recently inquired, was manufactured by the A. Schoenhut Company which went out of business in 1935. At present the dolls are not being manufactured by any agency whatever.

"The information behind the doll is that its construction was the brainchild of Albert Schoenhut, who was a member of a long line of toy making families in Germany, and came to America in the neighborhood of 1865, and invented the 'Schoenhut Toy Piano' which is still sold to-day.

"The principal feature of the Doll was the unbreakable nature of the parts and the indestructible metal joints. The joints were so mounted that the springs in them would compress if they were pulled rather than stretched. This made the life of the doll almost endless.

"After his original concept of the doll's construction Albert Schoenhut employed Italian sculptors to mould the faces for the dolls. They were first introduced circa 1907. At this time they sold at prices ranging from $5 to $25, depending upon the type of costume, and the size of the doll.

"After a life time of toy making Albert Schoenhut considered the doll to be his masterpiece, of which he was even more proud than his toy piano. So much was this true that his fifth son, Harry E. Schoenhut, who had a definite artistic nature, studied sculpture under the famous American portrait sculptor Charles Grafley, and later modeled all the heads which were used on the dolls.

"As the market for these dolls spread, they included such novelties as the bowed legs and large head of a very young baby up to a model of a child of perhaps 10 years. Although Albert Schoenhut died in 1912 the sale of the dolls continued and spread until the end of the World War when America was flooded with low-priced German dolls. The Schoenhut Doll just about held its own in the face of this competition but finally was put out of the running by the importations of Japanese merchandise which followed in the wake of the German flood of 1921. It gradually became unprofitable to manufacture them even for the very definite prestige value which they had. Consequently the manufacture was abandoned circa 1924. This is, in general, the broad history of the Schoenhut doll.''

Through the generosity of Mrs. Emma C. Clear, who loaned a unique and valuable copy of the Schoenhut Instruction Book, even more information of these fine dolls was made available. To quote from the catalogue '' 'The first American Perfection Art Doll' . . . no more loose joints—never needs restripg-ing and no broken heads. The doll is made entirely of wood, even the head is solid wood. The hands and feet are of hardwood painted in enamel oil colors, so that the doll may be washed with a fine sponge, or soft cloth. Two holes in the soles of the foot receive part of the metal stand that goes with each doll. None of the original stands seem to have survived. All parts are held tightly together . . all joints are very flexible, move smoothly, and will stay in any correct position in which the doll is placed. There are even wrist and ankle

Copyright 1912 by A. Schoenhut Co.

A sketch showing the Schoenhut Trade Mark

joints.'' Schoenhut dolls listed in this catalogue were:

(1) The regular baby doll made in four sizes, 14, 16, 19 and 21 inches.
(2) The infant, made in three sizes, 11, 14 and 17 inches.
(3) The infant with natural arms, in two sizes, 13 and 15 inches.

All the dolls wore trade mark buttons.

This Schoenhut doll of which the American doll industry is justly proud, is a real work of art. The Schoenhut head, with the sleeping eyes, is a marvel of workmanship. Even the eyes are made of wood. The peasant type face is very beautiful and is found on the dolls that have the carved wooden hair. These have become quite scarce. The ball Schoenhut doll heads were carved out of a solid block of wood, the little dolls also from a solid block. The head was hollowed out, the eyelids carved to a feather edge, and the eye balls inserted with only a cardboard to hold them, the eyes were of wood, and painted.

Mrs. Clear adds one more interesting item to this intensely interesting doll. These Schoenhut dolls are often spoken of as 'hand carved.' They were not. They were carved on a multiple machine, a carving machine, with cut-ters similar to dental tools, following a master mold, cutting into the solid blocks of wood. It was one of Mr. Schoenhut's sons who gave Mrs. Clear this information when he was introducing the dolls to the trade in 1911.

1. Group of Early Wooden Dolls. Queen Anne, Sanders after Ellis, Joel Ellis, Potatoe masher with candlewick arms, Gingerbread Doll from Lebanon, Penn.—Collection Janet J. Johl. 2. Wooden Dolls. Circa 1833—Collection Maude Eunice Willand. Photo by Charles G. Willand. 3. Goodie Plummer. Circa 1874—Collection Mrs. Nina B. Shepard. Ten inches tall, all wood with pewter hands and feet, black hair, curls wide and up and down. Dress of brick red calico, original, trimmed with tiny rick-rack. 4. A Doll similar to the Joel Ellis, Circa 1850—Collection Mrs. Nina B. Shepard. 5. Large wooden doll, 22 inches, Paper mache head—Collection Mrs. Florence Wadsworth. 6. Early American Wooden Doll—Collection Janet P. Johl. 7. All wood, peg joints, 16 inches. Netherlands Circa 1780. Blue glass eyes set in plaster—Collection Mrs. Nina B. Shepard.

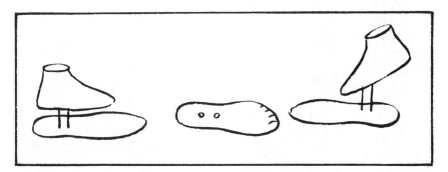

This doll body, cut in half, illustrates the inner construction and shows the steel spring hinges and swivel connections. One hole is put in straight to hold the foot in arresting position, flat. The other is oblique to hold the foot in tip toe position. Stockings and shoes had holes in the soles to correspond with those in the feet.

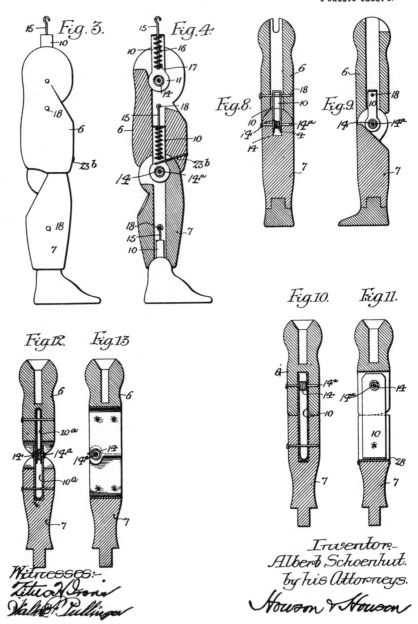

A. SCHOENHUT.
JOINTED FIGURE.
APPLICATION FILED JULY 3, 1909.

982,096.

Patented Jan. 17, 1911.

2 SHEETS—SHEET 2.

A. SCHOENHUT.

JOINTED FIGURE.

APPLICATION FILED JULY 3, 1909.

982,096.

Patented Jan. 17, 1911.

2 SHEETS—SHEET 1.

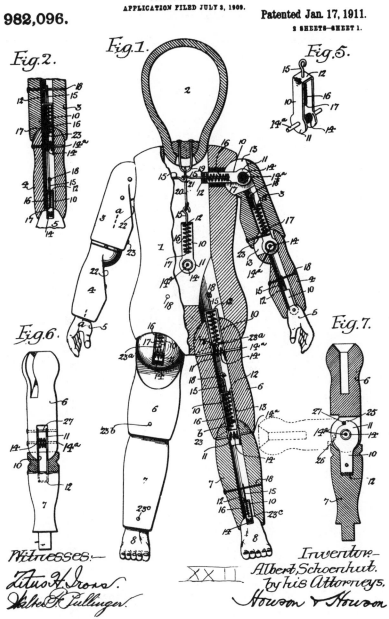

Fig.1.

Fig.2.

Fig.5.

Fig.6.

Fig.7.

Witnesses:—

Titus H. Irons.

Walter R. Pullinger.

XXII

Inventor—

Albert Schoenhut.

by his Attorneys,

Howson & Howson.

(No Model.)

H. H. MASON & L. W. TAYLOR.
Construction of Dolls.

No. 242,210.   Patented May 31, 1881.

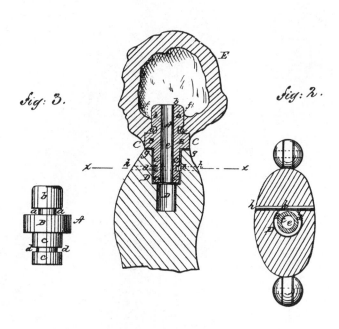

Fig: 1.

Fig: 3.   Fig: 2.

Witnesses.   Inventors:
Chas Nida   Henry H. Mason
H. Wattenberg   by Luke W. Taylor

Chapter IX

Courtesy of Helen Siebold Walter

Papier Maché Dolls with unique Hairdress. Probably German. Circa 1830.

OTHER TYPES OF EARLY DOLL HEADS

(Papier Maché, Gutta Percha, Wax, Wax over Composition)

IN 1484 a wood cut appeared in a volume dealing with medical subjects, which showed a doll maker standing beside a table on which were a number of wooden doll heads. It is known that at Nürnberg, Germany, dolls were made of wood at an early date, and that wooden dolls also came out of England with

81

disproportionately large heads. In France, the style advertisers, the fashion dolls, were often carved from wood, or molded from alabaster, or earthenware. Across the ocean in the new world, the settlers whittled crude dolls from wood for their children. It was not until the nineteenth century that doll heads of wood were supplanted, first by china, or porcelain, then by papier maché, by wax, and lastly by still finer porcelain and bisque. Of course, the use of wax for effigies and figures was known from a very early date and some of the first doll heads were of wax, although the number was comparatively small.

The invention of papier maché, in 1810, revolutionized the doll industry. In 1700 a Mr. Watson of Birmingham, England, was carrying on a papier maché business, and in 1772 a japanner named Henry Clay invented a heat resisting material suitable for japanning. The body of this material was produced by pasting sheets of paper together, one upon the other, over a metal mold, until the desired thickness was obtained. The mold was then removed. This process was known as paper ware in England until 1825, when the term papier-maché was applied. The word papier-maché means literally 'chewed paper,' in the French. For the more common uses, it is made from waste paper, ground to a pulp, after which it is mixed with glue or paste. In many cases ground chalk, clay and fine sand are added, with the result that the finished product is little more than a plaster, bound with a fibre pulp. When the mixture is dried in a mold, under pressure, the product is tough and plastic, and somewhat resembles wood. Papier maché is put to many uses, one of which is the making of doll heads.

Papier maché was first discovered, it is believed, in either Italy or France but it was used, definitely, in Sonneberg, Germany in 1810. The first papier maché doll heads, cast from sulphur molds were clumsy and crude but soon the new material gave evidence of the possibility of obtaining a more life-like expression for the doll. Crude caricature effects had been the result of trials to make doll heads from leather, in 1827, but it was soon found that heads from papier-maché could be made which produced a natural, human expression. When cheeks were tinted rose, and eyes were blue or brown, a most life like doll head resulted. Hair, colored black, and arranged in the fashion of the period could also be achieved successfully.

A not uncommon type of Papier Maché Head. Circa 1860. Probably German.

In 1850 a flesh colored model appeared in Germany, a baby doll known as 'Gelenktäufling.' The papier-maché dolls of 1830-1850 with papier maché hair, in elaborate detail, were the first real fashion dolls of later vintage. By the time of the Great Exhibition in 1855, lovely doll heads were on the market, practical substitutes for the china heads, which led eventually to the modern dolls of composition, an outgrowth of the papier-maché idea.

The composition head of gutta percha first made by Mlle. Calixto Huret, followed papier maché, and the rubber doll put in its initial appearance almost immediately after.

The papier maché, or composition, heads made in Europe, found their way to America, unmarked, so that the origin of many, is therefore, difficult to ascertain. Unending research, for instance, has not brought to light the background of a doll head, of composition, clearly marked SUPERIOR and with the number 1214 on the label. There is no listing for this doll in either the American or the English patent records. Yet it is not uncommon. A doll, circa 1850-1860, would not of necessity, bear a label, if it were continental. Mrs. Clear writes, "The 'Super-

Courtesy Mrs. Izole Dorgan

Front view of a Papier Maché Doll. German origin. Circa 1830-1840. 33½ inches high.

ior' still remains an X doll." She reports a very beautiful papier maché, circa 1855, with fine, classical features, which she believes is an imported head. Mrs. Estella Graham of Long Beach, Cal., writes of a most unusual papier maché doll head in her collection, with blonde curls all over the head and a round full face.

The first doll head patented in the United States, according to the records of the patent office, was the now famous Greiner, Patent #19,770, dated March 30, 1858, for an 'improvement in constructing doll heads.' It is very possible that Ludwig Greiner made doll heads before he took out his patent but he does not appear in the Philadelphia Directory until 1840 where he is listed as a 'Toy Man,' with the address of '441 Coates St., Philadelphia.' In all probability Ludwig Greiner was a German toymaker by profession, who came to America and settled in the Quaker City to carry on his trade. Mrs. Dora Walker, of Rutland, Vt., has an interesting papier maché head, which has a script letter 'G' inside the head and she has proffered the opinion that perhaps Greiner made doll heads and marked them in that fashion, prior to 1858. Patents, in those days, were easily obtained and not unduly expensive so it seems logical to surmise that when Greiner thought he had a good doll's head, with sales possibilities, he applied for the patent.

UNITED STATES PATENT OFFICE.

LUDWIG GREINER, OF PHILADELPHIA, PENNSYLVANIA.

IMPROVEMENT IN CONSTRUCTING DOLL-HEADS.

Specification forming part of Letters Patent No. **19,770**, dated March 30, 1858.

To all whom it may concern:

Be it known that I, LUDWIG GREINER, of the city of Philadelphia and State of Pennsylvania, have invented a new Improved Mode of Making Doll and other Figure Heads; and I do hereby declare that the following is a full and accurate description thereof.

The nature of my invention consists in applying linen, silk, or muslin to the heads, which process makes them so substantial that they will not break by falling.

The manner of preparation is as follows: One pound of white paper, when cooked, is beat fine, and then the water is pressed out, so as to leave it moist. To this is added one pound of dry Spanish whiting, one pound of rye flour, and one ounce of glue. This is worked until it is well mixed. Then it is rolled out with a roller to the required thinness. After it is cut into pieces required for the mold it is molded. Wherever there is a part projecting out—for instance the nose—it must be filled with linen or muslin. This linen or muslin must be well saturated with a paste, which consists of rye-flour, Spanish whiting, and glue. After the heads are molded, each head consisting of two parts, they are left to get about half dry. Then they are put into the mold again and the parts well saturated with the paste. At the same time the linen or muslin is cut up into pieces to match the parts, and is also saturated with this paste and pressed on the inside of the parts. Then they are left to dry again as before. Then these parts are put together with the same composition as the head is made from. After this, when they are perfectly dry, a strip of the linen or muslin saturated with paste is laid inside of the head where the parts were put together, and a piece is also put over each shoulder and extending over the breast outside. Then they are painted with oil-paint, so that children may not suck off the paint.

What I claim as my invention, and desire to secure by Letters Patent, is—

Strengthening the seams and projecting or exposed parts of doll-heads by cementing or pasting on those parts muslin, linen, silk, or other equivalent material, in the manner and for the purpose set forth.

LUDWIG GREINER.

Witnesses:
 G. W. PAGE,
 A. F. GREINER.

Mrs. Dorgan is inclined to the opinion that Greiner did not put either an 'L' or a 'G' inside the doll head he made.

No patent was granted to Ludwig Greiner in 1872, the extension being granted on the original patent of 1858, as No. 19,770.

"On many dolls I am not sure," Mrs. Emma Clear admits honestly, "On the Greiners I thought I was. Lately one came in that I would have said positively was *not* a Greiner. It was a little composition doll with common hair dress, similar to one marked

This Composition is

G L

Excellent

Perfectly Harmless

She had been a little mechanical doll that pushed a miniature doll buggy. When we undressed her we found one of the most perfect Greiner labels on the back of her head. The Greiner dolls carry two different labels, the first or earlier ones, 1858. Then later, 'Pat. Ext. 1872.' There is no difference in the labels for blondes or brunettes."

"The owner of the 'Perfectly Harmless' claimed that the doll was made in 1840. We have another one in now. The trade mark is the same size and in the same position as the Greiner mark, leaving the same kind of unfaded place on the head after it has come off. I presume the 'Harmless' means that a youngster could chew it with impunity. I do not know who made any of them."

Mrs. Gustav Mox of Santa Monica, Cal., reports a Greiner Head labeled "Greiners Patent Doll Heads No. 7. Mar. 30, '58 Ext. '72." The Greiner heads appeared for a period of twenty years. It is not too difficult to spot a genuine specimen but to say accurately the year in which it was made is something else. The better the condition of the doll head, the later the year, is one method, but by no means an infallible one. To date a Greiner is but another

Courtesy Mrs. Izole Dorgan
Back view of the same doll reveals a most interesting hair arrangement. German. Papier Maché. Circa 1830-1840.

of the mysteries surrounding the kingdom of dolls. Mrs. Bathe reports that she has seen all sizes, blondes and brunettes with various types of hair dress, and one enormous Greiner, as big as a baby's head, and in good condition.

A study of the patent specifications will reveal that it is not difficult to prove whether a doll is a genuine Greiner or not. These heads, which vary in size, and in facial expression, are usually marked with the original label, which adheres to the back of the neck between the shoulder blades. The patent covers the method of manufacture, and this method is the test employed to determine an original model. The specifications call for the heads to be made in two parts, front and back, and then joined inside by means of a narrow piece of muslin or calico cut out like a piece of tape. A collector need only put fingers inside of a Greiner head, and feel around, the muslin is readily felt, and usually may be seen. The nose is filled with linen or muslin, which is also cut up in pieces, saturated with paste, and pressed on the inside of the parts. Paper, flour, glue and water, along with Spanish whiting, make up the composition of these doll heads. Any others, not following these specifications, are not Greiners, regardless of what their fond owners claim.

Ludwig Greiner was no esthete. These famous dolls, as one collector aptly remarked, "remind one of an old aunt who has a cupboard full of cold fried chicken, and cream cookies, they are so gentle and placid . . . but many of them

1. & 2. Two interesting Greiners from the collection of Mrs. Cyrus Beachy. 3. Greiner Blonde. Later model. Label reads "Pat. Mar. 30, '58, Ext. '72."—Collection Janet P. Johl. 4. "Phoebe Trafton," unusual brown eyes. Greiner Head. Circa 1860-1870. Formerly in collection Mrs. W. Massey Blackburn. Now owned by Mrs. Greville Bathe. 5. "Abigail, Aunt Electa and Phoebe," all labeled Greiner. Collection Helyn Ewing Fowler. Photo by Eric Stahlberg.

have shoulders like Jack Dempsey." The Greiners do look well bred, well fed, sweet and placid. Some of them are almost beautiful, in the way that age brings forth a mellow beauty, not the beauty of the sculptor or the artist. They usually have high foreheads, and small noses and small mouths. Their eyes, which are either 'set in,' or painted, are wide open, and the hair, drawn back, almost invariably shows the lobes of the ears. These indestructible heads were sold separately, and industrious mothers usually made the bodies at home. These dolls never broke. They were sturdy and durable, made for hard play and not for ornamental use. They just wore out, and so they are often found in bad condition with scarred noses, home made worn and torn shoes, and bodies mishapen. Sometimes the hands and feet are of carved wood. More often they are of cloth or leather.

One western collector reported a china head doll with a brownish lustre finish, and real glass eyes, with typical Greiner features. Although there was no mark on the head, she felt this might be a Greiner. However, as there was some doubt as to the doll actually falling into this classification more study was definitely needed before positive identification could be determined. Is it possible that Ludwig Greiner had his famous doll head copied in china in Germany, as an experiment? Perhaps there are other similar doll heads hidden away in other collections. It would be interesting to know more about this doll.

There seems to have been just one patent taken out for the Greiner doll head, according to the records of the United States Patent Office. There were other patents taken out for composition heads between 1858-1880. Prior to 1875 there were the Judge, and the Hawkins and Brock heads. The Brock was thin leather, which was pressed into molds. The hair was dressed low and a little unusual in style, and painted. In 1865 Lucretia Salle of Illinois patented a doll's head to be made of thin leather and covered with composition. These patents are all worthy of perusal although many of them as far as it can be ascertained never resulted in actual manufacture.

Every serious collector of old dolls wants to possess a Greiner. This is particularly true of those interested in the field of American antique dolls. Inasmuch as only the head was made and was sold separately, the body makeup of these dolls is quite diversified and this very diversity makes for their interest. There is something satisfying about the facial expression of the Greiners, a something so akin to the rugged courage and perseverance that it is a part of the story which belongs to things labeled "Old Americana." One Greiner, a brunette head of the early period, seems to be more easily obtained than the other types. Many composition, or papier maché heads have been called Greiners erroneously.

But one inventor is always interested in, and spurred on by the achievements of another, and surely in the world of dolls, ingenuity has played a great part. If collectors could be persuaded to bring forth their old unclassified dolls for serious contemplation, the results might prove to be illuminating. Only through the study of the doll patents of a given period, and the possible application of the patent requirements to certain types of dolls, can the student hope for further knowledge of the doll through analysis, and even, in some cases, dissection. It cannot be stressed too strongly that in the world of doll research, all those interested in doll-ology must cooperate if more on the subject is to be brought to light.

The use of wax in the making of effigies and figures dates back to an early era, for wax is a most pliable object. In ancient Greece, plaster and wax were employed and the wax type of doll was called Dagynon in Ionic, and Dagys in Doric. In the fourteenth century the wax doll was known on the continent. Mrs. Arthur Goldsmith of Narbeth, Penn., reports a rare 400 year old Italian wax portrait doll in her collection.

The wax makers of the Middle Ages were called ceroplasts and very often the images they fashioned were used for revenge as well as for religious purposes. In the early days of civilization images of an enemy were made to work destruction, so that the wax doll, created for such a purpose, falls into the fetish class. This custom was employed by the New England settlers, and is known among the Scotch and the negroes, and undoubtedly, among many other peoples.

Wax dolls appeared in Germany, sometime in the seventeenth century, and a Daniel Neuberger of Augsburg, is credited with making many of the early wax dolls, which have been described as being 'as hard as stone,' and colored so naturally that they seemed almost human.

Glass and enamel eyes appeared in the wax doll heads, and also in the wax over composition type. To say definitely when the first glass eyes were invented is an impossibility although it surely marks one of the most vital forward steps in doll history. It has been said that there is a doll with eyes of Stiegel glass made by Stiegel himself; that the head of this doll is of wax, and the date given is circa 1750. It is extremely difficult to date any old doll accurately, but it is a known fact that Henry William Steigel came to the United States in 1750, bought a tract of land at Mannheim, Penn., built his glass house and then returned to Germany, evidently for further study, before actually beginning his industry. The first run of glass at Mannheim, Penn., was in 1765. It is perfectly possible that this wax head doll has eyes of real Steigel glass. Another wax head doll, really a wax over composition, which is difficult to date positively is the so called 'wire eyed' doll. It can be said with assurety that by 1825 this doll was in existence. A wire, passed through the doll body, from the upper thigh, just below the hip, connects with the back of two blocks of wood on which the eyes are mounted. When the wire is pulled downward, the eyes open. When the wire is raised, the eyes close. Another device used was one that had the wire protrude from the right side of the doll's head, just under the wig. When turned, either to the right or to the left, the eyes opened and shut. Both these types of wire-eyed dolls were earlier than the counterbalance device for doll eyes which appeared at the beginning of the nineteenth century in Paris, France, and greatly modified the customary implacable stare.

One authority gives 1823 as the approximate date for sleeping eyes in a horizontal position which were closed by means of a counterweight fastened to the eye-ball. Another gives 1826 as the date. Still another says that by 1826 the method of opening and shutting doll eyes was known. No authority gives the date for the first use of these weights. If the counterbalance was really well known by 1826, then it seems possible to date a wire eyed doll earlier than 1825, but how much earlier is the question. The introductory article in 'A Picture Book of Dolls and Doll Houses' of the Victoria and Albert Museum *of London* mentions "dolls with china faces and with eyes that opened and shut by the counter-balance movement." The date, 1824. If this eye movement was true of the china doll heads, then it must also have been true for the wax.

One thing is certain, and that is that glass eyes were evidently very difficult to manufacture, especially those of **violet and sapphire** colors, and these **have** become collector's items, rarely **found,** and much sought after. Brown eyes **are** perhaps older and **not** so common as light blue eyes, the latter having come into

Courtesy of Mrs. Frederic C. Ripley

Belle Hervey: A Pure Wax Head Doll

fashion after Queen Victoria ascended to the throne of England. At that time the brown eyed dolls lost favor in England, and were sent over to the continent and to Spain. This fact may help the collector to date a wax doll, and to place its source of origin.

In an article entitled *"The Age of Old Dolls"* which appeared in *The Magazine ANTIQUES*, May, 1936, Mrs. Frederic C. Ripley of Los Angeles, Cal., wrote: "Sally Taber, c. 1825 has emerging from her side, at the waistline, a wire loop, which, when pulled or pushed, caused the lady to droop her eyes modestly or raise them in an implacable stare." In this same article, Mrs. Ripley notes that "wire is a primitive device not commonly used," and also that "Wax heads with wax hair are very hard to place because of overlapping periods." Mrs. Ripley has in her own collection a pure wax head doll, named Belle Hervey, with hair growing out of the head, and lifelike eyes of blue glass. The hands and feet of this doll are of wax, and because the feet were covered with stockings for many years, they are still of the palest pink hue, and the toes have remained dimpled like those of a child.

Mrs. Mary E. Lewis reports two interesting wax dolls in her collection. One, circa 1860, has a solid closed head, but is wax over composition. It has blown, blue glass eyes, a bellow which plays a hymn, and curiously enough

bears a stamped mark, reading 'Patented in England. Patented in America.'
It is twenty six inches high. The other doll is of an earlier date and even
greater interest. Mrs. Lewis writes:

"The doll was originally from a collection of dolls belonging to the late
Queen Victoria and sold in New York City. The original dress was copied in 1917 for the Doll Show at the Emergency Aid of Phila., during the World War. Each strand of hair has been individually put into the wax head so it seems to grow as in a human head."

Mrs. Velvalee Dickinson reported a fine wax doll very similar to this, in the fall of 1939.

These dolls seem to be the truly English type, with the hair growing out of the wax, on the scalp, and also for the eye lashes and eye brows.

Mrs. C. H. Kelso of Kansas City, Mo., writes of a rare old wax doll, the head entirely of wax with each hair set in separately . . . so that it feels 'sort of spooky.' The body, of horse hair, seems to have been re-covered, during the passage of years and the eyes are of glass.

Courtesy Mrs. Mary E. Lewis

Mrs. Mary E. Lewis holding a Wax Doll, made in England, Circa
1825. Bought from a collection of dolls having belonged to the
late Queen Victoria and sold in New York City. Original Dress
copied in 1917 for Doll Show at the Emergency Aid of Philadelphia during the World War.

Mrs. Earle E. Andrews, of Winchester, Mass. has a very interesting pair of Bees Wax Dolls in her collection, which came from Lima, Peru, circa, 1847. These dolls sailed around Cape Horn on a six months voyage to Paris, France. They were originally owned by Isabella Jewett, whose father had been the United States Minister to Peru. The daughter of Isabella Jewett, Isabella Harris, relinquished them to Mrs. Andrews in 1937.

In 1849 Mme. Montanari was one of three leading wax doll manufacturers, and it was she who developed the method of imbedding the hair, the eyebrows and eye lashes into the

Courtesy Mrs. John Albright
Old Wax Dolls. Spanish.

wax, instead of using wigs and paint. Her dolls were of real, poured wax, made in all sizes. Even the neck and the head of the doll was of wax. and although not very durable, this doll was a popular creature of elegance and fashionable attire. At this same time M. Richard Montanari showed wax doll heads covered with fine muslin. Although never produced in great quantities, the plastic realism of the wax dolls made them favorites. But this had its drawbacks for wax faces had to be washed in butter. The warm sun melted them, and the cold cracked them. The age of the wax doll is not judged by the color of the wax alone but by the method of construction, and the materials used. Modeled with life like reality, these dolls represent the first use of wax as playthings of children.

Throughout the middle of the nineteenth century, wax head dolls were used, having the real hair, carefully coiffeured, and the glass eyes. Glazed porcelain was termed old fashioned for doll heads, and some manufacturers made a dull porcelain in flesh color, using the newly invented moveable glass eyes, and bodies of paper pulp. The papier-maché doll heads, which were received with popular favor because of their unbreakable and unperishable qualities, now received a thin coating of wax over their faces, and often on their

Courtesy of Mrs. Velvalee Dickinson
A Rare Montanari Wax Doll—1860

D. Checkeni,

Doll,

No 52,782.

Patented Feb. 20, 1866.

Fig. 1.

Fig. 2.

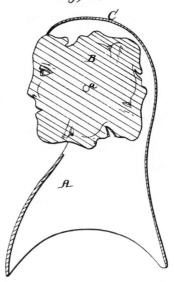

Witnesses;

Jos. A. Austin

R. Litzginld.

Inventor,

Dominico Checkeni

feet and hands. In the early models the eyebrows, lashes, lips and cheeks were painted *on* the wax . . . later the paint was beneath the wax. Stationery glass eyes were usually inserted.

It is said that doll heads of this type, with a pompadour hair dress, were made either in Virginia or Kentucky. But, of course, the great majority came to America from Europe and probably from Germany. Two well known heads of this type are the so called 'Punkin' and 'Squash' heads. Mrs. Izole Dorgan describes the former as having a round bulging hair arrangement, very orange-yellow in color. The latter were more flat, and had more intriguing heads. Mrs. Greville Bathe believes that both of these dolls are of German origin, circa 1840-1850, and that the Squash heads had a peculiar type of hair dress that "resembles nothing so much as a bright yellow hot dog, bent over the forehead, something after the manner of the pompadour of the early 1900's." The eyes of these dolls are glass and are very unnatural looking, because of their stiff, staring, fixed gaze. Most specimens are no longer completely covered with the wax, which has peeled off with the years.

Miss Eva Page Daly, of Albany, N. Y. reports a wax doll with a black band on her hair, wax head, drop shoulders and composition hands. At the upper waist line is a band of linen which covers a noise box. If pressed down on the shoulders, the doll makes a sound, and perhaps, back in 1870 or 1880 she was able to say 'Mama'.

UNITED STATES PATENT OFFICE.

DOMINICO CHECKENI, OF MARION, ASSIGNOR TO HIMSELF AND GEORGE N. THOMPSON, OF NEW HAVEN, CONNECTICUT.

FANCY DOLL.

Specification forming part of Letters Patent No. **52,782**, dated February 20, 1866.

To all whom it may concern:

Be it known that I, DOMINICO CHECKENI, of Marion, in the county of Hartford and State of Connecticut, have invented a new and useful Improvement in Fancy Dolls; and I do hereby declare that the following is a full, clear, and exact description of the construction, character, and operation of the same, reference being had to the accompanying drawings, which make part of this specification, in which—

Figure 1 is a perspective view of the doll, showing one of the faces, wig, bust, &c. Fig. 2 is a section of the same cut vertical through the center from front to rear, indicating the fore face and the axis or pivots on which the head turns vertically.

My improvement consists in making the doll with four faces and having its head revolve on an axis or pivots, so that either face may be brought in front at pleasure.

I make the bust A of wax or any other suitable material, in the proper form to sustain a wig which will serve for all the faces.

I make the head B of wax or any other suitable material, with four faces, as in Fig. 2.

I make the faces of any desired character of features, and suspend the head on an axis, as indicated at a, Figs. 1 and 2, or two pivots made of the crank form or any other suitable or convenient form, so that the head may be revolved vertically, so as to exhibit either of the faces as desired.

I make the wig C of the usual form, so as to cover all portions of the head except the face which is desired to be exhibited, substantially as represented in Fig. 1 and indicated in section in Fig. 2.

What I claim as my invention, and desire to secure by Letters Patent, is—
Making the doll's head with four faces and suspending it in the wig-frame in such a manner that the head may be revolved vertically, so as to bring either of the four faces in front at pleasure, when the whole is constructed and fitted to operate substantially as herein described.

DOMINICO CHECKENI.

Witnesses: JAS. A. AUSTIN, R. FITZGERALD.

The wax doll gained popularity because of its life like appearance, both in its complexion and its expression. But the collector should always note the difference between the wax doll that was made for a special purpose, and the ones which were manufactured on the continent in the eighteenth century, solely for commercial usage.

It is difficult to find any of the wax dolls in perfect condition because of the very fraility of the material. When restored wax dolls are lovely, although still fragile, despite the fact that modern wax is more durable than the older variety. Wax has a delicate bloom that even a finger mark will damage, and the question of the restoration of old dolls is always a very individual one, from the collector's point of view.

On July 5, 1881 an American patent was granted to Fritz Bartenstein of Huttensteinach, Germany for a wax doll, double faced. This doll was first made and patented in Germany, and although most unusual, is no object of great beauty. One of these dolls is in the collection of Miss Helyn Ewing Fowler of Northampton, Mass. It does not seem to be similar to a patent filed in 1866 by a man named Checkeni, in Connecticut, for a doll head of four revolving faces with different expressions. There is no Checkeni doll in any collection that has come to light so perhaps it was never manufactured.

UNITED STATES PATENT OFFICE.

FRITZ BARTENSTEIN, OF HUTTENSTEINACH, GERMANY.

DOLL-HEAD.

Specification forming part of Letters Patent No. 243,752, dated July 5, 1881.
Application filed October 28, 1880. (No model.)

To all whom it may concern:

Be it known that I, FRITZ BARTENSTEIN, of Huttensteinach, Germany, have invented a Doll-Head with Movable Double Face, of which the following is a specification.

My invention consists in a movable doll-head having two faces of different expression and being partly covered with a hood, in which it can be turned horizontally, so as to show either of the two faces while the other is hidden.

In the accompanying drawings, which illustrate my invention, Figure 1 is a side view, and Fig. 2 a vertical section, of the upper part of a doll having a laughing face and a weeping face, while Fig. 3 is a horizontal section, showing the mechanism for turning the head of the doll.

The hood, joined to the neck of the doll, covers the laughing face, and the head has a pivot, k, which can be turned in the body of the doll by pulling one end of the string u, which passes over a grooved pulley, r. This pulley is mounted on a prismatic spindle, s, guided at the bottom by a plate, h, and passing with its top into the pivot k. Two stop-pins, m and n, are attached to the circumference of the pulley, and another stop-pin, m, projects upward from the base-plate h, so as to prevent the pulley from making more than one-half of a revolution, by coming into contact with one of the stop-pins m or n. Two openings are provided in the body of the doll for the passage of the string u.

(No Model.)

F. BARTENSTEIN.
DOLL HEAD.

No. 243,752.

Patented July 5, 1881.

Fig.1

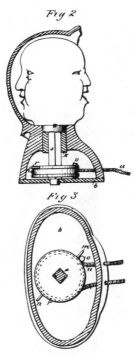

Fig 2

Fig 3

Witnesses
Al.McChurch
Henry Gehon

Inventor:
Fritz Bartenstein
pp. Ott.Hadden
atty

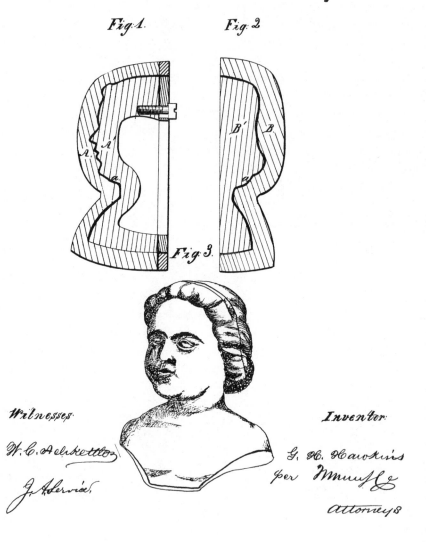

G. H. Hawkins,

Doll Head.

Nº 81,999.   *Patented Sep. 8, 1868.*

Fig. 1.   *Fig. 2*

Fig. 3.

Witnesses: *Inventor:*

W. C. Aehketten,   *G. H. Hawkins*

J. A. Servia,   *per* Mmufge

                        Attorneys

A group of old dolls showing Greiners and Papier Maché, composition, and several types of wax head dolls, including the wire-eyed.—Collection Janet P. Johl. 2. Papier Maché doll overlaid with wax.—Collection Mrs. Henry W. Bell. 3. "Hannah Greenleaf," German made, gessoed type wax doll often called "Punkin Head." Circa 1840-1850.—Collection Mrs. Greville Bathe. 4. A gray eyed wax doll with curls.—Collection Grace Woodworth. 5. A lovely wax doll. Circa 1850. Note legs and shoes—Collection Marion Weeks Casey.

Chapter X

GERMAN DOLL HEADS

(German Monopoly in Doll Industry—Multi-Faced Dolls—
Tariff Act—Markings on Doll Heads—
Recipes for Doll Making)

Three sizes of China Head Dolls. Modern. German.

FROM a very early date, doll making was a popular and successful industry in Germany and many doll heads and busts came from Bavaria, Prussia and Austria. A large proportion of home industry surrounds the doll made in Germany, and the makers worked hard and long, actually living and sleeping with the dolls during all stages of their manufacture. Coburg, Sonneburg and Holdburghausen, as well as the entire state of Thuringia, were noted as doll centres of manufacture, and especially for doll heads and busts of papier maché.

Before the War of 1870, all countries drew their supply of doll heads from Saxony, Germany. Unfortunately none of the china heads bore the name, or any mark, of the artists who worked on them, nor of the firm which manufactured them, to say nothing of any identifying label which told of the locality from which they originated. The French, while active, found the German competition extremely difficult so that from 1870 to 1914, the industry remained predominantly German.

As early as 1858, bisque doll heads won the Prix d'Or in Paris. The best known bisque head, was made until 1885, and was attached to a kid body, with an extended rump and narrow waist. The German bisque was fired first, then colored, and then re-fired. Germany also made a delicate pink bisque, the color ground into the body. These bisque heads may have been of French origin, the artistic endeavors of M. Jumeau, when the Prix d'Or was won, or they may

98

have been German copies, or German originals. No one can say with any degree of certainty. But the fact that the doll of 1858 was the exact same doll as that of 1870, makes one ponder the point of origin. The 1870 doll was accompanied by an elaborate French wardrobe, but the body was of German kid. It would scarcely seem plausible that Jumeau used a German kid body for his own doll heads, when he and his son, were also responsible for improved doll bodies. The German kid

Courtesy Verai de Ferré
Fagen
**Flemba—A Doll with
five faces.**

body is heavier than the French in texture, and not as thin, as supple, or as shapely.

There is no proof either that doll bodies, used with French heads, were of French kid, rather than of German. They, too, may have been German. The German doll heads of this period, were hollowed out, and over the top of the hole was fitted a little pasteboard, or a crown of cork, or plaster, the latter filling in the head hole completely. Upon these, the wig was either tacked or glued. Painted hair gave way to Tibetan goat hair, astrakan fur, mohair, fine lustrous silk and even human hair. The French continued to use elaborate coiffeurs for their fashion dolls, and the hair dress received the attention of beauty experts.

Once they realized the commercial possibilities of the doll in-

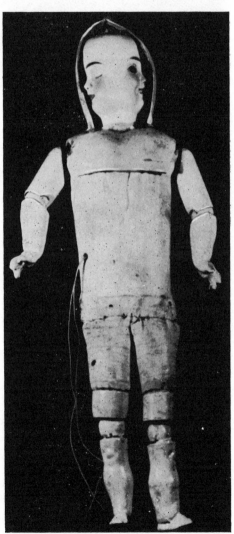

Courtesy Mrs. Izole Dorgan
A Doll with two faces

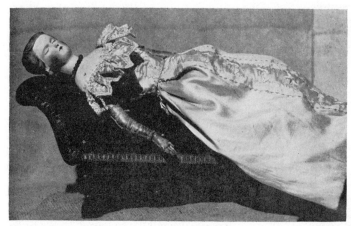

Courtesy Mrs.
Nina B. Shepard

**Suzanne, a doll
with two faces,
sleeping.**

dustry, the Germans started a mass production, and gradually began to cater to a world market producing dolls with which children could actually play. Never being a nation fortunate in fashions, for even their men folk preferred French styles, they left that phase to France. However, by skillful labor, the Germans soon monopolized the doll trade, which was more or less subsidized by their government.

Courtesy Mrs. Nina B. Shepard

Suzanne awake

Between 1870-1880 dolls with two, three and four faces were common. It seems logical to believe that the regular bisque doll head was employed, and that new molds were made for the additional facial expressions. These dolls appeared with waking and sleeping faces, laughing, crying, pouting, or with normal smiling expressions. The face rotated in a little hard wood, and the doll was almost always of German bisque.

A two faced doll was recently on exhibition at the *New York Historical Society* with a reversible head, a bonnet hiding the head not in use. Verai de Ferré Fagen, of Bridgeport, Conn. reports a unique doll in her collection "with five faces which form a metal ball which turns inside a head over which there is a wig. There are five separate noses and mouths but the eye of one face also forms the eye of the other. Thus she is awake, she winks her left eye (The right or open eye being the same one that forms the left eye of the wide awake expression). In this face she boldly sticks out her tongue, she sleeps, she winks the right eye (the closed eye is the same as the right eye in the sleeping expression, while the open one for this is the right eye of the crying face.) She cries with her brow wrinkled, tears showing and lips puckered.'' There is no marking on the doll but Miss Fagen believes it to be either French or German. Because it represents such an ingenious idea, it is probably of German origin. Mrs. Izole Dorgan raises the question ''Is a true multifaced doll one without a pair of eyes for each head?'' Whatever the answer a doll of this kind surely has its place as a unique specimen.

At a recent Doll Show held in New York City, a four faced doll, carved in darkwood, was shown, that alternately cries, laughs, sleeps and assumes a placid expression as its head revolves in its socket. This doll, believed to be one hundred and fifty years old, is from the collection of Mrs. Amy Coburn Lyseth of Worcester, Mass., and is a splendid example of a primitive type of head. In this same exhibition there was a three faced, laughing, crying, sleeping doll.

Mrs. Nina B. Shepard of Granville, Ohio, has a two faced French doll, with its neck on a spring. This doll, which is of bisque, circa 1850, is sixteen inches tall and was sent in a consignment of toys to the Rinewelt Toy Store in Mansfield, Ohio in 1850. The store keeper gave this doll and another similar one to his two daughters.

It is said, an actor invented a 'Doll with Forty Faces' in 1913, made of wood and paper with a head on a revolving disc and eyes and mouth on a similar disc. With every turn of the disc the expression of the eyes and the mouth changed and the doll could laugh or cry, frown or smile, accordingly. Whether this doll ever appeared is hard to ascertain. It does not seem to be in any collection to-day.

An interesting article entitled ''Dime Store'' by John K. Winkler and Boyden Sparkes, which appeared in the *Saturday Evening Post*, February, 1940, had to do with the life of F. W. Woolworth, and gave considerable insight into the doll world of 1890. In this article a letter written by Mr. Woolworth after he landed in Liverpool, and went immediately to Staffordshire to select pottery, had this description of that particular English locality. To quote, in part:

> ''Stoke-en-Trent,
> Saturday March 1, 1890

''This is the center of the potteries, over 600 of them in the county of Staffordshire. Some of the finest china in the world is made here, some of the poorest. We have been in 25 potteries the last three week days, but have not bought anything yet, but expect to next week.''

The article then told how Mr. Woolworth accompanied by B. F. Hunt, the buyer for Horace Partridge & Co., America's largest firm of toy importers went to buy dolls in Sonneberg, Germany. To quote:

''On our arrival at Sonneberg the whole town was there to meet Mr. Hunt, as he is a great favorite here for several reasons. One is that he buys more dolls than any

other importer that comes into Sonneberg, and another is he makes friends wherever he goes. After the handshaking, kissing, etc., were all over, we took the bus to Grug's Hotel. Sonneberg is headquarters for dolls for the whole world, as nearly every doll of every description is made here or within a few miles from here, and this is the market."

"March 9.
"It seems as though the whole toy trade of America is represented here. As we walked along the street we could look in the windows of the houses and see the women and children at work making dolls, while the men drink beer. Nearly every doll is made in private houses. We could see some of the women and children molding the legs, others the heads, some putting the hair on, another making the shirts, others putting in the eyes, and one would be painting the finished doll. After they are finished they are put in long baskets and taken to the packers, where they are put into boxes of one dozen each and put into large cases and shipped to all parts of the world. The poor women do most of the work, even to lugging them to the packing houses."

"March 14.
"It is no longer a mystery to me how they make dolls and toys so cheap, for most of it is done by women and children at their homes anywhere within 20 miles of this place. Some of the women in America think they have got hard work to do, but is far different than the poor women here, that work night and day on toys, and strap them onto their backs, and go 10 or 20 miles through the mud with 75 pounds on their backs, to sell them. The usual price they get for a good 10-cent doll is about 3 cents each here, and they are obliged to buy the hair, shirts and other materials, to put them together, and they probably get about 1 cent each for the labor they put on them.

"The streets here are filled with women with baskets on their backs filled with dolls and toys, and they walk in the middle of the street when the mud is ankle deep, in preference to the clean sidewalk. We saw a poor little girl that could not have been over four years old with a basket strapped on her back larger than herself, and Mr. Hunt asked her where she lived and she told us a place about five miles from here, and she came alone. We gave her some money and she looked at it as if she never saw any of it before. It is an ordinary thing here to see a dog and a woman hitched together or cows and women drawing a heavy load of goods.

"We can find out more about the toy and china business of America here than at home. Here we find out what the other firms are buying and what they pay for the goods. I have found out where these Sailor Dolls that we sold so many of are made here . . ."

In this same year, 1890, the United States passed a Tariff Act, section sixth of which reads "That on and after the first day of March, eighteen hundred and ninety-one, all articles of foreign manufacture, such as are usually or ordinarily marked, stamped or labeled, and all packages containing such or other imported articles shall respectively be plainly marked, stamped, branded or labeled in legible ENGLISH words, so as to indicate the country of their origin, and unless so marked, stamped, branded or labeled they shall not be admitted to entry".

A study of Section 304 of the Tariff Act of 1930 (U. S. C., 1934 edition title 19, sec. 1304) is worthy of additional attention for it is in effect at the present time:

"SEC. 304. MARKING OF IMPORTED ARTICLES AND CONTAINERS.

"(a) MARKING OF ARTICLES.—Except as hereinafter provided, every article of foreign origin (or its container, as provided in subsection (b) hereof) imported into the United States shall be marked in a conspicuous place as legibly, indelibly, and permanently as the nature of the article (or container) will permit in such manner as to indicate to an ultimate purchaser in the United States the English name of the country of origin of the article. The Secretary of the Treasury may be regulations—

"(1) Determine the character of words and phrases or abbreviations thereof which shall be acceptable as indicating the country of origin and prescribe any reasonable method of marking, whether by printing, stenciling, stamping, branding, labeling, or by any other reasonable method, and a conspicuous place on the article (or container) where the marking shall appear;

"(2) Require the addition of any other words or symbols which may be appropriate to prevent deception or mistake as to the origin of the article or as to the origin of any other article with which such imported article is usually combined subsequent to importation but before delivery to an ultimate purchaser."

This section then lists exceptions for any article from the requirements of marking under conditions and cites also the additional duties for failure to mark, such as delivery withheld until the marking, and penalties for improper markings.

Shortly after this Tariff Act was in effect the socket doll came into vogue, and the shoulders were no longer attached to the head, but instead there was a ball shaped throat, with a hole in it, through which elastic string was drawn and attached to the inside mechanism of the body. In 1904 a doll trust was reported in France, and the Republic made a determined effort to push her own doll trade. Germany came into sharp competition, because of cheaper labor, but nothing was made in Germany as lovely as in France at that time. Only the exports to the United States kept up the doll industry.

Cheap china heads coming from Germany were very plentiful and so also were the metal heads. China heads were less expensive than the sleeping eyed bisque heads. Metal heads, besides being reasonable, were also unbreakable. Both types were largely used to replace the bisque when it broke. The heads were generally imported without the bodies as the import costs were high.

Courtesy of the Boston Antique Shop, Boston, Mass.

A Salesman's Sample Board

Mrs. Emma C. Clear remarks that she cannot remember seeing any factory marks on the metal doll heads but perhaps at the time these metal heads were in vogue, no one paid much attention to the markings. Two metal German heads do bear the names Juno and Minerva, respectively, and are accompanied by trademarks, both clearly perceptible. The metal heads, Mrs. Clear explained, were made by a stamping machine, the two halves being stamped out, then soldered together and finished. A lot of 'tin head' dolls with sleeping eyes, still exist. There is even one with the pompadour style of head dress modeled in the metal. Some have glass eyes, oval shaped, that do not sleep. Usually the sleeping type have an opening in the top of the head to which the wig is attached. Eyes are also painted on. In actuality these dolls are not tin but are brass or zinc.

China heads were cast in two piece molds, except for the Parians. The later bisque models did not have the pierced ears of the earlier types, the style going out in the doll world as it did in the world of fashion. By 1908 the china head dolls were becoming less popular in the northern part of the United States, but not in the south.

A metal doll head patent was issued to John B. Dane and Charles S. Cannon of Elizabeth, N. J. April 10, 1919 for "sheet metal front and back sections permanently secured at vertical point—back section has inclined opening."

Many of the pre-war German heads of china, bisque and metal, had interesting markings. One German word on the back of several of the bisque doll heads has become the subject of discussion. It is the simple word HANDWERCK which some believe means 'hand work'. Others however feel that this is only a trade mark, or perhaps the name of a German doll maker because it is often found with the word Heinrich—HEINRICH HANDWERCK—translated in English to Henry Handwork. Mrs. Clear suggests that it may be a handicraft name with nothing whatsoever to do with dolls, and that there is no more hand work on this type of doll than on any other head. She remarks that the words are written as if they were a man's name, a full name with letters all the same size and type, and from this she concludes that the signature has nothing to do with hand work. A German grammar rule prohibits the use of the letters CK after a consonant, or after S, and as hand work is spelled 'Handwerk' in German, and a handworker is, 'Handwerker', perhaps Handwerck is just some one's name. "Handwerk" may also refer to one's profession.

Controversially the definition of L. C. S.'s of the American Embassy in Paris (1939) is this, but the source of L. C. S.'s information is unknown. To quote: "Handwerck is a German word meaning hand work and not a trade mark. On a dolls head it may simply imply that the cheeks were painted by hand. However in the making of a bust, statue or even a doll's head, there is an enormous amount of necessary handwork. First an artist makes a model of clay or wax, or of modern composition known as plasticine (wax and glycerine). A plaster cast is taken and a plaster mold made from the cast. This must often be retouched by the artist. Then another mold is taken and cut off in two parts. There are several sorts of molds. Sometimes a complicated group will need as many as fifteen separate molds, but this is far beyond the needs of a dolls heads. Two parts of the doll head are now in plaster. China clay is pressed by hand into each half to the desired thickness and this is a delicate operation for there must be no air and no seams. The clay must fit perfectly into the hollows. The mould is then put together, 'sealed' and when the head is dry the mould is cut off and the head decorated and baked. Like most statues and busts it is hollow and is not hollowed out.''

Mrs. Clear feels that this statement of L. C. S. covers statues and has no bearing on dolls. She has this to say: "The mold is made from the model. Casting is a delicate operation. There must be no air pockets and the clay must fit perfectly into every hollow. The head is taken out of the mold as soon as it is dry enough to handle freely. The head is thoroughly dried, and the seams are carefully dressed before it is fused. Some heads are fused twice, the first time in the biscuit or unglazed stage then again after glazing. Some are glazed after drying, and before the first fusing. At this stage the heads are white. Decorating is another process. The heads are painted with mineral paints, that melt and fuse into the glaze. These paints would be destroyed at the high temperature necessary to fuse porcelain. Sometimes they can be successfully decorated in one firing, often two or three firings are necessary.''

Both of these comments are interesting. As for the word 'Handwerck', a careful study of the markings on the doll heads will indicate that it is perhaps wisest to assume that it is a workman's name rather than any indication of very carefully executed hand work.

SOME OF THE MARKINGS FOUND ON DOLL HEADS

Schultz Mark (a turtle) 17 Germany

Waltershausen—1916—Germany

Omen Louise Germany

Simon & Halbig Germany

Heinrich Handwerck — Simon Halbig Germany

Henbach 300 12/0 Koppelsdorf Bavaria Germany

Henbach 250 3/0 Koppelsdorf Germany

1894 M DEP 2 Made in Germany

50 R- D.E.P. 18/0 X

201 14/0 DEP

A. O. M. 259 D. R. G. M. Made in Germany

J. D. K. 260 (Crown mark of old Germany) Made in Germany

C M Bergmann Waltershausen 5 Germany 1916

99 11 ¾ DE P Handwerck Germany

119 13 Handwerck 5 Halbig

Kiddiejoy A 2½ M

165 2

193 D 8 Made in Germany

6 78 Heubach 50 3-0

2 0/0

150 A. No. 1 Germany

Armand Marseille 390 A8M Germany

Armand Marseille 390 a 4/0 M

Armand Marseille 390 n DRGM 246/1

Armand Marseille 370 M 5/0 D.E.P.

Armand Marseille A 10/10 M

(Armand Marseille have been making dolls for many years. The modern German dolls of this firm carry numbers 390 and 391)

1902 No. 103. 16cm Minerva. Trade mark, the goddess with a helmet. Germany Patent Applied For.

S and C Germany

D R G M 374830 1374 Floradora A G M

Juno Trade Mark a crown. Front of shoulders

Bisque Head AA

Rubber Head 85

O L C 3 Made in Germany

K W 4

Heubach 250—4 Koppelsdorf Thuringia /

1900 1 Trade Mark a horse shoe

1. Five Interesting Dolls, Head of Waffle Flour by Kellogg Brown, attempt at American bisque during World War, celluloid head by Marks Bro.   Circa 1917, Head marked Nippon, possible Japanese attempt, German "Globe Baby" DRGM. Hartman, Pre-War.—Collection Janet P. Johl.   2. Bisque head and shoulders.   German.   Note circular filled in area socket section, usually left open.   Marking on head "Kiddie Joy."   A 2½ M.   Probably a product of Armand Marseille, a German house established between 1884–1890 in Wurzen, Saxony. Operative up to present war.—Collection Janet P. Johl.   3. Gibson Girls, probably German origin.—Collection Mrs. Ruffin A. Smith.   4. "Elsie," a bisque head with bisque hands replacing original ones of kid.   Ears pierced.   Circa 1881.   Boston, Mass.   Probably German.—Courtesy Miss Julia Caverno, Northampton, Mass.   5. A Doll Mold.—Courtesy Lewis Wiggin.   Photo by Eric Stahlberg.

06½0 D E P   Trade mark a flower.
Germany
Jutta Jointed
AB, 1362 (very deep letters)
1912 4 Made in Germany
(This has 4 dots in circular arrange-
ment.)
Simon 9 Halbig K R. Five Pointed
Star between the two letters.
J with a dot over the J
Mabel O Germany
Gebruder Henbach 8192 Trade mark
indistinct.

F Y 1003
G O D 93 — L DEP
Alma 5/0
J D K 201
Roseland A0M
2076 Baby Head Heart shape mark
with dot over the heart. Five pointed star with letter C in the center.
Floradora A5M Made in Germany.
585 Letter X with S P O B the S in
the top part of the X the other letter following around.

Almost all these markings above are found on bisque heads. Some are definitely marked *Germany*, or *Made in Germany*.

Others bear only the numbers with no reference to the place of origin. Some of these markings were very difficult to decipher so the spelling in every case cannot be considered absolutely correct. A repetition of the letters D E P, J D K, and D R G M is to be noted, but its meaning is not known. For a little further study into these markings it may be wise to consider a few in detail as regards the doll bearing the marks. For example:

(1) Heubach 60 3 0 is a German bisque, pink tinted with a blue ribbon in her hair, and her head tilted to one side, her face happy and smiling.

(2) 119-13 Handwerck Halbig 5 is a socket neck type bisque, with pierced ears, no eye lashes, but with teeth and two holes in, the rear of the head. It is interesting to note here that teeth and eyelashes are usually found on later dolls. Almost invariably the dolls with pierced ears, herein noted, were marked handwerck.

(3) Kiddie Joy A 21/2M is an Armand Marseille product with no eye lashes but with teeth and with a bisque square shoulder instead of a socket type.

(4) 165 2 is a character face reminding one of the American Billiken doll with no teeth and no eyelashes.

The marking—'*Germany Patented Applied For*'—is found on many white, china head dolls, with a Peter Pan type of collar in china, edged in gold lustre. This doll also comes with its name in, gold lustre across the front . . . Pauline— Edith—Mable—Agnes—Helen—Ethel—Daisy—Florence—Marion and Esther are but a few of the named varieties. Most of the baby dolls seem to be classified by the use of the letter 'O'.

These few descriptions may prove helpful. There are certainly plenty of names and markings to be found on the later bisque heads. This list is by no means complete. Many may be just trade names used for assembling the heads from the various potteries, and for selling purposes. They may mean little, or nothing, or a great deal. But certain firms are easily told by the type of doll they put out. This seems to be true of Armand Marseille, for the facial expression of this doll does not change greatly. Surely the work of an artist stands out as a distinctive feature, just as an individual handwriting does. The resemblance is in the sculpturing, more often than in the bisque.

In a most enlightening book called *"Toy Manufacture"*, issued in London in 1921, J. T. Makinson discusses doll heads at length. In his preface to his book he remarks "This book believed to be the first serious volume in the English language to present information on commercial toymaking, is the work of a practical craftsman who has had a very wide extensive experience in both German and English workshops. From his wide practical experience he has been able to give a large amount of information that will be new even to that public to which it makes its special appeal".

Of twenty samples examined by J. T. Makinson, of ordinary doll heads made from a paper pulp composition, the ingredients used were pretty much the same. "The Japanese" says the writer "are experts in manufacturing papier maché that is exceedingly tough and hard being made of rice paper, and so pure white. The composition for larger dolls must be stronger than for the small . . . consisting of 10 parts prepared paper pulp, 2 parts whiting, 5 parts rye flour (or ground rice) all made into a paste by means of water, added. Sometimes a small amount of glue is used but this is not necessary. A popular composition in France consists of 4 and $\frac{1}{2}$ pounds of wood pulp, 1 and $\frac{1}{2}$ pounds china clay, 2 pounds of whiting, 3 pounds of plaster of paris, and 1 pound of liquid glue."

Plaster of Paris however is apt to make a doll head brittle, and so is not strong enough to stand the knocks it receives from the play of small children. Says J. T. Makinson: "The 'secret' preparation for heads used on German dolls is this: (1) 25 parts water, 18 parts dry pulp, 17 parts whiting and 3 parts swelled glue: (2) 2 pounds paper pulp, 1 and $\frac{1}{2}$ pounds flour, 1 pound whiting and $\frac{1}{2}$ pound unslaked lime."

"Mix together and pour over it starch paste, hot. Then mix into a smooth paste, allow four hours to settle and stir again. It must now be left for three days and the excess liquid poured off. This is repeated three times. The paste left can then be moulded and pressed to any shape, and when set can be turned in a lathe. Draughtsmen utilize it for various toys."

"Papier maché heads are cast in plaster of paris moulds and the manufacture was kept a secret until recently when the writer divulged it: China clay 5 and $\frac{1}{2}$ pounds, paper pulp 4 and $\frac{1}{4}$ pounds and plaster of paris 5 pounds. This is cheap to make, dries out well, shrinks a little and moulds easily. A plaster of paris mould will make 30 heads, and then requires drying in the oven. Thousands of moulds are in use. A favorite with the six penny line of German dolls is a good hard composition made by mixing 15 parts water with 5 parts wood pulp, 5 parts whiting and 1 part hot glue. In Austrian houses a similar compound was employed with a 5 % plaster of paris added."

In regard to the making of molds for dolls heads, Makinson has this to say, taking the English character doll for an example "The artist should model the features so that the common doll face is avoided. The original sample may be molded in clay and from this a gelatine matrix (half mould) of each side cast in a suitable pair of boxes. When finished or set the gelatine matrix may be employed to obtain several very fine sand and plaster casts, the latter are then used as a core for the type metal moulds. One of the plaster casts may be thickened up all over as equally as possible, this thickening can be accomplished by pouring over it successive coats of plaster and then the thickened up pattern can be molded in sand each half separately. A comparatively thin two part is obtained, when cast off the mould is split and the casting set up to dry. A wax core can be melted out by warming, care being taken to warm from the open end first. All the wax is reclaimed and used again. For the chilled system of moulding dolls heads, a composition is required that can be hardened on the skin in a reasonable time by heat, or by making cold. The material must cast with ease. With a fine surface and further should be unbreakable.''

''A rough experimental mould of any bottle shaped profile may be the best method to find out, in pouring and mixing the consistency of the mixture, the mass of the mold and the questions of the applications of heat or the cooling of the mould. If wax were used, the two halves of the mold would be placed together and the hot wax poured in, the molds being slightly hot to ensure perfect contact as well as absence of chilling and consequent cracks. The mold may then be cooled down on the outside by cooling or dipping in cold water and before the interior wax sets, may be poured out leaving a shell. All wax is reclaimed and used again.''

This technical, and very brief culling, from the Makinson book gives the doll collector but a glimpse into the intricate world of doll head making. It is indeed hard for the amateur to follow these steps, but a deeper appreciation of all that occurs to a doll, before it reaches the shelves of the collector, but adds to its interest.

It seems fitting to close here, quoting, in part, from one of Mrs. Gustine Courson Weaver's poems:

> ''Dolly's'' such a magic word,
> Most enchanting music heard;
> Takes us back to Mother's knees,
> And forgotten Christmas trees;
> Bedrooms where we used to play,
> Sunshine, carpets, curtains gay,
> Hills of wild-flowers nodding sweet,
> Dewy grasses on bare feet;
> Green umbrella o'er our swing,
> Singing wild birds on the wing;
> Sugar cookies tasting fine,
> Humming bees in wild grapevine;
> Child in town or city's street—
> Cold of Northland, Southland's heat—
> Hugs them—corn-cob, rag, or wax—
> Dressed in cotton, silk or flax,
> Magic Dolly—East or West—
> Which child of us loves you best?—
> Folk of centuries agree—
> ''Dolls—have—Immortality!''

> ''Dolls *have* Immortality.''

Chapter XI

DOLL BODIES
UNCOMMON DOLL TYPES

(Wooden, Wax, Gutta Percha, Kid,

Peddler Dolls, Mechanical)

Collection Janet P. Johl

German Doll Bodies during experimental stages. Wood, painted flesh color. Note Disproportionate legs and arms. Heads are of a later period. (Also German).

WHEN one begins on doll bodies the ground becomes more uncertain than in the matter of doll heads. Many doll bodies were home made, from whatever material available. However, certain definite facts do exist regarding doll bodies, and here again the trail leads back to Germany, the most famous doll country.

The old, high German word for dolls was 'tocha'. The middle high German was 'tocke'. The word changed after the fifteenth century to 'docke'. Tocke apparently meant a little block of wood, and as the primitive German dolls were simple wooden objects, the word was aptly chosen. Early examples of doll bodies date back to the thirteenth century and a number of specimens have been unearthed in the soil of old Strasbourg. In the Middle Ages, doll makers were known as coroplasts. The earliest dolls were of clay, and impersonated women dressed in contemporary fashion. There were no dolls representing children. Illustrations have been found showing the early doll makers at work, revealing, too, the possibility that a knowledge of moving arms and legs, was in existence, and proving profitable.

110

In an article entitled "*The Story of the Doll—the Child's Oldest Plaything*" appearing in the English magazine, *Games and Toys*, May, 1938, the writer "Ulysses" has this to say. "In the early days the manufacture of dolls in Germany appears to have grown up in and around Nürnberg—in Nürnberg alone there were seventeen workshops devoted to the manufacture of dolls and it is recorded that the council of the city on November 17, 1600, gave "permission to Barbara Breitner, of Bamberg to display dolls of her own making in the market place near the Schönen Brunnen."

Although in the year 1700 only 6 master doll makers were registered in Nürnberg, doll making had undoubtedly become a part of family life, and the dolls were carved in the homes. Later, as the industry developed, formulas were kept secret within families, and were passed down from father to son. Almost all of the work was hand work, heads and limbs made separately, and later eyes were made in the basements where no light could penetrate. The old Nürnberg toy dolls were made entirely of wood and covered with cloth, the heads carved and painted."

The French doll was held in esteem at an early date because of its highly artistic appearance. In the market stalls of the Palais de Justice, in Paris, during the fifteenth century, many exquisite articles of luxury were offered for sale, and among them were 'charming and attractively dressed dolls'.

In the sixteenth century dolls played an even more important role. Emperor Charles V, despite his hatred for France, had dolls sent to his little daughter, from Paris. Others of the nobility also obtained French dolls for their children. No definite authentic example of these early French dolls seems to be in existence, except through the medium of prints and the world of art. In the seventeenth century the French Fashion Dolls were freely used.

Whether these earliest dolls were of German, French or English origin, they must be looked upon as quite simple and rather primitive objects as far as their features, and bodies were concerned. Coming from the hands of the working people, they were not always artistic, and often not proportionate.

The earliest American dolls, too, were probably carved of wood, and existed even before the equally early rag doll. Some of the so called American dolls are undoubtedly English, of the Queen Ann type of wood, turned on a lathe and built up in plaster, or some early composition. Many of the old wooden dolls had arms of candlewick, and with the passage of time, the wood has taken on a waxy shine, from much handling, until it almost has a velvety sheen, and then it is called *patine*. The old jointed, pegged body, wooden dolls are occasionally seen in collections, and are treasured as examples of primitive Americana, primitive, in this instance, dating from the arrival of the white settlers. Miss Marion I. Perkins of Providence, R. I. the creator of the modern 'Peggity Doll' writes: "The inspiration for Peggity Dolls came from seeing a very old stiff wooden doll in my Great Aunt's garret, forgotten and loved by no one. Then the thought came, why not make little wooden jointed dolls that could be loved and could sit in tiny toy colonial chairs and sleep in canopy four poster beds, and enjoy wearing the quaint gowns of the period." Dolls of

---

* American wooden dolls and Fashion Dolls are discussed fully elsewhere. The Pantin receives a brief notation elsewhere.

cloth, whose bodies contained the letters of the alphabet were often made from
the linen pages of a child's book.

Wax dolls belong to the world of very old dolls, for the art of modeling
wax is so ancient that it comes down from a past that is beyond history. The
ease with which wax can be worked, and its charm, has ensured its use through
generations. In Bolivia, South America, primitive wax specimens have been
found. Wax dolls of the Haussa, in Africa, bear little resemblance to human
beings, although they have for adornments nose ornaments of glass beads. At
one period in Greek art wax dolls were quite common toys for the children.
The Egyptians made wax figures for their deities, and Pliny records that about
300 B. C. colored portraits in wax were made from plaster molds. Spanish art
boasts of many beautiful specimens made during the Middle Ages, and Italy
was using wax to reproduce her church figures. In the fifteenth century, Andrea
del Verrochio, and Orsino, were the first to make figures simulating human
beings. These were created on a wooden skeleton with wax faces and hands,
glass eyes and natural hair. Wax dolls appeared in Germany in the seventeenth
century and very lifelike models were produced. Those who could afford it
molded in wax. George Herzog, of White Plains, feels that Austria held the
first place in the waxwork business, especially in creating likenesses of individuals
to be given to friends as gifts. Antoine Benoist became quite famous for his
life size portrait of Queen Anne of Austria, and miniature reproductions of
prominent persons found a ready market. It seems safe to conclude that these
wax figures and replicas were the forerunners of the popular wax head doll of
the 1850-1880 period, and undoubtedly inspired such museums as that of the
famous *Waxworks* of *Madame Tussard* of London.

The son of Antoine Benoist met with competition in Johann C. Creutz, who
resided in Paris, and called himself Curtius. He persuaded his niece, Marie
Grosholtz, to come to Paris, and she learned to model wax heads from life, and
even gave lessons to Elizabeth, sister of Louis XVI. An exhibition given in
1789 was immediately successful. It was Marie who married Monsieur Tussard,
and moved to London, in 1802, taking with her the entire and remarkable collection originated by her uncle.

So the wax doll leads into a number of fields that do not actually belong to
a discussion of the doll, except to point out how the wax doll gradually evolved,
and the various methods of making wax dolls which varied according to the type
of doll, in regard to the all wax head, the wax over composition, the manner of
joining the head to the body, the hands and the feet, and the kind of body used,
and its stuffing.

Mrs. Emma C. Clear who works with the problem of the restoration of old
wax dolls, writes: "There are two kinds of wax in common use in the old dolls.
The commonest are the wax over papier maché. The French type were poured,
they give more detail and the molds are more perfect. A combination of the
two processes requires much thought and time. Poured wax, reinforced with
papier maché from the inside gives all the details of the poured wax and has the
strong underwork to keep it from collapsing under heat and pressure."

In telling of an old wax doll, Mrs. Daniel Hampton notes that such a doll
requires great care, and above all an even temperature. She gives this bit of

advice, of value to other collectors. "In too warm a temperature, the doll will melt, and if it is too cold, it will crack, particularly in the dry climate of Colorado. I have solved the problem by keeping pans of water in the doll cases to assure the wax dolls of their self preservation in the dry western air."

As has already been noted the beautiful wax heads made in England had no rivals in France, or in Germany, but the bodies were of wood, or kid or cloth, stuffed with rags, or bran, and were apt to be long and stiff and not jointed, with arms short in proportion to the bodies. Practically all of the wax over composition dolls, had cloth bodies, and many had composition hands and feet.

A doll can easily be a composite, with heads and arms and feet put together at any stage of its career.

In the early eighteenth century, wax peddler dolls were popular. These, and other English peddler dolls, not wax, were miniature copies of the vendors who went from house to house to sell their wares, in the days before there were any established stores. These dolls, also called "Haberdasher Dolls" were faithful replicas of picturesque English characters, even to duplicating, in tiny, detail the objects they had to offer. One private collection has a peddler doll with over a hundred things in her basket.

Vol. I, No. 5 of *Doll Talk* had an interesting little article entitled "Famous Peddler Dolls."

Courtesy Victoria and Albert Museum, London, England.

Peddler Dolls

Peddler dolls, a fascinating fad in the 18th century, are again coming into their own as a valuable hobby. So rare are these ancient figures that they are really of museum class, yet there are enough in existence to make a search for them intriguing.''

"These picturesque characters represent the street vendor of London, a century or so ago when from dawn to midnight they could be found hawking their many wares. Like their prototypes they even have a peddler's license, always in full view. Another characteristic is the red cape and black silk bonnet worn over a small lace cap. This garb is generally supposed to be the insignia of the Peddler.''

"Though most of these dolls are found in English Museums, a few are to be found in the United States. A Doll Hobby Club member, Miss Jennie L. Abbott of Massachusetts, is the fortunate possessor of two which are extraordinarily interesting.

"Miss Peddler, dated 1850, is in a perfect state of preservation as she has always lived in a glass case. Her china head has been covered with sponge which gives the appearance of an old, old woman. Her basket is filled with lace and needlepoint and many other lovely things, but perhaps the best thing is a tiny doll.

"These dolls depict the old men and women who sold their wares on street corners.''

"The tallest is about one foot high. Their baskets contain miniature copies of innumerable objects—musical instruments, candle-sticks, knitted and crocheted scarfs, Kitchen utensils. One doll, made in Wales, is dressed in Scotch woven wool and in her hand are knitting needles about one-half inch long on which she is knitting a sock. Another doll pictures as a peddler a crippled veteran of the Crimean War.''

Doll Talk also had an interesting account of these Peddler Dolls, part of an article by Amy Louise Woods in the Sunday issue of the *Worcester, Mass. Telegram* for January 31, 1937. A unique peddler doll, dating 1790, was described with 'sharp glass eyes and a nose that veers slightly to the left. Her wares are numerous: buttons, ribbons, needles, pins, rings, mirrors, brooms, mops, and any amount of household items.'' To quote further from *Doll Talk*:

The Largest Private Collection.

"One of the largest private collections of Peddler dolls is that of Mr. and Mrs. Dewitt Clinton Cohen of New York who have nine of these rare figures. Several are 1780 dolls and all are very interesting. There is a Welsh lady in her queer leek hat who stands patiently knitting. Another, a man, is a veteran of the Crimean War wearing a turban and red breeches. There is a beautiful lady, almost too regal for a street vendor, and a practical-minded house wife selling household utensils. Each is a treasure in itself and the entire collection is exceptional.

The dolls themselves are as varied as the articles in their baskets, for their makers were not factory-minded. Each doll represents hours of patient work and clever needle-work. The dressing of these dolls was as much a hobby of the 1800's as paper flower-making and burnt wood art was in the early 1900's.

The clothing of these dolls was carried out with great care and exactness but in filling the baskets or boxes, the imagination was allowed to run riot.

One may stand hours before a group of these figures and feel sure they have seen every tiny article; one may even write down a list of the contents. But come again another day and many new things will be discovered which were unnoticed on the first trip. In fact, one cannot see all the intricate little articles without taking the boxes apart; one box contained one hundred twenty-five different objects.

Occupied Place of Honor

As these dolls were made by ladies for their own pleasure and pastime, they were never in any sense toys. Instead, they occupied the place of honor on the mantel of Victorian parlors, their freshness preserved under thick glass globes. For this reason, there are quite a few peddler dolls in excellent condition.

Like all antiques, copies and reproductions appear from time to time; so is it in Peddler dolls. One appeared not so long ago who was so well copied that she could almost pass for an original.

It looks as though the century old Peddler doll is emerging from its undeserved obscurity to take its place as a modern favorite."

Mrs. Stewart Campbell of Bristol, R. I. tells of an extremely rare pair of English peddler dolls, ten inches high, bearing the trade mark of the "Whites of Milton"—circa 1810." She also mentions a rare pair of Shell Peddlers, with wax faces and wooden bodies.

From the most primitive types of wooden and wax dolls, the doll continued to improve although the bodies remained queer for a considerable time. They were of leather, of canvas, kid or rags, stuffed with any handy material. In 1850 Mlle. Calixto Huret began to use Gutta Percha, which preceded the use of rubber, for dolls.

Gutta Percha, discovered by accident in Singapore by Dr. Montgomerie of England, comes from the Malayan, meaning Gum (gatah) and Percha, (tree). It is a milky juice which is obtained from the Malay Gum Tree and resembles caoutchouc, which is an elastic tenacious substance. It is imported in oblong masses formed by rolling thin layers together in a soft state. When purified it is semi-transparent and tough. The stiff formless doll, and the doll with the leather bag for a body, gave way to Gutta Percha for a short while. On the earliest dolls Mlle. Huret* used heads of porcelain with a spherical part at the end so that the head could be turned. The center of the gutta percha business was located in the streets around Le Passage Choiseul. At ordinary temperature, it is non-elastic, but from 200°-212° Fahrenheit it becomes elastic and ductile. It is soluble, but not by the same agents as rubber, and is very useful in the ornamental arts for a number of reasons.

(1) It will not return to original size after being extended.

(2) It has no stickiness when softened by hot water.

(3) When under heat, it can be rolled out very thin and later, when cooled, still retain its original toughness and flexibility.

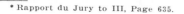

* Rapport du Jury to III, Page 635.

Courtesy Mrs. Edward A. Vossahlik

A Gutta Percha Doll

Lastly articles can be manufactured from it by molding, stamping, embossing or casting.

Mrs. Edward A. Vossahlik, of Hopkinton, Mass. has a Gutta Percha with kid hands and a very expressive face. This doll was formerly owned by the Jukes family of Winthrop, Mass. who were originally from England. Mrs. Clear, in writing of a Gutta Percha sent her for restoration, has this to offer "It was as brittle as an old piece of rubber, and the face was stove in against the back of the head, but the features were intriguing as was the hair dress. It snapped when you tried to bend it. I thought for a time that I would have to break it into small sections, and dress it down after gluing them to the base, but I decided to try various solvents and softeners. We finally solved it. Then we straightened the features back into place, modeled the shoulders, and refinished it. It is a regular Puritan old maid, but with the fanciest hair dress. I know that no woman with such a face would have submitted to that hair dress. Since then we have had four others, one with the original arms and legs of the gutta percha but none as interesting as the first."

The experimentation with materials for doll bodies went on, bodies of rubber, of leather and of canvas appeared but none proved so popular, or remained popular up to the time of the composition body, as the use of kid, which after all is only another name for leather. In this field the French greatly helped toward doll body improvements.

M. Brouillet, who was located on Rue St. Denis. No. 116 also made 'dolls that could stand without support or sticks'. By 1849 dolls were decidedly better, and the efforts of the manufacturers were not in vain. The house of M. Bru brought perfection to the doll by adding an internal organ which permitted the body to bend forwards, backwards and sideways. The kid body had a groove in the upper leg and the bust was part of the chest. Wobbly hands and feet were

borrowed from the Japanese and the hands were often very beautiful. This doll was jointed and could assume quite natural positions, the arms fitting in well. Most of the other dolls, made during this period, were constructed in stiff angular forms, some in one piece with awkward, ungraceful limbs.

By 1855, according to the 'Rapport du Jury l'Exposition' there were three famous doll houses of which Jumeau was listed first, and M. Voit de Hildburghausen, second. In the same year M. Fr. Greffier presented 'Poupeés Genres', which were known as 'babies', and showed Japanese influence.

The French Patent Books in the New York City Public Library, have this on the Bru dolls.

"December 12, 1867. Bru, representing Martinet, Paris. Poupeé-surprise, a tête tournante et a deux visage. (turning head and two faces)

Courtesy Mrs. Velvalee Dickinson

Papier Maché of late 1820's

"December 9, 1868. There is a *certificate d'addition* (for the same inventor for doll with turning head.)

"February 15, 1869. Bru, representing Mugard, Paris, same address. Perfections in doll making.

"May 18, 1872. Bru, dame, representing Hebre, Paris—magic doll called *poupeé a surprise.*

"February 19, 1876. Statuette of rubber.

"October 14, 1878. Bru representing Gebre, Paris. Moving dolls—baby dolls—in rubber (caoutchouc—India rubber). Addition Nov. 5, 1878.

"Bru, jeune, March 1879 represented by Hebre, same address. Type of baby doll in kid."

Three sets of indexes and catalogs for the period 1827-1880 revealed nothing further on Bru, but checked with each other.

The German kid bodies were very well constructed, but stiff, and the doll could not be placed in a sitting position easily. The bodies made in England were much more pliable and the construction was better suited to a child's play. Legs and arms could be bent with ease and the doll could be seated in a realistic attitude.

The French doll, with the kid body, usually had the type of doll head which opened all the way to the neck, and had cork fitted over the hollowed out head. The wig was glued on to the cork. A mechanism at the base of the neck permitted movement. The bodies were made of white kid for the finer types and pink for the more common dolls. All parts of the body were cut out of single or individual pieces of kid to assure accuracy of form. The arms were first attached to the body and then the legs. The joints at the shoulders, elbows, thighs and knees, were intersected by a small iron wire which permitted the parts to move, or to be held, in any desired position. The mechanical parts of the body were made by men, and the other parts by women. In the second

TRADE-MARK.

THE FIRM OF J. D. KESTNER, Jr.
KID BODY BISQUE HEAD DOLLS.

No. 29,129.   Registered Nov. 10, 1896.

WITNESSES:

Gustave Dieterich.

George Moise.

PROPRIETOR.

The Firm of J. D. Kestner, Jr.;

BY *Briesen Knauth*

ATTORNEYS.

half of the nineteenth century the kid bodies, white or pink or brown, were cut out by machinery, sewed together into a bag and stuffed with bran and saw-dust. These kid bodies influenced the manufacturers of doll heads, for the heads needed holes so that they could be sewed onto the kid bodies, and holes were put in the doll heads for this purpose, about this time. However dolls are often found which have the heads glued onto the kid bodies. The kid body with wooden jointed arms, painted, is said to pre-date the kid body with the bisque head. There was also a type of material, something like oil cloth, that was used about this time. The older French dolls had the wasp waist type of bodies and the body was much more shapely than the German. In fact the Germans were experimenting with bodies of wood at the time the French were producing the kid body, and surely these wooden doll bodies, painted flesh color, are anything but proportionate.

Miss Eva Page Daly, of Albany, N. Y. mentions that the wood-painted German dolls were the forerunners of the all plaster jointed dolls. The exact date for these dolls is quite difficult to give but it may be safely said that they all belong to the time when the doll industry was an active one, and when manufacturers were experimenting with the best kind of body to present to a doll minded public . . . 1850-1860 might be called the starting point, and there is no date to mark any end, for the doll is always being improved.

The manufacture of 'La Poupeé de Luxe' started in 1862 with the elder Jumeau's beautiful French made doll head. Paris had no rival in the art of making exquisite doll costumes. From the smallest fragment of cloth, the nimble fingered dressmakers could produce a tiny, but elegantly perfect gown.

The French dolls of this era were dressed in the most elaborate and beautiful costumes. From their curled and coiffeured wigs, to the tips of their pointed shoes, they were exquisite and dainty, proof that France had no rival anywhere who could produce such beauty and perfection in costuming as the French doll displayed. The degree of completeness was carried to such an extreme that dolls actually wore real jewels; and lace and shawls of such great value were often imported from far away lands. These dolls were known as "Les Grandes Dames," and garbed in the finest of silks and satins; boasting the latest in fashion attire and accessories, they were indeed propaganda heralds of France's claim to being the fashion centre of the world.

As the manufacture of the French doll improved, the combination of the two factors, the beautiful doll face, and the chic costuming, definitely gave the French doll a place in the eyes of the world, despite the competition of the German doll producers, the skilled German craftsmanship, and competent German handling of the fast growing industry. French dolls, well proportioned, appeared in about fourteen sizes, made of carton moule with arms and legs of India rubber or carved wood. They were offered at modest prices. By 1880, there were eight famous toy shops operating in Paris, but with the exception of the Jumeau dolls, it was the German market that really controlled the doll world. The well known Kestner plant in Germany put out every type of fine doll, jointed, kid, lady dolls and baby dolls. From year to year they enlarged their line, adding flirting eyes, or more naturally shaped bodies, always improving the doll. It was this company which made the first Rose O'Neill Kewpies for the American company of Borgfeldt. Dolls from this factory were still coming in from Germany when the war broke out in Europe. The trade mark for the Kestner Company is given to help the collector check specimens.

RENEWED.

UNITED STATES PATENT OFFICE.

THE FIRM OF J. D. KESTNER, JR., OF WALTERSHAUSEN, GERMANY.

TRADE-MARK FOR KID-BODY BISQUE-HEAD DOLLS.

Statement and Declaration of Trade-Mark No. 29,129, registered November 10, 1896.
Application filed October 10, 1896.

STATEMENT.

To all whom it may concern:

Be it known that we, THE FIRM OF J. D. KESTNER, JR., domiciled and doing business at Waltershausen, Thuringia, Germany, have adopted for our use a Trade-Mark for Dolls, of which the following is a full, clear, and exact description.

The said trade-mark consists of the representation of a crown with streamers pendent, and is generally used in the form shown in the accompanying drawing, wherein a king's crown is used, from which depend two streamers bearing the letters "J. D. K." and "Germany," and is generally colored blue.

The said trade-mark may be used in connection with various words, characters, and devices without materially altering the character of said trade-mark, the essential feature of which is the representation of a crown with streamers pendent.

This trade-mark was adopted by us about the 24th day of December, 1895, and has been continuously used by us ever since.

The class of merchandise to which this trade mark is appropriated is dolls, and the particular description of goods comprised in such class on which it is used is kid-body bisque-head dolls.

The said trade-mark is used by being printed upon the dolls, but it may also be otherwise marked or affixed to the dolls and the coverings in which they are sold or used in connection with any means whereby the said dolls are advertised to the public.

THE FIRM OF J. D. KESTNER, JR.
ADOLF KESTNER.

Witnesses: THOS. EWING MOORE, R. WYON.

An outlined description of dolls appearing during this period may be helpful to the collector in dating a given doll.

The Dolls were usually made in ten stages, progressing in the following manner.

(1) A Head of Bisque . . . (Possibly wax from England).
(2) A bust of paste or wax . . . or bisque depending upon the type of head and its manufacturer.
(3) Teeth of enamel or straw.
(4) Eyes of enamel glass, or painted.
(5) Hands. Wood, paste or kid. Feet usually kid.
(6) Hair, crimped, curled, or beautifully coiffeured.
(7) Complete toilette. Stockings-body linen.
(8) Gown . . hat . . shoes . .
(9) Accessories. Often a wardrobe trunk to accompany French lady doll.
(10) Inspection. Packing for shipment.

Each division went to a special department and to a separate person.

Quite some time elapsed before the paper pulp, or unbreakable composition material saw usage in the doll body, and in the construction of limbs and arms, although to-day this is probably the most popular kind of doll manufactured. The evolution of the doll body takes the student step by step along the way, leading from one material to another, and from one improvement to another. The doll is always moving along with civilization, and perhaps in this twentieth century, it serves and fulfills a greater purpose than ever before.

A chapter on doll bodies must, of necessity, be almost as composite an affair as the doll itself, for heads and parts were once sold separately. If a doll shop chanced to be out of matching arms or legs, the purchaser just took what came. When breakage occurred bodies were often switched, just as is sometimes done to-day. Because of the odd make-up of many old dolls, it is extremely difficult to ascertain their age. Facts can be presented about doll bodies, and that is about all.

An interesting doll that belongs to a discussion of doll bodies is the Walking Doll, known to both the Egyptians and the Greeks, in the fourth century, B. C. It is believed that the children of this era played with mechanical little toys whose actions simulated those of human beings, in walking, and arm movement. It took men centuries to perfect such a doll, but by 1352 there were clocks, such as the famous one in Strasbourg, with automatic figures. By 1716, costly, and very ingenious, dolls, displayed a variety of actions by means of clock works, concealed within their bodies. Germany again came to the fore, and mechanical toys became the specialties of Augsburg and Nürnberg. Traveling performances showed dolls which nodded their heads, moved arms and legs and gave a fairly good imitation of a person walking. Later the Swiss added, to the doll body, a concealed music box, and as the music played, the doll went through its rythmic movements.

About the time that the earliest settlers were arriving in America, Europe was quite familiar with life like dolls which went through a variety of motions. But it was not until the nineteenth century that the doll was really manufactured as a plaything for children. As early as 1823 there was a patent for a talking doll which said, 'Mama', and, 'Papa', the mechanism working by lifting one arm for one word, and the other arm for the other word. In 1826 contrivances were invented which brought the walking doll into existence as a toy rather than a mere automaton. In 1827, the inventor of the metronone, Malzel, took out a patent, in Paris, for a doll which could say, 'Mama', and, 'Papa', when squeezed. This was probably the first talking doll that was a success. It was not until 1862 that any patent was taken out in the United States, at Washington, for an automatic doll. But in that year, July 15th, E. R. Morrison of New York took out Patent #35,886 for "an improvement in automatic apparatus" and it is believed that this patent applied to the Autoperipatekos, or Walking Doll, and that the doll had a bisque head.

Mar. 23, 1869 A. W. Nicholson of Brooklyn, N. Y. took out patent #88,197 for a 'Walking Doll'. Henry C. Work, of Brooklyn, N. Y. took out Patent #140,605 on July 8, 1873 merely for a 'doll', but this 'doll' proved to be an ingenious idea, more simple than the Nicholson invention. Beneath the skirt of the doll was concealed a wheel which had on it four pairs of legs. Only two pairs of feet were visible, beneath the voluminous skirt, which was fashionable after that period. Because the skirt was so full and trailed behind, the doll was balanced, despite her wheel. There were a considerable number of walking dolls patented between 1862 and 1900, and, since the beginning of the twentieth century, many walking dolls have been invented varying in size, and ingenuity. Lovely dolls from France, exquisitely gowned, literally walked and talked their way into the arms of little girls. But how many dolls were actually manufactured is hard to surmise, surely not as many as were patented. By the late eighteen hundreds there were de luxe dolls, opening and shutting their eyes, walking and talking. Of the talking dolls, circa 1850, only a few seem to be left. More of the walking dolls are to be found. Mrs. John C. Albright has a mechanical doll which stands on a velvet covered box concealing a music box. When the music plays the doll begins to move her head from side to side and brings one hand up to smell a wee bouquet of flowers held securely, while with the other hand she gently fans herself. Her body is of papier maché, her arms of wire, with bisque hands and her head is also of bisque.

Many of the mechanical dolls have the Jumeau heads, while many more have heads made in Germany. Velvalee Dickinson, of New York City, has several of these mechanical dolls, with both French and German heads, men and women dolls, which go through a number of fascinating movements to the slow, tuneful melodies of their individual music boxes.

J. A. H. ELLIS.
Doll-Joints.

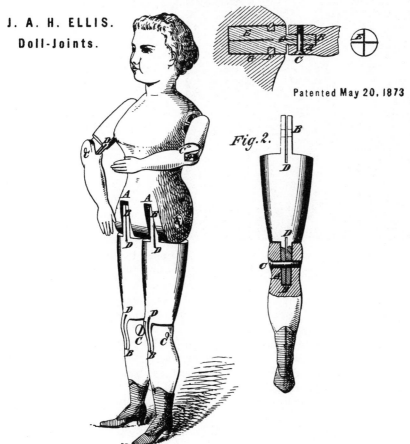

Patented **May 20, 1873**

Fig. 2.

Chapter XII

DOLLS OF UNIQUE INTEREST
REPLICAS

*(The First American
Made China Dolls)*

Courtesy Helen Siebold Walter

The Martha Washington Doll wearing a duplicate of the original hand painted costume now in the Smithsonian Institution. The doll by Mrs. Emma C. Clear. The costume by Miss Walter.

One of the most beautiful dolls that ever came out of Germany, is said to be in the image of the Princess Augusta. Several of these dolls are in existence in this country, and the stories concerning them are contradictory.

Mrs. Emma Teskey, of Pittsburgh, Penn. has a beautiful doll standing twenty-five inches high with blonde curls and braids about her head and pink cheeks. Mrs. Teskey called the doll 'bisque', until she was advised by several members of the local doll club, at one of the regular meetings, that the doll's head was undoubtedly of Parian.

However, Parian was not discovered until 1846 and according to the history of this particular doll, which is a carefully compiled record, the doll commemorates the marriage of Princess Marie Luise Katherina Augusta Von Weimar and Wilhelm 1st, afterward Emperor of Germany.

Here is Mrs. Teskey's story. Shortly after the royal wedding in 1829, this doll was given to Sophie Bittner, a young girl living in the German city of Frankfort-am-Main, who later became Mrs. Teskey's own grandmother. The

122

doll was passed on to Mrs. Teskey's mother who gave it, at Christmas time in 1882, to Mrs. Teskey when she was seven years old. The mate to the doll is said to be in the Children's Museum at Thür-ingen, Germany. Mrs. Teskey does not know how he came there, whether he belonged to her family, originally, and in time was given to the Muse-um, or whether he was given by some one else. To the best of her knowledge and her study, there is no similar *pair* of these dolls in existence. She has searched in many museums in large cities, made innumerable inquiries, and friends traveling have looked carefully in many large Euro-pean Museums, all to no avail. Since Mrs. Teskey has no daughter of her own, the doll will eventually go to her grand daughter Carol Jean Teskey.

Most interesting is the Iron Cross of Germany which is molded, in black, into the bisque, or parian, as is the ribbon on which the cross is suspended. The German Iron

Courtesy Mrs. Emma Teskey

The Princess Augusta Von Weimar, or The Princess Augusta?

Cross was first given for distinguished service in the War of Liberation, 1813, under Friedrich Wilhelm, III. It was revived in 1870 in the Franco-Prussian war and again in the World War in 1914. Women of the nobility may wear the cross, which always has the date of campaign and the initials of the reigning sovereign.

Mrs. Teskey's doll has arms of leather, the fingers of the hand stitched. The body is of cotton stuffed muslin, and the feet are encased in blue boots. Eighteen beads form the black coronet around the head. The original robe of yellow velvet that fell from the shoulders of the doll, over her gown of silver brocade, has been replaced by another, a copy of the original which Mrs. Teskey made of materials from old frocks belonging to her grandmother, her mother and herself. The doll has a very complete wardrobe, in the style of the early nineteenth century, consisting not only of gowns, but of parasols, jewelry and hats to match the dresses.

Courtesy Mrs. Izole Dorgan
Two Dolls similar to the Princess, one without the Iron Cross

This is the story of Mrs. Teskey's Princess Augusta. The story, as well as the doll, has been handed down to her right within her own family. Yet, there are other persons who believe that this doll is *not* the Princess Augusta, born in 1811 and married in 1828, but another Augusta . . . Augusta Victoria, born in 1858 and married in 1881 to Friedrich Wilhelm Victor Albert, Emperor of Germany and King of Prussia, Wilhelm II, the grandson of Wilhelm I, and the son of the Princess Alexandrina of England, daughter of Queen Victoria. It is interesting to note that both the Princesses bore the name of Augusta, and both were daughters of Dukes named Friedrich. Perhaps this may account for some of the conflicting theories surrounding the true identity of the doll.

There is living in New York City a gentleman who once served in the household of Augusta, wife of Wilhelm II, in Germany. When he saw the blonde doll he immediately recognized his former mistress, though he did not know a replica of the Princess had ever been made. Mrs. Catherine Richards Howard writes that she has been told that a German Museum has this type of doll, dated 1860, also that she has seen several of these Princess replicas, and where the clothing is termed "original," the style is nearer the period of the '80's, than that of the '30's.

Mrs. Howard also has a brunette doll from the same mold. Her doll has deep blue eyes of blown glass, and dark chestnut brown hair. Gold dots join the coronet. The original Augusta Victoria was a blonde and in doll form her eyes were set in blue glass and her ears pierced. However Mrs. Howard believes that this brunette doll is the same except for the hair color.

Mrs. Dorgan has two dolls of this type exactly like the blonde Princess except that one of the two does not have the Iron Cross molded in her chest.

There still remains Mrs. Teskey's story which seems to be the only one surrounding this doll that has actually come down through one family for three generations. The other dolls do not appear to have so carefully a recorded history, although perhaps some may have a story that has not been told, to date.

It has also been said that the portrait of Princess Augusta Victoria, painted at the time of her marriage to the German Kaiser, is very like this doll. One thing is certain and that is that the doll is exquisitely beautiful. That alone should suffice to give her a place of honor in any collection.

Mrs. Emma C. Clear, who recently produced the first American china head doll, and who is engaged in creating replicas of famous dolls, includes the Princess doll in her list as follows:

"H.R.H. The Kaiserin Augusta Victoria. Marble white Parian portrait doll of the young Kaiserin on her wedding day. High blonde curls with a chain of black beads through them. Earings. Shirred blouse of the Parian with a little neck ruff and the Maltese cross in black and gold on a black ribbon around her neck."

So much for this intriguing doll. Perhaps some one can cast further light by coming to the fore with further historical information.

The beautiful replicas which Mrs. Clear has succeeded in creating are worthy of full mention for they represent an outstanding achievement in the world of dolls.

The first of these replicas, a lovely lady of long ago, is Jenny Lind. When she recently made her bow to the world of dolls collectors at once recognized not only the beauty of the doll but the fine craftsmanship that went into her creation. It took time and study, disappointments and perseverance, and untiring efforts to reproduce this copy of a lovely old doll, but Mrs. Clear labored on.

A little over two years ago she located the correct clay, both the German and the English, but no one seemed to find the right mixture, or the correct fusing temperature. Finally, just before Christmas, she struck it, and found that 2300 degrees, hot enough to melt ordinary ceramics to a puddle, was the right degree for doll heads.

Mrs. Clear was delighted and wrote enthusiastically of her find. "We have the china down pat now and can get any shade and texture from the Purest Parian to the lustres and white chinas. I held my breath over the first firing of the heads. We brought out four lustres, three Parians and several white chinas, all perfect".

But the way of the artist-creator is not strewn with roses . . . it is a hard path to tread . . . one full of discouragements. "We have struck a snag" wrote Mrs. Clear a few weeks later, "China decorating, our newest work, is entirely different from any other medium. If I want a certain shade in oils or lacquers I obtain it by blending, just a bit of this and that, until I have what I want. Not with the chinas; With them, it is like working in the dark. The soft irregularity that passes for art in placques and china decorating, simply will not do on fine doll heads. The best china paints obtainable are not fine enough and do not have the flow. Even an expensive new air brush does not solve the trouble. At last we set our research man on the problem. He thinks that we will have to grind and mix our own colors. But with china, it is not possible to tell what the result will be until after it is fired, and then it is too late to do anything about it . . . and heads are too expensive to experiment on."

Courtesy Mrs. Catherine Richards
Howard

A Princess Doll with dark chestnut
brown hair

Somehow the experimenting went on, and soon more news arrived from California. "The china is going smooth as silk and the problems on the colors are gradually working out."

"The head's have to be fired at least twice, occasionally three or four times. I am not following the models exactly. For instance, the old clay often had imperfections, like the bits of flint and air bubbles and black heads, in old Chelseas. Evidently in those early days it was necessary to grind the clay by hand and probably the sifters were poor. The original Jenny Lind head for instance was squint eyed, but the real Jenny did not have such eyes. Neither will the new Jenny Lind doll for we shall make her as lovely as we are capable of doing. For feet, we had to get old silver, gold and copper lustres to match the antiques in the various color combinations. After some difficulties the third trial was perfect. Now they are going along smoothly and the modeling is splendid. Craft work is a real joy . . . there is no speed nor high pressure, but the craftsman must have ability and the power to think logically; that is what makes the work so fascinating."

That all the workers, and especially Mrs. Clear, have this exceptional ability is evidenced by this first American China head doll, the Jenny Lind replica. It is indeed a lovely doll with exquisite shoulders and finely molded features. The creamy white china is as interesting, as the pink lustre finish, if not as delicate. Doll collectors claim that there are several models for the original Jenny Lind doll but the artists who were talented enough to do these originals did not think them important enough to sign them. They died unsung and unhonored, and, in addition, from the prices still to be found in many of the old heads, poorly paid for their efforts, and perhaps even unpaid. In order to distinguish the originals from the replicas, Mrs. Clear has a registered trade mark, so that all her replicas will be known for what they are . . . beautiful examples of modern art.

There are many varied dolls called "Jenny Lind" and almost as many and varied stories about them. When the 'Swedish nightingale' was brought to these shores by P. T. Barnum the public received her with open arms and her popularity was so great that her likeness appeared, it is said, in dolls and glass bottles. Her name was used on all kinds of commodities and products.

Mrs. Izole Dorgan reports a Jenny Lind in rubber. Mrs. Catherine Richards Howard mentions a "Jenny Lind with dark hair drawn down quite low over the ears, and a funny flat knot low in the back."

Miss Gertrude D. Collins of Great Falls, Montana sent this information about the original Jenny Lind doll. "When the great singer visited New York in 1850, a wax doll was manufactured in her likeness to commemorate her first appearance at Castle Garden. She retired from the stage when she married M. Otto Goldschmidt. In 1861 she re-appeared and England celebrated her return to the stage by making her likeness in a doll of china. As she had always desired black hair, the doll was made with black hair. Jenny Lind dressed the dolls in material of her own dresses and gave them to her friends."

It is also said that the *Commercial Advertiser*, published in New York City, August 24th, 1850, had the news that a Jenny Lind doll arrived on the packet ship, Albert Gallatin. The Swedish nightingale came to the United States on

Loaned by Mrs. Emma C. Clear

The First American China Doll makes her bow . . . a replica of the 'Jenny Lind' Staffordshire in creamy white china, or in pink lustre. 24 inches tall.

Sept. 1st, 1850 to sing at Castle Garden and many a little girl happily possessed a doll named for the famous singer, whether the likeness was an exact one or not.

All the legends surrounding Jenny Lind are intensely interesting. Miss Gertrude Collins had a fine dressmaker copy a gown for her Jenny Lind doll. after the oil portrait of the real Jenny by Eduard Magnus. Miss Elma Fuller, of Bristol, Vt. reports a china Jenny Lind doll that she believes is quite rare. "My doll is small, about 12 inches tall with a 5 inch head. She is an old doll and her coloring is rather pink. The story is told that Jenny Lind was a sandy blonde and wore a black wig for concerts because her natural hair showed up drab in poor light. That seems to be why the Jenny Lind dolls have dark hair."

Mrs. William Harvey, of Cortland, N. Y. has some Jenny Lind dolls which she classifies as 'rare Staffordshire'. Mrs. Clear calls her replica "Jenny Lind Staffordshire." An outstanding authority on the great singer, who prefers to remain incognito, says that the Jenny Lind dolls are shrouded with mystery, although he has heard of rare Staffordshire ones, but has never seen one.

Mrs. Ruffin A. Smith of Birmington, Ala. reported a doll called Jenny Lind which she described as having a waist joined by gussets kid feet and hands, golden hair, the blue scarf in bisque around the head. This definitely answered the description of a doll known as the Princess Louise of Prussia. Folded in the hollow of the head was found a thin scrap of paper with this poem penned upon it.

"TO MY DOLL UPON A SHELF"

How like the color of a sweet June rose,
The pink upon thy rounded cheeks of bisque,
Blue eyes, golden hair, mouth in sweet repose,
Placed carefully, so there be no risk
Of broken fragments on a polished floor.
If I like thee, could have kept my youth,
My dreams, all lost so long before,
Where, with magnanimity, I could reason why
My love for thee was unrequited,
I stand and gaze and wonder with a sigh,
If we two can ever be united,
Perhaps through Memory's magic page,
I yet may hope to vanquish jealous age."

In the world of dolls, it is possible to say with W. S. Gilbert, in 'Pinafore' . . . "Things are seldom what they seem." A Jenny Lind doll turns out to be a Princess Louise. Mrs. Catherine Richards Howard terms the Blue Scarf Doll "Dresden Bisque".

Mrs. Izole Dorgan feels that the so called portrait dolls were not posed for by individuals but rather were taken from photographs and sketches. A study of various Jenny Linds will reveal the diversification. What one individual calls a Jenny Lind another terms a Victorian. Who really knows?

Mrs. Dorgan tells also of a work table doll, circa 1865, a wooden doll with china head and legs, with a dark, rich pink complexion and a Dresden hair arrangement, truly resembling Jenny Lind. This doll, of the Peddler type, was 'dressed in a few odd pieces of merino calico ribbon' and full description as to how to dress her were given. She held two papers of needles, a thimble, a pair of scissors and a ball of cotton. Measuring eight inches from head to foot, this was a Utility Jenny Lind Doll. The top of her head served as a pin-cushion, a ball of wool hung from the back of her belt, and pockets assured a place for the things necessary to a Work Table Lady.

Following Mrs. Clear's replica of Jenny Lind, are other replicas of equal interest. Here is her list as the dolls have appeared.

(1) Jenny Lind, *the First American China Doll.* 24" tall. Pink lustre, copper lustre shoes, gold trimmed. In white china.

(2) Elizabeth Parian. Blond Bisque head on Parian shoulders. High blond curls with a turquoise and gold lustre comb. Earrings. High ruff of the Parian. Hand carved corsage in rose and green lustre. 20" tall.

(3) The Mona Lisa. An exquisite doll of the Biedermeier period in pink lustre. Slender, aristocratic face. Hair dropped low over the ears and drawn to a bun. The most beautiful shoulders that we have ever seen on a doll. Just the shadow of the throat muscles in the lustre. 32″ tall.

This doll was modeled from the original in the Williams Collection of Beverly Hills, Cal. by Martha Oathout Ayres, one of America's best classical sculptors, who has made the 'International Blue Book', 'Who's Who in America', 'Who's Who in Art', and Leading Women of America'.

(4) Louise of Prussia, blonde bisque with a bisque scarf around her head. Scarf

Courtesy Gertrude Collins

Replica of Jenny Lind

and shoes in pink or blue. 18″ tall. Blue glass eyes. This doll was copied from the original in the Collins Collection of Great Falls, Montana.

Miss Gertrude Collins found her 'Blue Scarf' doll in an antique shop in Los Angeles. It had been taken by the proprietor because she wanted silver and in order to obtain the one, she had to take the other. Miss Collins first saw the doll sitting in a large silver fruit dish in the window. On inquiry she found that an elderly woman in need of funds, was disposing of a life time collection of dolls and old silver, that she had owned the doll for 70 years, and called it her Beulah Doll because her mother had rocked her to sleep and sung 'Beulah Land' as she drifted off, the doll clutched in her arms. The body was of kid, old and falling to pieces, and very dirty. The pale blue wool dress dropped to mere rags with cleaning. So the beautiful head was put on a new body, and arms and legs added to match the delicate Parian head. "Now it holds a high spot and is admired by all."

(5) H. R. H. The Kaiserin Augusta Victoria. From the Schmidt Collection, Los Angeles, Cal.

(6) Victorian Lustre. Lovely, placid face with wide eyes and forehead. Hair plain on top with perpendicular curls. 26″ tall.

This is a pink lustre from the Negus Collection of Fullerton, Cal. A beautiful placid face, cute hands with outstanding thumbs and flat heeled shoes. The original doll has poorly dressed joints as is often the case in the mold joints of old dolls. The modern replica has joints dressed down so that they cannot be found, thus showing the improvement in the workmanship of to-day.

(7) The little Mona Lisa, a small doll in pink lustre of this lovely model done at the request of eastern collectors. 16-18″ tall.

For those who either do not like large dolls or do not have room to house them.

(8) "Curley Top", 16″ tall. May be had in either china or pink lustre. Pretty, doll face with rows of curls coming to points on her forehead. Light brown, honey blond or black hair.

The original is from the Denham Collection, Monterey Park, Cal. A very pretty type of doll, more attractive than rare.

(9) "Spill Curls", a pretty doll face china with an elaborate hair dress. Curls spill down her neck and each side of her throat. Honey blond, light brown or black hair. The hair band may be in light blue lustre or painted to match the hair. 22″ tall.

The original is from the Moebus Collection, Lima, Ohio.

(10) Another little Parian in a deep bonnet which is caught back in the centre with a ribbon rosette. The original is from the Lewis Collection, Beverly Hills, Cal.

(11) The greatest work has been done on the Martha Washington. This is the first original doll by an internationally famous sculptor. The doll is a result of the study of all that Mrs. Ayres could find in the library on the First First Lady and thus is a composite of all the various portraits. The doll will be of marble white Parian, silver curls, and lace cap . . . Martha Washington at sixty years of age. Mrs. Clear served as a model for the hands, as Mrs. Ayres felt that they suited the character of the doll as to capability, skillfulness and correctness of age. This is the first time that doll hands have been cast with the fingers spread out in a natural position. They are perfect even to the delicate veins and life lines.

The long slender fingers do not touch each other but clasp when brought together. One doll collector wrote enthusiastically of this doll, "Mrs. Clears' 'Martha Washington' is the most beautiful doll in the world".

Courtesy Mrs. Emma C. Clear and Mrs. Nellie Upp
Mrs. Emma C. Clear with her Replicas

Miss Helen Siebold Walter, of Staunton, Va. sent the following data. "The original hand painted costume, in oil, worn by Martha Washington when she was the First Mistress of the White House, now in the Smithsonian Museum at Washington, D. C. is of soft faded salmon silk, and shows the wild flowers and insects of North America. Through the courtesy and co-operation of the National Museum this original costume has been duplicated in individual hand painted and hand made costumes for the Martha Washington doll. The five undergarments are of linen and lace. The outfit is entirely hand made and includes the lace scarf and Martha Washington bag, which is a duplicate of the original in the National Museum which was made by the first First Lady herself. It is of brown satin with wreath of hand embroidered, multi colored, flowers and sequins. Within the wreath is the name, 'Mrs. M. Washington", in the child like hand writing of the First First Lady. The bag is filled with rose leaves, from an old rose jar, as a fragrant memory of Martha's own rose garden, where she gathered the leaves for drying and spicing."

About to make his debut is George Washington who is now in the hands of the sculptor, and who will be a companion piece to the First First Lady. Mrs. Clear writes that 'The George Washington Doll is ready for casting, a fine man's figure that stands alone. The sculpture work is very fine. The hands are modeled so that one will rest on the back of Martha Washington's chair, and the other is designed so that it may hold something, perhaps a cane."

"The legs have the buckled dress shoes of the period and are beautifully modeled to wear short, lace trimmed pantaloons. The wig is of Parian. This doll presented a number of serious problems which were ultimately worked out and now we feel that the pair—Martha and George Washington, do indeed cap anything we have done to date".

"Besides our talented Mrs. Ayres, we are fortunate in having Hazel Francis Raines, whose profession is that of a portrait painter on porcelain, as our decorator. She is, I believe, the best in her field on the west coast, and she has won first place in figure work on porcelains at the California Fair for three successive years. Mrs. Winnie Woods has mastered the use of the panograph and is able to turn bodies and corsets out almost as fast as they are needed to fill incoming orders. Mrs. Wood figured out the correct proportions for the doll bodies and then mastered the tool, the panograph. She is the only member of the crew whose work we never have to check."

"We have added a new decorator, Antal Schonig, Austro-Hungarian artist and painter, probably the last active one of the old European trained great ones. They have something that the best of this generation do not have. Mrs. Raines is a pupil of Schonig, also of Punch. They are the only two left of the great ones. Franz Bischoff, the two Aulichs, Klein of Dresden and Berlin."

Despite all the work accomplished and that lying ahead, Mrs. Clear, modestly, begs, "Do not give me too much credit. It takes the co-operation of a mighty fine group of artists to turn these dolls out. I am just a sort of director."

But that Mrs. Clear also experiments successfully is revealed in another of her enthusiastic letters.

"Take, for instance, Dresden work in tiny flowers of glazed china. I did my first recently on an Elizabethan Parian head with high ruff, hair ornament

Courtesy Mrs. Emma C. Clear — Photographer Conrad
A group of replicas. Note head of Martha Washington.

and little bouquet of flowers. I had carved the flowers before of solid clay.
It is difficult, as one slip, and the piece is ruined. You have to change your
design. I cut those tiny leaves and petals, with no tool but a pen knife . . . I
had no other. The clay is rolled very thin like pie dough, and then cut. I held
my breath until they came out of the kiln. The first attempt was perfect. Now
I have to rig up other tools for it took me six hours to carve four wee flowers.''

"Mr. Clear, who has an inventive mind, has been working for the past year
on perfecting a body stuffer, for the saw dust filled dolls. Our sawdust comes
from a sawdust specialist and it is ground wood, which is made up for the
industrial and chemical plants. We tried several kinds of saw dust before we
found the right kind . . . one that would pack tight, hold its shape and be clean,
not gummy. No one makes enough bodies to need a machine to stuff them and
when this type of doll body was popular—years ago—labor was so cheap, it
did not matter. But now, it is quite different and a half a day to stuff a doll
body is costly.''

"Mr. Clear has made us a body stuffer that 'is a honey'. It does prettier
and smoother work than could ever be done by hand . . . It is an auger working
in reverse, in a brass shaft in the bottom of a hopper. The feeding end sticks
out about 6 inches and is belted to a motor. It gets right down to business and
pours the nicest stream of sawdust . . . a really practical and cute gadget doing
in five minutes a better and neater job than a good worker could do in an hour,
or a poor one in half a day.''

"We are not calling our discovery, our ability to reproduce these replicas
in china, lustre, Parian or bisque, anything in particular. Just finding out
something that other countries have known and kept to themselves is not really
such a great accomplishment. We would not have bothered had we been able to
import satisfactory parts. It was the wretched quality of recent importations,
and the fact that they would give us no models except those found on the cheaper
dolls that led us on to experiment. It is impossible to import dolls cheaper than

Courtesy Gertrude D. Collins

The Blue Scarf Doll, sometimes called Queen Louise of Prussia.

to make them, even with the duty of 150% and the one cent extra for every moving part. All our dolls will be copyrighted and dated.''

''I believe that we can do anything in America that has ever been done before, but it is not easy, the work is hard, the financial reward not yet sufficient to induce people to learn the real crafts. We shall continue to make our replicas. True they are not old, but we believe that they are lovely enough to stand on their own merits. We are not trying to imitate the old dolls but to capture their beauty and charm, and give them the advantage of modern technique.''

Another person interested in ceramics who is making interesting and authentic arms and legs of china and porcelain is Mrs. C. H. Kelso of Kansas City, Mo. who writes ''I am doing a lot of experimenting and I want you to know that I find my work in the field of dolls, fascinating.''

The more students of ceramics who engage in serious and concentrated efforts to produce china doll heads, arms and legs, the sooner the doll world will know the back ground of the old china dolls, for the one must lead to the other.

Chapter XIII

AMERICAN MADE DOLLS
1858-1913

(Patent Listings-Goodyear-Darrow-Dotter-
Goldsmith-Palmer Cox-Billiken-Chase
Stockinet-Kewpies)

Courtesy Robert D. Chase
Chase Stockinet Dolls

A glimpse at a partial list of doll patents taken from the U. S. Patent Office Records reveals the beginnings of the industry in the United States. As many of the patents issued do not seem to have materialized into the actual doll head or doll body, and as many others were listed under the classification of toys, it has seemed advisable to show only a certain few, which in themselves should give a sufficient introduction to the early years of doll manufacturing in this country.

Patent No.	Date	Patent Issued To	Description of Patent
19,770	3-30-1858	L. Greiner, Philadelphia, Pa.	Constructing Doll Head.
46,270	2- 7-1865	L. E. Sallee, Decatur, Ill.	Method of constructing doll head
52,142	3- 1-1866	F. E. Darrow, Bristol, Conn.	Manufacture of Dolls
52,782	2-20-1866	D. Checkeni, Marion, Conn.	Fancy Doll
81,999	9- 8-1868	G. H. Hawkins	Dolls Heads.
85,589	1- 5-1869	G. H. Hawkins	Manufacture of Dolls Heads
113,532	4- 4-1871	J. Lacman, Philadelphia, Pa.	Doll
129,086	7-16-1872	G. Benda, Coburg, Germany	Doll Head
139,130	5-20-1873	J. A. H. Ellis. Springfield, Vt.	Doll Joint
144,373	11- 8-1873	Izannah F. Walker, Central Falls, R. I.	Rag Dolls with Painted Features.
149,831	4-21-1874	W. E. Brock, New York	Manufacture of Hollow Doll's Heads and other figures.
187,173	2- 6-1877	Lazurus Reichmann, New York	Doll's Head
214,830	4-29-1879	Frank Martin, Springfield, Ill.	Doll Joint
235,218	12- 7-1880	Charles T. Dotter	Doll
235,300	12- 7-1880	George W. Sanders, (Assigned to W. H. H. Slack, Springfield, Vt.)	Joint for Dolls
242,210	5-31-1881	H. H. Mason & L. W. Taylor, Springfield, Vt.	Construction of Dolls.

Patent No.	Date	Patent Issued To	Description of Patent
243,752	7- 5-1881	Fritz Bartenstein, Hutten-steinach, Germany.	Double Face Wax Doll.
267,212	11- 7-1882	Charles C. Johnson, Spring-field, Vt.	Doll's Head.
268,020	11-28-1882	George W. Howard, Washing-ton, D. C.	Doll
278,420	5-29-1883	Stuart Eldridge, Yokohoma, Japan. (Assignor of one-half to E. C. Hine & R. W. Beyrich, Brooklyn, N. Y.)	Doll
332,248	12-15-1885	Philipp Goldsmith, Covington, Ky.	Doll Body with Corsets.
371,751	10-18-1887	Wolf Fletcher, Covington, Ky.	Method and Means of stuffing dolls.
480,094	8- 2-1892	Solomon D. Hoffman, Moscow, Russia	Composition for and method of making heads and limbs of dolls.

These few listings reveal the fact that at quite an early date the doll entered the field of industry, in America, as a profitable item, and also that at an early date there was competition from Germany and Japan. Glancing over this partial list, it is easy to see that the doll minded persons were of an inventive nature, for almost every kind of doll was tried . . . perhaps this period of trial and error, accounts for the fact that many dolls, for which patents were issued, never appeared.

'According to *"American Made Dolls & Figurines,"* in the report of the Bureau of Statistics of Labor in Massachusetts, it mentions that "the oldest existing manufacturing plant of toys and games for children was established in 1835", and that, "all statistics of toys and games establishments were included under the heading of miscellaneous manufactures in 1875". No reference is specifically made of dolls. Victor S. Clark in his work *"History of Manufactures in the United States"*, covering the period from 1860-1893, says: "Dolls were a large article of manufacture in New York, Boston and Philadelphia, although their porcelain and china heads were generally imported.'

UNITED STATES PATENT OFFICE.

NELSON GOODYEAR, OF NEW YORK, N. Y.

IMPROVEMENT IN THE MANUFACTURE OF INDIA-RUBBER.

Specification forming part of Letters Patent No. **8,075**, dated May 6, 1851.

To all whom it may concern:

Be it known that I, NELSON GOODYEAR, of the city, county, and State of New York, have invented a new and useful Improvement in the Preparation and Manufacture of Caout-chouc or India-Rubber; and I do hereby declare that the following is a full and exact description thereof.

The nature of my invention consists in so compounding caoutchouc with other substances that the composition thus formed, when subjected to the heating or curing process described in the patent of Charles Goodyear, dated June 15, 1844, and in the reissue of said patent, dated December 25, 1849, will form a hard stiff substance hitherto unknown.

The indispensable ingredients used in my composition are caoutchouc and sulphur, and when only these two ingredients are used the best proportion will be about equal parts, by weight, of each of them; indeed a much less proportion of sulphur will not suffice. But though the combination of so large a proportion of sulphur with the caoutchouc will not produce, when cured, a hard substance, a still better result will be obtained by the introduction of magnesia, lime, carbonate of magnesia or lime, or sulphate of magnesia or lime into the composition, in which case the following proportion will be found a highly advantageous one—viz., one pound of caoutchouc, half a pound of sulphur, and half a pound of magnesia or lime, or carbonate of magnesia or lime, or sulphate of magnesia or lime.

Courtesy of Mrs. Izole Dorgan

An Old Rubber Doll in the Likeness of Jenny Lind

The Scientific American of 1867 describes 'the stuffed bodies of dolls made in New York, Boston, and Philadelphia', and states that 'the heads were purchased from France and Germany'.''

Miss Jennie Abbott, of Westfield, Mass. has a most interesting article entitled "Old Rubber Toys a n d Dolls", in *American Made Dolls & Figurines*. To quote: "Rubber toys are also distinctly American in origin, dating from Pre-Columbian times when the Amazon Indians played with bouncing rubber balls."

"According to the "Dictionary of American Biography", Charles Goodyear, inventor of the first successful process for making soft rubber began the manufacture of rubber toys in 1837. In his book 'Gum Elastic', Mr. Goodyear writes that the manufacture of rubber dolls in the U. S. was licensed to B. F. Lee."

"The directories of New York City from 1821-1870 list Benjamin F. Lee, a merchant, the first mention of rubber goods in this connection being in 1850 and continuing through 1870."

"Doll's heads, the modeling of which resembles that of china and composition heads of the 50's and 60's, are in existence as well as a portrait doll of Jenny Lind, the famous Swedish singer who visited the United States in 1850."

"Hard Rubber was patented May 6, 1851 by Nelson Goodyear, brother of Charles, patent #8,075. Dolls are said to have been made bearing the mark "Goodyear-May 6, 1851" the mark referring to the material from which the doll was made and not the doll itself. This same mark is found on old hard rubber buttons and other articles."

Velvalee Dickinson, of New York City has, in her collection, a Goodyear Rubber Doll.

About 1865 a factory was started in Bristol, Conn. which made dolls of untanned leather. Beginning on a small scale it became a corporation in 1867, under two men, Franklin E. Darrow and John A. Way. On May 1, 1866 the firm took out a patent for "Improvements in the Process of Manufacturing Dolls &c., from Rawhide."

UNITED STATES PATENT OFFICE.

FRANK E. DARROW, OF BRISTOL, CONNECTICUT.

IMPROVED PROCESS FOR MANUFACTURING DOLLS.

Specification forming part of Letters Patent No. **54,301,** dated May 1, 1866.

To all whom it may concern:

Be it known that I, FRANK E. DARROW, of Bristol, county of Hartford, and State of Connecticut, have invented certain new and useful Improvements in the Process of Manufacturing Dolls, &c., from Rawhide; and I do hereby declare that the same is described in the following specification, so as to enable others skilled in the art to make or pursue the same, the nature of which consists in the employment of any suitable liquid by the use of which the rawhide is saturated or steamed just as it is about to be introduced into the die and press and pressed into shape, and will perfectly retain the shape given it by the mold.

The process is simply as follows: The rawhide is first cured in the usual way. It is then cut into blanks of suitable size for the purpose desired. Then take a box of concentrated lye, (about one pound, usually found in stores for sale), put it into about two gallons of water, then place said blanks in a suitable apparatus into which steam made from said composition or liquid may enter, and thereby saturate or steam said blanks, when they may be taken therefrom, one at a time, and introduced to the die and press, and pressed into the desired form or shape. When taken therefrom it will be hard and perfectly retain its shape or form into which it has been pressed while in its flexible or elastic state. There may be other liquids by means of which this effect may be produced.

The particular object of saturating or steaming is to produce an elastic or flexible state of the rawhide during only the time occupied in pressing it into its mold or die.

I have found by the use of alcohol the same result may be produced; but it will be seen that it is too expensive. I therefore believe that the process particularly described will be found to be the best and cheapest.

I believe I have described the process so as to enable others skilled to use the same to produce the same effect.

What I claim, therefore, and desire to secure by Letters Patent, is—

The process of saturating rawhide for forming it into a desired form or shape, substantially in the manner, as and for the purpose described.

FRANK E. DARROW. [L. S.]

Witnesses:
LEONARD BLAKESLEE,
BENJ. F. HAWLEY.

To quote again from *American Made Dolls & Figurines* "John A. Way conceived the idea of making rawhide belts for conveying power in factories because this material would not stretch. It is worth noting that the first experiences with it were quite favorable. But the factories thus equipped soon discovered that rats were very fond of rawhide and so these belts were apt to be gnawed by these rodents and ruined. This finally led to the bankruptcy of the company which stopped business in 1877."

One of these Darrow rawhide dolls is in the collection of Mrs. Nina B. Shepard, of Granville, Ohio. Mrs. Shephard writes "I doubt if there is another rawhide doll of this factory in existence after much communication with a descendant of the early factory owner."

Mrs. Greville Bathe of Philadelphia, Penn. notes that a Philip Lerch, Toymaker, was first listed in the Philadelphia directories in 1864, at 358 Dillwyn Street. Dillwyn Street has long since disappeared and, undoubtedly, was one of the little old streets of old Philadelphia. Again, in 1866, Philip Lerch is listed as a maker of 'Doll Heads', at 5 Witmers Alley. "There never was a Witmers Alley', writes Mrs. Bathe, "It is probably a misprint for "Wilmers Alley". By 1868 Philip Lerch becomes Lerch and Co. Doll Head Makers at 347 N. 4th St. This he remained until 1870 when he seems to vanish from any directory. There is no patent record taken out for Doll Heads by a Philip Lerch but, according to *American Made Dolls & Figurines* there was a trade mark 'Lerch and Klag, Philadelphia." Very often a listing appeared in a directory long before a patent for the same doll was taken out . . . and sometimes the patent was not taken out at all. L. Greiner appeared in the Philadelphia directories as early as 1840, it is said, and yet his patent for 1858 was the first doll patent issued by the U. S. Patent Office. Mrs. Nina B. Shepard has a Lerch & Klagg doll, 1875 in her collection. Mrs. Dorgan reports that the Lerch doll looks very much like the Greiner.

Emil B. Goldsmith, Vice-President and Treasurer of Sports Products, Inc., of Cincinnati, Ohio, wrote that it was his father who introduced the doll industry to this country, with the establishment of a doll factory in Covington, Ky. where doll heads, made of papier maché were manufactured, and doll bodies, were stuffed with sawdust and sewed together. Workmen from Germany molded the heads. Imported kid bodies were used for the domestic made papier maché heads, and also for porcelain heads imported from Germany. Wax heads for window display were also made and sold all over the United States. When the factory was moved to Ohio, the manufacture of doll heads, bodies and wax figures was abandoned, and the present company is now concerned with athletic equipment.

It is thought by some authorities that a repair shop started in 1875 by Wolf Fletcher, later became the Goldsmith factory for dolls, in Covington, Ky. In 1885, Philip Goldsmith took out a patent, #332,248, for a "doll body with corsets", and in 1887, Wolf Fletcher took out patent #371,751 for a "method and means of stuffing dolls".

Mr. Emil Goldsmith was kind enough to send this additional information. "In the year of 1875, and until 1894, (the year of his death) Philip Goldsmith manufactured dolls in Covington, Ky., beginning his career with a partner who dropped out of the business in 1878. No. 710 Madison St. was the first location of the factory which occupied two floors about twenty five by seventy five feet each. The only access to the second and third floors was an iron outside stairway. In these humble quarters, this young American added white sheepskin bodies to wax doll heads, hands and feet. Some of the wax parts were imported, some were made on the premises. In 1885 Mr. Goldsmith branched to a different type of doll, the wax window display just beginning to be considered a business necessity by retailers. In cutting the sheepskin for the doll bodies, much scrap material accumulated which turned Mr. Goldsmith's mind to baseballs. Therefore in 1877 the manufacture of baseballs was added to that of dolls."

"In 1890 this pioneer introduced a new art into the Americas, the making of Bisque Dolls, formerly imported from Europe. However by 1893 the outlook for the doll business was becoming increasingly poor because of keener foreign competition, and more and more time was directed to the manufacture and improvement of baseballs.

(No Model.)

P. GOLDSMITH.
DOLL BODY WITH CORSETS.

No. 332,248.   Patented Dec. 15, 1885.

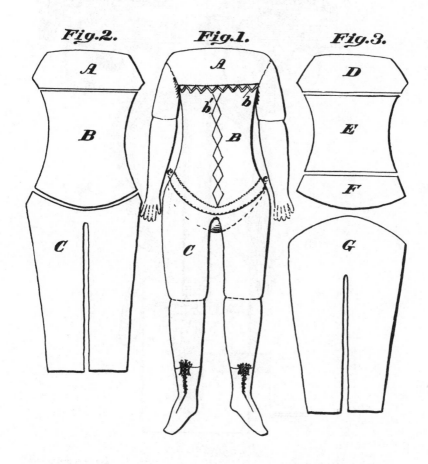

Fig.2.   Fig.1.   Fig.3.

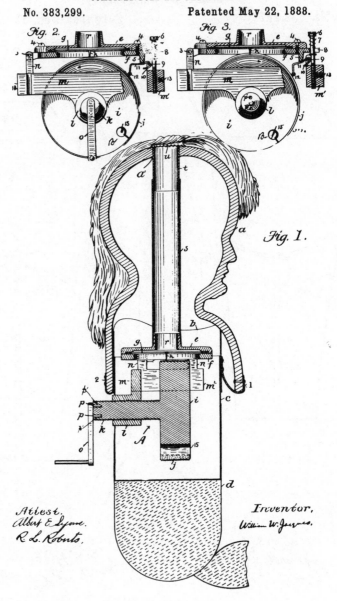

W. W. JACQUES.
COMBINED DOLL AND PHONOGRAPH.
No. 383,299.   Patented May 22, 1888.

Fig. 2.   *Fig. 3.*

Fig. 1.

Attest.
Albert E. Lyone.
R. L. Roberts.

Inventor,
William W. Jacques.

F. D. MARTIN.
Dolls.

No. 214,830.   Patented April 29, 1879.

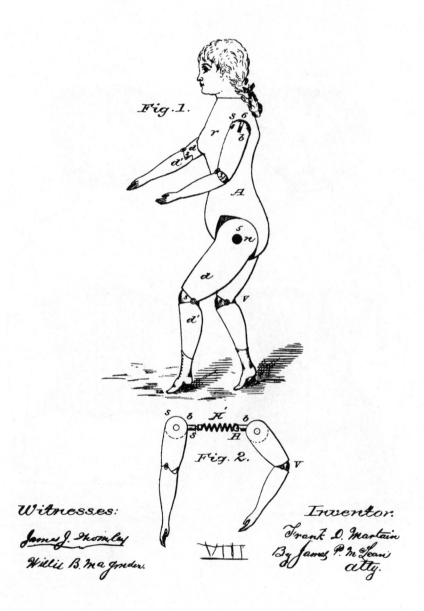

Fig.1.

Fig.2.

VIII

Witnesses:
James J. Thornley
Willis B. Magunder

Inventor:
Frank D. Martain
By James P. McLean
atty.

(No Model.)

C. T. DOTTER.
Doll.

No. 235,218.   **Patented Dec. 7, 1880.**

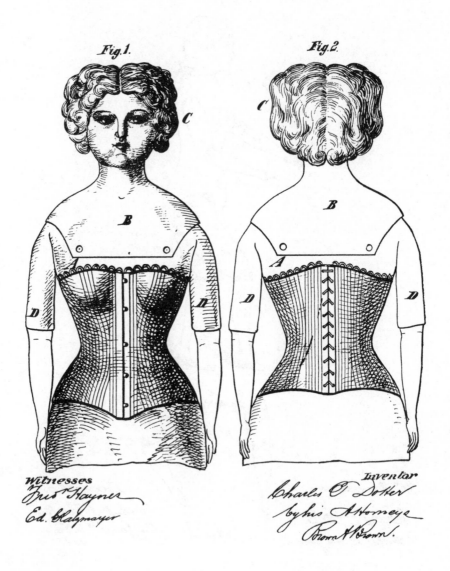

Witnesses
Fred. Hayner
Ed. Clahmayer

Inventor
Charles T. Dotter
by his Attorneys
Brown & Brown.

W. MILLER.
Doll.

No. 164,582.

Patented June 15, 1875.

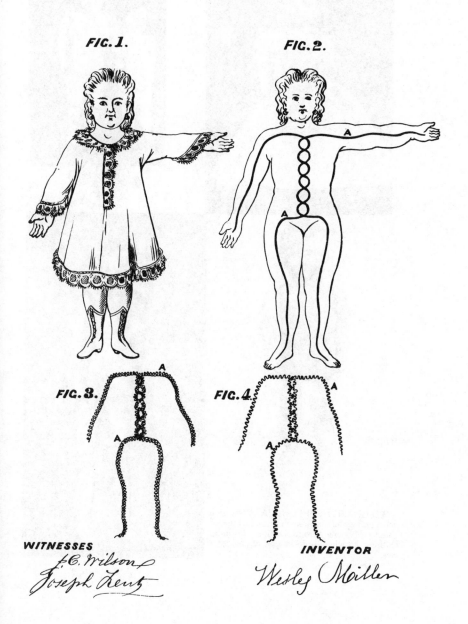

FIG. 1.

FIG. 2.

FIG. 3.

FIG. 4.

WITNESSES

J. C. Wilson

Joseph Lentz

INVENTOR

Wesley Miller

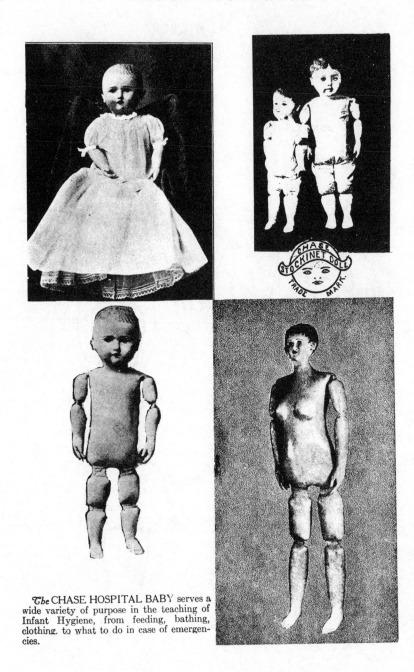

The CHASE HOSPITAL BABY serves a wide variety of purpose in the teaching of Infant Hygiene, from feeding, bathing, clothing, to what to do in case of emergencies.

Creation of Martha J. Chase, orders began to come in and soon they came from all parts of the globe, even from royalty. One doll was made, adult size, to use in a hospital training school and so a new industry developed. Now the dolls are made so they may be immersed in water and used also in child welfare work."

"The Chase Hospital Baby is durably constructed, thoroughly waterproof, and equipped with a set of internal tanks so that it will meet all technical requirements. It is made in five different sizes. They are:

In reply to an inquiry about these dolls addressed to the M. J. Chase Co. at Pawtucket, R. I. the following reply was received. "Mrs. Chase first started making the cloth dolls around 1889 but at that time made them only for her children and the neighbor's children. In 1893 she took one of her dolls to a large department store in Boston to fit it for shoes. While there the buyer of the doll department saw it and asked her to make some for his store for the Christmas trade, which Mrs. Chase did, and so started the commerical end of the Chase Stockinette Doll. In 1910, Mrs. Chase was asked by a hospital to make a life size doll for hospital training work which she did, and that was the beginning of the business known as the Chase Hospital Dolls. In 1913 she made the smaller sizes of dolls for hospital training work and better baby work . . . and thus evolved the Chase Hospital Babies. These dolls have been sold the world over. There is one in the collection of the late Queen Marie, of Roumania. The business is still going on but since Mrs. Chase's death, 15 years ago, it has been run by her family. It is now being run by her children. Very truly yours, A. M. Sheldon, Mgr."

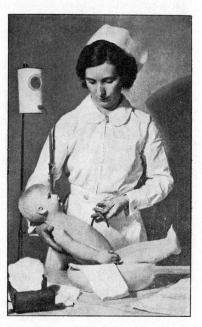

Courtesy Robert D. Chase

Nurse demonstrating with the Chase Hospital Baby. The complete care of children is practiced on this doll by nurses and prospective mothers.

The slogan for the Chase doll has been "The Maintenance of Prestige". One of the old circulars described the doll as "a 'rag doll', with hard raised features, as clearly defined as those of a bisque. Dainty and winsome in looks, with a soft 'cuddly' body it is yet as durable a doll as is made . . . virtually unbreakable. It is found everywhere, from the playrooms of our Western plains to those of European royalty." A later advertising circular states that "If Stradivarius made dolls, he would make the Chase Stockinet". A description of how the doll is made is described in this same circular as follows:

How Chase Dolls Are Made

"The manufacture of the Chase Stockinet Doll, from the first stroke of the shears to the last painted eyelash or lock of hair, is fascinating to watch. It is hand made by trained craftsmen of specially woven stockinet, stuffed with clean white cotton batting, till it has the natural life-like responsive body of a young child. It is painted with the purest and best paint obtainable and completely water-proofed so that it may be bathed at will, kept sanitary and perfectly safe for the child to handle. In fact the child can take it right into the tub.

The mysterious shapes and forms which the shears cut out are quickly sewed into arms and legs, with elbows and knees and fingers and toes. They are then stuffed with cotton batting till hard and firm as flesh and blood.

The head also is made of stockinet and cotton. But the remarkable thing is that the delicate features are all so real and beautiful—raised like the features of a bisque doll, formed and hardened by a special process so that a child cannot crush them.

When finally assembled the doll is sent to the studio where it is thoroughly water-proofed from head to feet and then painted to look like a real girl or a real boy, with pink ears, smiling eyes, wavy hair, round cheeks and pudgy nose."

There can be no doubt that this doll is something of a tradition among American families. It is practical, sanitary, washable, indestructible and lovable. For years, children have played with it because they are able to scrub it and throw it about, and it always comes back for more rough treatment, regardless. Outside of child play, this particular doll meets the basic requirements for such educational usage as that of kindergartens, day nurseries, orphanages and children's hospitals. The treatments to which the Chase Baby is subjected are many and varied and extend from the routine practice of daily hygiene to emergency and first aid and sick room treatment. The Chase Baby performs an indispensable service in teaching the modern technique of child care, and in augmenting class room instruction and explanation by actual demonstration and repeated practice.

There is no patent for the Chase Doll. Labels sewed on the dolls read, "The Chase Stockinet Doll. Made of Stockinet and Cloth Stuffed with Cotton. Made by Hand. Painted by Hand. Made by Especially Trained Workers." The trade mark is printed either on the left leg of the doll, between the knee and the hip, or under the left arm. It is a round, moon shape face with the words "Trade Mark" under the face, and 'The Chase Stockinet Doll' name worked into a sort of bonnet.

Through the generous cooperation of Callista O'Neill the story of the famous Kewpies, in Rose O'Neill's own words, was made possible, a lovable little story that explains why the Kewpies were so popular, and continue to be so.

"How the Kewpies Happened"
(As Rose O'Neill explained it)

Well, the idea grew from the baby brother when I was a little girl.

I was forever playing with him and making drawings of him, watching all his little looks and gestures and unconsciously storing up all that babyism which came out later in the Kewpies.

The Kewpie topknot was that little wisp of hair that stands up on the pillow after the baby has been asleep.

The smile, the bright, kind little eye, the round tummy were all the baby's. **The tender clown.**

Rose O'Neill) COPYRIGHT 1940

'The very next day I began to make the verses and drawings which went into the magazines . . . . and soon after I modelled the dolls which went whooping around the world. And they have all gone on creating themselves and having fun in their own way ever since.

In the drawings and verses I elucidated the Kewpie Philosophy.

It seemed that the Kewpie quality was not only to be smiling and round and ridiculous, but rather profoundly wise and kind.

The little elves described themselves to me in that dream with the chirping song (their voices are like tree-toads and crickets). They sang:

'The Kewpie wights
Stay up at nights,
All gayly singing rumpty-tum.
Like puddings they are pleasant sights,
Well rounded at the tumpty-tum.'

But it developed that they were not only well-rounded at the tumpty-tum but well rounded in the heart and head.

The Kewpies hold that to correct a fault unamusingly is impolite, and to do a good deed in a tiresome way is a misdemeanor.

In short, the gist of the Kewpie philosophy is to do good deeds in a funny way. The Kewps put a quirk into a good deed that makes it as entertaining as if it were naughty.

And here's the Kewpie Philosophy in a nutshell:

'Philanthropists need
A spice of wit,
Or else they make
Dull work of it.

But the Kewps' idea,
If understood
Is to make you laugh,
While they do you good.'

Of course the exterior appearance of a Kewpie as it is observed in the Kewpie dolls and their pictures expressed the Kewpie philosophy; the bright little sidelong

Children dear and Grown-ups, too: You've had my Kewpie dolls in various materials for years, but for a long time it has been my dream to give you a soft Kewpie – a hug-Kewpie, – a Cuddle-Kewpie! And now here it is. Gay and hoppy, Soft and floppy. 'Tis a Funny Fellow with a Smile, for The Kewps' idea, If understood, Is to make you laugh While they do you good. So I am sending him out to cuddle the hearts of the uncuddled world. Snuggled among the cushions of her snuggly corner he makes a jolly-hearted young girl even jollier hearted.

Courtesy Rose O'Neill
A Letter from a Kewpish Elf
Copyright 1929 Rose O'Neill

Courtesy Rose O'Neill

Cuddle Kewpies
Copyright 1928 Rose O'Neill

eye like a convivial sparrow; the carelessly waving top-knot, the absence of severity in the almost absent nose, the well extended smile, the wings, and the well rounded heart and brain exemplified by the well rounded tumpty-tum.

The Kewpie is the protector and lover of children. Somebody called him Saint Kewpie, the patron saint of little tads.

And don't you think it's fun that if the children are to have a private patron saint of their own, it should be a tiny saint, an elf saint: little enough to be 'toted' about by a baby, and funny enough to make a baby chortle?

Of course the softness of the new cloth cuddle Kewpie doll expresses in a high degree the softness of Saint Kewpie's feeling for children.

But he keeps a friendly eye out also for Uncles, Aunts, Parents and Grandmas, big boys and girls and Grandpas. He's broad in his views.

I have had a passion to express all the Kewpish babyism and elfism in the dolls as well as in the drawings, the wisdom, the kind funniness, the funny kindness.

And it is there in all the doll Kewpies, the good little smile, the jolly tumpty-tum, the tricksy sidelong eye, the waving top-knot, the infinitesimal wings.

But I needed a Kewpie doll that was **soft to the touch.** A doll with a caress in it. A hugling that would hug you back. A cuddling Kewpie.

And now at last I've got him, and I rejoice mightily in feeling that the Kewpie Philosophy has become tangible in the cuddle Kewpie, and he's already going forth—not really a doll but a message of Kewpish good will to cuddle the hearts of an uncuddled world.''

The latest creation of Rose O'Neill is her baby Buddha Ho-Ho, of which Callista O'Neill writes as follows:

''Years ago Rose O'Neill created the Kewpie Smile and now she has brought forth a Laugh, the overpowering laugh of her baby Buddha Ho-Ho.

''The Kewpie smile went all around the world with the ineffable Kewpie Doll, carrying its irresistible baby-funniness mingled with all-embracing human-mindness.''

''And now she has created the supreme laugh.''

''Her little laughing Buddha has come to keep the world remembering how to laugh. And he is being welcomed like embodied sunshine.''

''Rose O'Neill, says she has carried the idea of that laugh for years meaning to materialize it for the world.

THE Great Success of the Arnold Print Works' Cloth Animals and Dolls during the past two years has led to a continued offer of the same popular figures this year with the addition of several new subjects, among which are

Palmer Cox's Celebrated

"BROWNIES"

Drawn by Palmer Cox — Copyrighted and Patented January 15, 1892.

Twelve Brownie Figures on One Yard of Cloth, Price 20 cents.

Other Household Pets

represented on this page are offered as follows : "Tabby," "Bow-Wow," "Tatters," "Jocko," "Pickaninny," "Little Red Riding Hood," "Owl," "Jointed Doll," "Rabbit," "Rooster," "Floss," "Hen and Four Chicks" and "Six Soldiers."

These come on one-half yard of cloth at **10 cts. each**. All the rest of the smaller Figures come four on half yard at **10 cts.**, or eight on a yard at **20 cts.**

Directions.

These figures are printed on cotton cloth in natural colors and marked accurately where to CUT OUT AND SEW TOGETHER. Stuff with Cotton or Bran and put pasteboard in the bottom to make them stand up.
ANY CHILD CAN DO IT.

CAUTION.

Be sure that the Trade Mark that is at the side of this paragraph is stamped on every piece of cloth with the figures.

These can be had of your dealer. If he has not got them, show him this advertisement and he will get them for you.

NONE ARE GENUINE WITHOUT IT.

The Arnold Print Works

Is one of the largest manufactories of Prints and Dress Goods in America.

Probably many of the Print Dresses that are worn in every home came from these mills, which is the best guarantee for the quality of the articles offered on this page.

For Sale by your Dry Goods Dealer.

ARNOLD PRINT WORKS,
NORTH ADAMS, MASS.

PAT-PARACHUTE
Captivating Parachute Dolls

The parachute type of doll is not exactly new for several years ago a very inexpensive doll was on the market, of Japanese make, which when thrown up into the air opened an umbrella like parachute and floated down to earth with "the greatest of ease." Mrs. Mary E. Lewis reported that newspapers in New York City, for Feb. 20th and 21st, 1941, mentioned that an airplane would leave La Guardia Field on Feb. 22nd for one hundred cities in the south, over which would be dropped parachute dolls, with capsules tied to their legs, and a written message within the capsule. Sponsored by the British American Ambulance Corps, the first person delivering the message to the mayor of the city would receive a monetary gift. These dolls were in red, white and blue.

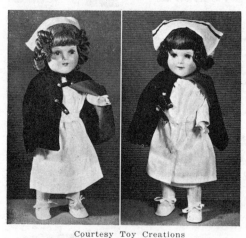

Courtesy Toy Creations

**The Nurse is again in vogue . . . even in
the world of dolls.**

The parachute jumper doll is undoubtedly a lot of timely fun for the modern child, for its main purpose, and accomplishment is its ability to make many successful "forced landings." There is a fascination about it as it glides slowly to the ground. Another doll of interest is the deep sea diver which, equipped with an electric lantern, can light his way down to the depths. A bulb pumps air through his rubber tube so that he is able to dive and rise at will.

Chapter XIV

THE WORLD WAR
INFLUENCES THE WORLD
OF DOLLS

*(War Benefit Dolls——English
And American Dolls)*

Courtesy of Grace Woodworth
German Bisque Baby Dolls

IN 1913 the wholesale valuation for toys exported from Germany to the United States was nine million dollars, and Germany was computed to be supplying two thirds, and over, of all the dolls made in the world.

By this time, dolls had reached the stage where they were pretty much alike, with bodies of kid, or jointed composition, or, of the baby doll type. There was a constant supply of metal and china heads, of rather an inferior quality, from an artistic point of view, and these replaced the finer bisque. Doll hospitals bought the parts needed for repair work and either hooked or glued them on. Fine hair or wig weaving was done by the beauty parlors. Almost all of the doll supplies came from Germany, for the German people had a monopoly in doll making, particularly as far as doll heads were concerned.

In Germany the doll industry was considered a 'key' industry, and the government would not even permit some of the factories to export doll heads separately. It is interesting to note that in 1913, the German Christmas shoppers were urged not to purchase brunette dolls for their children but rather to buy 'Teutonic Blondes'. The advice was based on the theory that dark haired dolls were not representative of the German ideal for feminine beauty, nor did they teach the children the value of 'inborn racial unity'. The fact that a 'doll knows no nationality and every nationality' was evidently not known in Germany in the pre-World War days.

151

1914 came all too quickly for the doll industry and the World War brought about drastic and dynamic changes. Doll supplies were cut off overnight. The Doll Hospitals found that they would either have to make, or restore, broken parts by their own ingenuity, or go out of business. Other countries, seeing an opportunity for new business, attempted to enter the doll world. France enjoyed what was known as 'The Renaissance of the French Doll'. Italy and England concentrated on "art dolls' while America, in addition to supplying a large portion of her own requirements, commenced to export considerable quantities of 'Unbreakable dolls'. Japan began to produce a very cheap, imitative line for the foreign market. Mrs. Emma C. Clear reports a Japanese copy of the royal Kestner baby that was so perfect an imitation that at first she thought it was a genuine Kestner. "Japan took the German models with no regard for the copyrights", comments Mrs. Clear, "America did the same but our work was much coarser."

During this same time, dolls for adults again began to appear, and War Benefits helped the artists sell their work. Sculptures, or dolls, appeared in cloth, silk, plaster and wax. The foremost exponents of this new form of artistic expression included such well known artists as Erna Pinner of Frankfort, and Lotte Pritzel of Munich, Germany, Katherine Paar of Vienna, Austria, and Marie Vassilief of Poland. American soldiers brought home French War Dolls dressed as officers, in felt, with high boots and slender, mincing figures, beautifully made.

Mme. Paderewski, the wife of the famous pianist, sponsored character dolls for Polish Relief, dolls inspired by the Vassilief dolls which were of ethological interest, because they showed the folkways of the Polish people. The Paderewski dolls were designed and made by young Poles to help their native land. Originated by a young Polish girl in Paris, a penniless artist, they represent every province or section of Poland. Two little dolls, Jan and Halka, duplicated in large quantities, were known as the 'Waifs of Cracow'. These dolls wore medals which read:

"Health and Happiness to you, kind doll lover, who by taking into your heart and home one of my little doll waifs of Poland, have fed a starving mother or child in that 'saddest land'—Helena Paderewski."

The sale of these Paderewski dolls aided the impoverished families of Poland and have become collectors items to-day. The dolls stand eighteen inches high, their bodies are sawdust filled, their faces of cloth with embroidered features and blue eyes. Bright colored streamers adorn the hair of the lady dolls, and gleaming, beaded, holiday belts are worn by the men. A collection of Polish dolls, including two of these Paderewski dolls, was recently exhibited at Velvalee Dickinson's in New York City.

During the World War, the earthenware people in the Potteries in England made pot heads with a certain degree of success. There was a definite shortage of china heads which the Potteries considered as a side line. This pottery, or 'pot' head as it was called, was not the same as bisque but quite a new product. England did not attempt to manufacture any celluoid products at this time. When the war was over, the making of these doll heads ceased, for some reason or other, and the pot head trade returned to Germany. However with the exception of the Baby Doll, which the Germans specialized in, the English continued to make dolls.*

This is what the Chad Valley Co. Ltd. of England had to say in part in a letter written in 1939 prior to the declaration of war against Germany, "As far as English dolls were concerned we are the original English makers of what is known as the soft type of doll's head, which are made up by full pressure heat with Buckram canvas and felt and afterwards paint by our own artists. We have never made any other type of head except of course the easily made flat faced dolls which are sold here and in America.

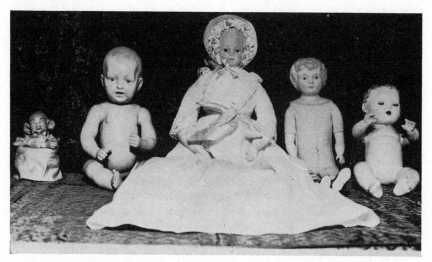

Collection Janet P. Johl

The Yellow Kid. The inspiration, it is said, for the cartoon figure "Happy Hooligan." American. The Parsons-Jackson Baby. Circa 1914. American. Considered the finest and most durable baby doll. Interesting baby doll. Circa 1880. Chiffon over wax, over celluloid half face. Back half of head is cloth. Lovely facial expression. Blue glass eyes. Probably German. Metal Head. Circa 1904. Pink Kidolene Body. Unbreakable. This specimen came originally from an old store in Indiana that had passed from father to son. Arms hand carved. German. Dy-Dee Baby Doll. Modern. Rubber. Popular. American.

"There is however in England to-day one manufacturer who is making pot heads but the principals are of German origin and we do not think them particularly successful. With the exception of Baby Dolls, the English trade for dolls fortunately is now confined to English manufacturers . . . the tendency is to buy still less from Germany."

With the World War the American Doll Industry actually came into being. From the total of nine million dolls that came through the United States Custom House, prior to the war, in 1909, there was a drop to less than half a

* Previous mention has been made in detail of the English dolls made by the Potteries during the World War . . . and the propaganda doll of Sevres.

million in 1918. During the war years the main thought in the minds of the doll makers was to cast, or imitate, the German models no longer available. Because of this, there are some very interesting war time heads, made in America. Kellogg and Brown of Los Angeles, Cal., made doll heads of waffle flour, or some similar cereal. At least it was edible. Mrs. Clear tells how she bought some ten thousand of these heads when the company went out of business. The weavils liked the mixture so much that it was necessary to buy antiseptics to use on the heads, until at last, in despair, she gave those that were treated away, and destroyed the remainder.

In 1918 the Marks Brothers, of Boston, Mass. put out a celluloid head that was unbreakable, and also a rag doll and a crying baby doll, the latter having first appeared prior to 1918. There was even an American attempt at bisque. The features of this doll were very lovely, but the bisque was mottled and poor. It could not be compared to the beautiful creations of German manufacture, falling short in detail and finish.

Mrs. S. Camille Tenney, of New Haven, Conn. reports that the American sand could not produce the same fine, smooth finish, in the bisque, as the sand used in the doll heads of foreign origin. A doll which has been classified as an American war time effort, but which bears in marking so much similarity to the English made product in Mrs. Tenneys collection that its origin is questionable, is a charming head, marked "N T I Hancock Girl" and a small c/c at the left. The inside of the head is lined with a very thin material. This doll has a lovely, delicate, molded face, with a pointed chin. The features, especially the brown eyes, are somewhat Oriental but the facial expression is most life like. The bisque hands and feet are coarse and clumsy and may not have been made by the same Pottery as the head, or perhaps the mixture was different. The body is cloth, treated so that it resembles oilcloth in texture. Mrs. Tenney's doll has in addition to the N T I Boy marking, the fact that the doll originated in England.

It is an established fact that during the World War period the Potteries made dolls, but how many kinds, or what types of dolls were made, is still unknown. The existence of the few specimens already discussed is proof enough that these war years were experimental ones, especially in the United States. As early as 1914, American ingenuity was at work in the world of dolls.

On December 8, 1914 a patent was issued in Washington, D. C. for a splendid baby doll, now known as the 'Parson-Jackson Baby', and considered the finest and most durable of the American baby dolls. The description used to advertise these dolls said that they were of tough composition, not paper but very light, that their arms and legs were held in place by easy working, oil tempered steel springs, that their joints were ball, and the doll could float in water.

F. W. PARSONS.
DOLL.
APPLICATION FILED FEB. 26, 1912.

1,120,331.

Patented Dec. 8, 1914.

2 SHEETS—SHEET 2.

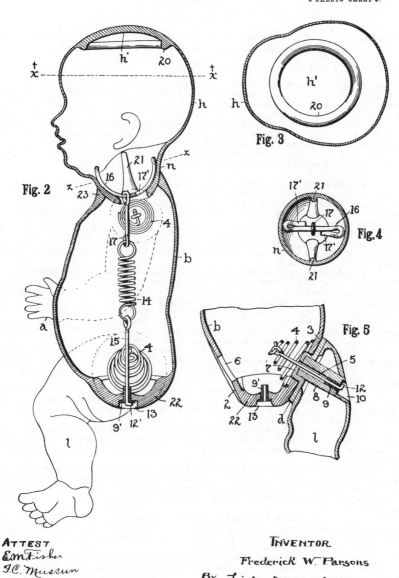

Fig. 2

Fig. 3

Fig. 4

Fig. 5

ATTEST
E.M.Fisher
J.C. Mussun

INVENTOR.
Frederick W. Parsons
By Fisher & Moot
ATTYS.

UNITED STATES PATENT OFFICE

FREDERICK W. PARSONS, OF CLEVELAND, OHIO, ASSIGNOR TO THE PAR-
SONS-JACKSON COMPANY, OF CLEVELAND, OHIO, A CORPORATION

DOLL

1,120,331.   Specification of Letters Patent.   **Patented Dec. 8, 1914.**
Application filed February 26, 1912.   Serial No. 679,818.

To all whom it may concern:

Be it known that I, FREDERICK W. PARSONS, citizen of the United States,
residing at Cleveland, in the county of Cuyahoga and State of Ohio, have invented
certain new and useful Improvements in Dolls, of which the following is a
specification.

This invention relates to an improvement in dolls, and the invention consists
in a doll having the construction and combination of parts substantially as shown
and described and particularly pointed out in the claims.

The object in view is to provide a doll of exceptional durability, particularly
in the places and parts heretofore found to be weak and defective.

What I claim is:

1. A hollow doll body having side facings at its ends at different angles to a
vertical plane and inclined toward the front, arms and legs seated on said facings
and having transverse bores with outer recesses, wires through the said bores
terminating in said recesses and helical springs in said body having said wires engaged therewith.

2. A doll body having a head provided with a substantially ball and socket
connection therewith, a yoke adapted to confine the head rotatably on said body and
fastening devices for said yoke comprising a spring having a wire rotatably engaged
in the bottom of said body.

3. A doll having a body with holes in its sides and ends and members having
substantially disk-shaped face portions with bosses at their center centered in said
holes and tubes socketed in said bosses, and wire connections rotatably mounted in
said tubes, and having spring connection inside said body.

4. A doll having a hollow body and hollow limb members, said members having tubes transversely through their upper ends and separate tubular bearings
therein, and springs having wires provided with bent ends engaged with said bearings and serving as retaining means for the said limbs.

5. A doll having a head with a circular tapered neck having ribs inside tapering
from base upward, in combination with a body having a socket seating said neck
and means to fasten the head rotatably in place comprising a substantially semi-
circular yoke fitting the inside of said neck and disposed between said ribs.

6. In a doll, a body having a separate head, and means to rotatably secure
said head in rocking relation with said body, comprising spring tension connections and a curved yoke provided with stops to fix the working relations of the
tension connections therewith.

7. A doll body having a hollow limb-member, a tension device to rotatably con-
nect said parts, and said limb-member having a cupped bearing-plate and a rein-
forcing tube at the joint to relieve the main strain of the tension device from the
limb-member.

8. A doll having a body with a seat at its side with a circular opening into
said body, a member provided with a raised annular projection seated in said opening, a spiral spring surrounding said projection and means connecting the inner end
of said spring through said projection with said member to hold the member in
operating position.

9. In a doll, a hollow body having rotatable members and means securing the
same in place comprising helical springs having their wider portion seated against
the inside of the body, and wires anchored in the outside of said members and en-
gaging the smaller end of said springs.

10. A doll body having flat annular facings at its outsides and ends and members faced to seat thereon, wires engaged transversely through the upper portions
of said members and rotatably mounted therein, and helical springs on the inside
of said body seated at their base against the same opposite said facings and the
said wires extending through said springs and engaged with the smaller ends
thereof, whereby said members are held in place under spring tension.

In testimony whereof I affix my signature in presence of two witnesses.

FREDERICK W. PARSONS.

Witnesses: F. C. MUSSUN, H. T. FISHER.

In 1919, in America there were a number of attempts to make successful war time dolls. American metal heads with moving eyes appeared. "Featherweight aluminum doll heads were advertised with these words, 'No more German Bisque. No more Japanese clay heads. Unbreakable flesh tinted 'Gie Fa' dolls.'" There was a tin baby doll, just a plain looking doll with plenty of sound when the joints moved. A new bisque head was advertised as American one hundred percent. This head was made by the Fulper Pottery Co. of Flemington, N. J. which was founded in 1805. There were other advertisements that the Fulper Co., made heads for many of the doll company. A letter to the pottery brought this reply.

"We have your inquiry in regard to doll heads which we manufactured a number of years ago. The only thing we can tell you is that we manufactured bisque doll heads . . . the same as Germany made years ago—but discontinued making same after a few years because the same doll heads were again made in Germany. On account of increased costs it was impossible for us to compete with the German made doll heads . . . Yours very truly. Fulper Pottery Co. J. M. Stangl, Pres."

American Made Dolls and Figurines, notes that these Fulper Bisque heads were "cast in the molds of the Armand-Marseille (German) Company", and were "sold largely through the Horsman Company of New York. Fulper heads can be distinguished from the German by the quality of the clay used, the American being coarser and the finish not as soft. The Fulper trade mark is on the back of these heads."

Another doll of this era was of stockinet and unbreakable. It looked like bisque but in reality the face had received many coats of paint and been sand papered. By 1920 the American doll makers were learning to improve the old methods and had developed a new composition less expensive than the German. Eyes were inserted through the neck, instead of by means of a hole on the back of the head. The Mama voice was better. There was a look of originality in the American product that the continental lacked. But the newness of the American doll could not compare with the finished fineness of the European. Also the American mechanisms were often not stiff, nor fine enough. Eye work on the imported dolls was all hand work. Not so the American. Most parts were put in by machinery, and no tools nor implements for resetting, or correcting, were furnished. Many parts could not be replaced because the domestic product was not made well enough.

But unlike the European in this industry, the American doll kept changing. New, and, sometimes, radical patents appeared, some good and some not, but the industry kept moving on progressively, constantly improving, until to-day there are many fine American dolls, the acme of loveliness, that will give way to-morrow to something newer and, perhaps, better. For that is the American way.

HOW TO SET A VALUE
ON A DOLL

By IZOLE DORGAN

How to evaluate a doll is a difficult matter but one which must be considered, not only from the point of view of the dealer, but also that of the collector. No one wants to pay too much to obtain a specimen . . . and no one should want to pay too little. The evaluation should work two ways, so that the ultimate result is the satisfaction of all parties concerned. Mrs. Izole Dorgan was good enough to write an article on this subject. As she is often called upon to appraise a doll, or a collection of dolls, she is equipped, through knowledge and experience, to help in answering this important question.

"When one is appraising dolls, the whole performance must be stripped of sentiment. The doll has to stand firmly upon its own feet, or wobble as the case may be. Very few of the dolls that collectors here in America value, are bona-fide antiques. The greater number of the really charming examples were made in the forties and fifties of the last century. About the oldest dolls we get are the Queen Anne's. Played with in America, Queen Anne's are practically all of historical value, as so few of them turn up with unimpeachable old American background. Most of the specimens in our present day collections have come from England, recently.

"For reasons best known to the doll makers of that time the forkish looking hands attached to the abnormally short arms, are made of bamboo. The doll, if representing a highborn lady will be wearing the bouffant skirt and padded under petticoat of the period. Her silks and taffetas will be stiffened with a crepey paper much the same sort as the paper we used when the leg-of-mutton sleeve was in bloom. Very fine examples of these dolls, beautifully and originally gowned with the added spice of having belonged to the family of Lord Nonesuch or Lady So and So have sold within the last year for sums ranging from one hundred and twenty-five dollars to one hundred and fifty. Perfect specimens, beautifully dressed and pedigreed.

"When trying to arrive at the market value, we doll people are at a disadvantage. We cannot consult the prices bought at the last auction sale, of similar specimens in some notable gallery. Whole collections are rarely sold at one time, though two or three dolls may appear with other highly diversified articles. Such figures have little or no value to us in appraising dolls. A price would have to be based on a large sale, well attended by collectors and dealers. But a big sale of dolls that might take place on a rainy day, with few attending it, could throw the prices, disproportionately, off. Buying in this manner does not help to stabilize doll prices, or make it possible to estimate accurately the values of certain types. Common sense is the best guide to 'buyer and seller.'

"Age, condition, Rarity, History, and clothing are all factors that enter into value.

(1) Age

The age is predicated on the material of the head, the style of hair arrangement, the age of the material of which the body is made and the age of the materials with which it is stuffed. Always bearing in mind that hair do is not infallible, because if a certain style was a good seller, it was continued ad infinitum.
That is the reason that the other points have to be considered together with the
style of the hair arrangement. Certain types, such as papier machè were discontinued when the more practical composition heads appeared. They classify
easily.

(2) Condition

"First 'proof,' meaning not played with and safely conserved against the
ravages of time. Second, head, body, arms and legs, must be perfect.

"Third, china must be free from all flaws caused by impurities in the paste
or in firing. Clothes should be of some material of the same period and well
and attractively made. The whole doll may show some signs of wear if it is a
'played-with' doll. Fourth, the head must be perfect, of good quality and the
body must be examined to note the conditions, and if arms and legs are chipped
or missing. How the doll is dressed is always a detail but the doll itself is the
greater feature of importance. When legs and arms are chipped or missing,
the seller is really disposing of *only* a head . . . not a complete doll. No matter
how elaborately a doll has been modeled, if it is chipped, if the china has flaws,
if the wax has cracked or peeled, the doll is definitely outside of the veteran collector's world.

(3) Rarity

This group includes beautiful and unusual dolls. At the moment collectors
are not attracted by the grotesque.

(4) History

When we strip dolls of sentiment in appraising them, only an authenticated
pioneer history, or ownership back to some distinguished source counts. Your
great Grandmother's doll, if otherwise undistinguished, is simply a doll of her
period. Romantic tales connected with dolls rarely sell them to any great advantage but they do make fine lecture material. The history of the doll, to be
valuable, must link with the history of the country, or, of distinguished people.

"Beware of histories.

"I remember with great glee a doll that a friend of mine picked up in
Europe for me. She dated around 1800 and was made of jointed wood and
very, very interesting. I had a great many wooden dolls at the time, so, when
one of my friends admired her greatly, we swapped. My friend rushed to her
desk, got a piece of paper and a pencil and demanded the 'history.'

"I had to admit that there was no such animal.

"Three years later viewing the same collection I was amused when my friend, pointing out the self-same doll, gave me a very complete and amusing 'history,' with it.

"History is a trap and a pitfall to many a budding collector. One learns to be wary.

(5) Clothing

"Clothing is not just a dress that is becoming to a doll. It should be a bit of fabric contemporary with her, buttons, tapes and all, it should be a garment that when contrasted with later day models, tells a story. A true story.

"We cannot all afford the perfect specimens but we can strive for them, and appreciate them when we do get them.

"We must now go back to the question I ask collectors who wish to dispose of their collections. Where are you going to sell? And how? Values fluctuate. In a country as big as ours, luxuries sell at better values in some cities, than in others. Certain types of dolls are more common in some localities than in others, and so it goes. Not very long ago, doll prices were higher in the Middle West than anywhere else, because half a dozen collectors, with more money than good sense, were buying every fine doll offered to them at fantastic prices. They bought hundreds of dolls . . . all of the finest dolls in the country came to them in time. It harmed doll collecting because it limited the collecting to a very few who could afford any price asked. That epic is closed.

"China heads came to this country in the fifties and sixties by the ton. A good large head cost fifty cents to one dollar . . . A very fine head made by one of the finest potteries in Europe would, of course, cost a great deal more. It was the really fine dolls with their trunks, their dozen or so costumes, hats, gloves, parasols, jewelry, lace and cashmere shawls, etc., that brought the prices and they were usually procured on the 'trip abroad' and not imported for sale.

"All wax dolls with inset hair are not Montanari's. They were being made, by other firms, until some thirty-five years ago. One of my friends was sent one for her older daughter . . . the younger by two years could not have one because the factory had closed. Beware of primitives unless you are a very experienced collector indeed, or buy them from reliable people 'who can document them to your satisfaction.'

"The rage for Parian is understandable. The paste first made in 1845, and used for classic figures soon began producing the pretties . . . spring, summer, autumn and winter, flower girls etc. Our first and finest heads were the personal efforts of potters who used the head mould and added the bust. These are limited in number because they were not a manufactured article. The classic appearance of most of them is no accident. The high prices paid for these rarities is understandable. But there is another genre of Parian that was factory made in quantity. Although we do not obtain them here in large numbers, they still do not qualify as rarities.

"No one can appraise a doll without seeing and handling it. It just cannot be done. And as values fluctuate, an appraisal made in 1920 can not set the value for 1941."

Chapter XV

THE STORY OF THE
BYE-LO-BABY

(A Great American Doll)

Courtesy Grace Storey Putnam and the Geo. Borgfeldt Corporation.

The Bye-Lo Baby, modeled from a three day old infant, in 1920. Manufactured in 1925. This picture shows the original wax head as cast from the heavy plaster mold.

GRACE STOREY PUTNAM, the artist who stopped her sculpture to create a doll that became famous, has been good enough to tell in full how the 'Bye-Lo' Baby came into actuality, a story that is remarkable for its sincerity of purpose, its struggle toward attainment, and its ultimate success.

"Although I studied art only intermittently in earlier years, my whole life was spent among artists both in the United States and abroad, for my husband was a well known sculptor. When through his unfortunate illness I was forced to face the necessity of providing for myself and my children, it was my knowledge of art, my notebooks crammed with art theory, with explorations and decisions as to form and color, that served me best . . . for in regard to the 'Bye-Lo Baby', the tree with its roots and trunk, was art, and one of the blossoms was the dolls.''

"When my little daughter was three years old, I decided to make a doll for her, a life size rag baby doll. We named the doll, 'Peter Pan', and dressed up it was realistic. Then, when my little girl was five years old, and Peter Pan was something the worse for wear, I fashioned another doll, this time out of new material, rather than of odd bits of cloth. This doll was a vast improvement over the other in the modeling. We named her 'Helen Pan' and she was so lifelike, she actually fooled people although she was rather irregularly formed, and had no mechanical exactness.

My friends decided that I should make dolls for the market and I did wish to do something of the kind to relieve a financial strain. I made two or three dolls for my friends, and filled a few orders, but each doll was done in an agony of spirit . . . the sewing was so stiff and difficult, and the modeling with cotton such an ungainly thing to do, that I had the deep realization that I should be using clay for my medium as a sculptor would do, and not be wasting good time with dolls . . . except perhaps for my own little girl. Then came the opportunity for my husband to have a studio in Rome . . . and later one in Paris. In Europe we were both able to study art and he gained many wonderful honors and awards, but the strain was great and his health broke. A few years after we had returned to the States, I was faced with the problems of caring for myself, my daughter, and an infant son.

FOUR DECADES OF AMERICAN DOLL MAKING: 1. Can't Break 'em Doll (1900), 2. Campbell Kid (1911), 3. Bye-lo Baby (1923), 4. Betsy Wetsy (1937).

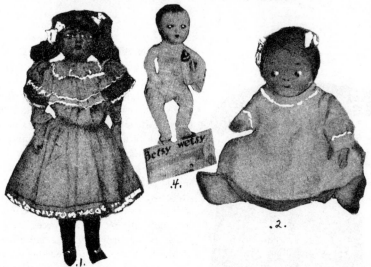

As soon as I was broken into my new work, I started the portrait of the baby again . . . this time in plasteline. I wanted to do a three months old baby, one that was not too new, and yet would still retain that early little helpless appearance. Now I was creating a baby, it was not even sculptury; it was not a doll, it was just a baby. Everything depended upon the personality of this tiny baby, and it all had to be in the face . . . no part was to depend on the ensemble as is true of many dolls.

"I was now following babies around, jotting down things about them in my little note book . . . the nose of one infant, the eyes or mouth of another . . . but still the baby face did not quite hang together. I entered my second year of teaching. As I write this, it seems utterly ridiculous that my doll should have taken so long to create but later on I learned that it was not strange at all. On Christmas Day, of my last year of teaching, I decided that the doll was to be the whole thing and I began to plan every step, so that I could leave my position in the spring. I continued with the modeling, and although, to my eyes, the baby was still dull looking, I kept fanning the sparks of my faith in it.

"I began to go to hospitals to see babies, and to the homes of young mothers to watch them bathe their infants . . . but I did not find the baby I wanted. Instinctively, I knew that I would recognize the right baby on sight . . . I'knew that I must be able to say "Did you ever see anything so cunning in all your life?" Recommended by a neighbor to the Salvation Army Nursing Home, I went there and found a nursery full of newly born babies. I spent much of my free time at this nursery making sketches of the babies and taking notes. I found myself more and more attracted to the newly borns . . . their tiny helplessness fascinated me, and soon I began to model my baby head in the image of these new arrivals. There was such an elemental appeal about them. I felt that if I could get over to others, forcibly and clearly, how basic a thing an elemental appeal can be, if I could catch and imprison the human emotion aroused at the sight of a new born baby, I could be sure of success.

"So a newly born baby was the thing! But many of the new babies were most disappointing . . . little red monkeys, or little old men . . . wizened and wrinkled. Some had large expressive eyes, some too big a nose, some had no chins, others looked too much like dolls, and the little Caesarian babies were too perfect . . . I wanted a baby with a fat, broad, and squashed little face. Then in the Salvation Army Nursery came my 'Red Letter Day'. I shall never forget it. The phone called me to the Salvation Army Nursery Home to see a three day old baby. It happened on my day off from teaching and I sauntered over. They brought it out wrapped in a blanket . . . they put it down on a pillow and parted the blanket. I fairly gasped . . . there lay MY BABY (a little girl born out of wedlock, poor little thing). I really trembled with emotion, it had been such a long search. This baby was fat as butter . . . it had the cutest little face . . . and what I had been dreaming to find . . . a wrinkle in its nose where there were the tiny rolls of fat. I ran for home and brought back my clay. In half an hour I had the work under way. I was never more inspired in my life. My work in the past had primed me for this . . . it was done with the ease of forgotten toil'.

"At first I modeled a deep mask of the face and the head was gradually tipped forward and the clay built up underneath the back of the head until I had pretty nearly three quarters of the head done. I obtained the rhythmic swing of the lines and forms of the face, and was charmed with these irregularities . . . the baby never moved and went soundly to sleep so I could work steadily for about two hours. I finished one side of the face and most of the other. Two days later I returned to the Home . . . I looked at the baby with dismay . . . it was still cute but the wrinkle had gone out of its nose and it had changed a lot. I could only use it for the ears and the back of the head . . . I finished the head and took it home to do what remained from memory . . . I felt numbed, bewildered . . . I could scarcely believe my eyes . . . it was done at last . . . after so long a time.

"Now the head needed to be protected; concealed in plaster. I was quite familiar with casting fo. I had often helped my husband but never had actually done it myself. I would not trust anyone else with the head and decided to do the work myself. With some fine, fresh, tested plaster and Toft's book on casting I began the ticklish work. Wax paper was put about the back of the clay head which had been allowed to dry to become a little harder. Then the lower part of the back half of the head was buried in fresh clay and a wall built around the face part. Into this clay receptacle containing the face I poured the creamy plaster, blowing away the bubbles, and jarring the table in the end to shake loose any other bubbles so they would rise to the top. When this plaster set, the whole model was turned over, plaster and all, and the back of the head cast in two pieces. At last I had a big heavy overmold. It had to be strong for all it might go through in the future. I nearly collapsed when it was done, the strain was so great. All I wanted was a good mold. My brother took a wax cast from it, for he was an expert at that. Then the wax head was tinted with my oil paints, and the cheeks and lips made rosy. I formed a soft roughly made body, dressed it in some old baby clothes . . . and well . . . it *WAS* just like a real baby.

In the summer of 1920 I landed in New York City and went to my brother. I gave myself six months time to put over my idea. I carried my big thick plaster mould with me and the wax-head model of the "Bye-Lo" doll, only it was not named as yet. I began to take the doll about to the manufacturers. They shook their heads over it—it was too realistic—too new looking. It was too like their own babies when they were tiny. They appreciated the idea and all my work, but they were afraid the public would not care for it . . . Some of the manufacturers even looked askance at the doll and said they wouldn't dream of putting such a doll on the counter. The eyes were not large enough and it seemed to make no difference that they were half closed baby eyes . . . I became weary of dealing with men, it was only women who saw the real value of the baby.

"I forgot to say that my first idea was to have the baby manufactured in rubber . . . but it was to be a rubber doll such as had never appeared before . . . with a face as soft and flesh like and as daintily tinted as a baby's face . . . like a pink rose petal, and yielding to the touch. The U. S. Rubber Co. considered the idea for some time and then rejected it saying they were curtailing their manufacture of toys . . . of course this was all before the time of lovely rubber dolls, such as may now be purchased.

"It was all taking so long and was so hard on me and the children. A small loan from a friend enabled me to live in New York City with my family. I did some designing and made efforts along art lines. Instead of the doll helping to make a further pursuit of art possible for me, I was now taking care of it with art.

"During the time I was working on the baby head, another field of art had opened for me . . . in out-of-door sculpture, but always the doll would come up at the wrong moment and I was obliged to finish the production of the Bye-Lo as it assured my son's education . . . I knew I could go on with my art work later.

"Then came another Red Letter Day . . . I was led, through a friend, to
F. A. O. Schwartz, the head of a large toy store, He was
interested in the doll

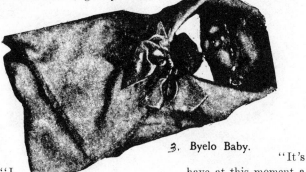

3. Byelo Baby.

"It's
wonderful", he said, "I   have at this moment a
little new daughter   THREE DAYS OLD." What
a thrill it gave me.   The lawyer took me at once
to see the President of the company and he, too, instantly realized the doll's
possibilities and before I left they arranged for me to sign up for a 10 year
contract with them . . . so that when they invested in the doll I would not at
any time take it away from them. I found them fine to deal with in every way.
We did have to go through some rather deep water until the doll was actually out
on the counter. Plaster heads were now made from my big mold, and plaster
heads were soon on their way to Germany where the dolls' heads were to be
made in bisque—up in the mountains where there had been toy makers for
generations. The bisque heads were to be shipped to the United States and then
the dolls were assembled, dressed and packed, and shipped from Borgfeldt's big
toy factory in New York City.

"I modeled a plasteline body . . . but a soft one proved to be better. At
last I designed one, but the shoulders and arms had to be well matched, the
legs had to be crooked or bent, and the lower legs and feet had to curl in. At
last I had the right kind of a body and applied for the patent. There were
long delays about the heads . . . the first samples in bisque had shrunk from
the original and the lines or creases in the face were intensified. The model
had to be softened. It was two years after I signed the contract before the dolls
made their entrance into the world. I thought I would actually starve before
the bisque baby began to take hold.

"The doll received the official name of "Bye-Lo". The buyers began to
comment upon it but many refused to place any orders. Men did not seem to
like it at all, just as they do not care for their own new babies until they are
old enough to smile at them. I thought so often if I could only get the baby
out where women and children might see it, my troubles would be over. But
there were exceptions . . . and there were women buyers . . . and they raved over
the Bye-Lo. Some of them . . . one or two who had lost babies of their own had
weeping spells and that set the men in a dither. Finally the uncertainties passed.
The first bisques that came from Germany were quite lovely. In time the bisque
colors faded and became grayish and pale. But the German eyes were almost
human.

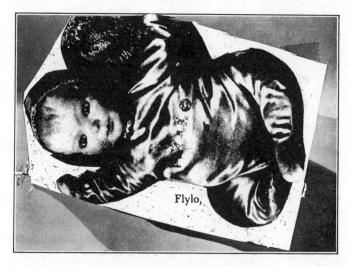

Flylo,

Courtesy
Geo. Borgfeldt
Corp.

"Five years after I left California and came to New York City, my Bye-Lo was a success and a huge one. Out of real poverty I climbed upward financially. It was almost too much; I needed a simple life, rest and freedom from care. I felt a great disappointment in the manufacture of the dolls. The faces of the bisques were so dainty and lovely with their soft German glass eyes and yet the model had been 'Softened', that is the clay had been smoothed over the creases I had so carefully molded. Also we were not to have the ball-and-socket neck so that the baby head could roll a bit. It was simpler for the manufacturer—and less expensive—to make a round neck with a rim at the bottom that could be sewn into a cloth body."

"The modeling on the baby's face and cheeks, back near the ears, had to be flattened out so that it would draw easily from a two piece mold instead of a three piece one. This gave the baby face, on the side, a long rigid appearance when sitting upright with the neck showing. The original baby seemed to have no neck at all, except the fat little rolls at the side and back."

"That first Christmas, the Borgfeldt Co. could not supply the market and Germany could not get more heads to them in time. People stood in line to buy the doll and it was soon called, in the trade, the 'Million Dollar Baby'. Several years passed and success was sweet. Then came the depression casting its shadow over all. The bottom fell out of the doll market, money was lost at every turn. It was all confusion and a conglomeration of fruitless efforts, until at last, in 1934, things began to appear better and the Borgfeldts decided to bring back the 'Bye-Lo Baby', in composition, with the indestructible head that had developed to a high extent, bisque having gone out of demand because of its breakability. Every effort was made to give the doll publicity and renewed sales. One dealer, in Cleveland, sent a basket with five life sized Bye-Lo's up to the quintuplets. Some newspaper took a picture of the five babies and the five dolls to-gether, alternating them, and asked the public to tell which was which. But just as the doll was ready to re-appear, the Shirley Temple doll came on the market, and took the country by storm."

"The Bye-Lo still sells and now it seems to be becoming a collector's item which is gratifying to me for I gave the very heart of my life to it and would not mind if it had a little niche somewhere in doll history . . . .

"And so this is the story of the Bye-Lo doll, but in reality a very small part of it. It took time to create the doll. The original live baby thrilled me. I felt I had caught the emotion in my model of the Bye-Lo and, therefore, I felt sure that if it could come through mass production without losing too much, it would have a contagious thrill for others. I knew that for some it would be the little-baby-that-might-have-been, or, the sad little baby that-could-never-be. I was always sure of its success for it stood for a symbol of life . . . the little new baby just arrived in the world. It 'ran true'—because it was so much a part of me, a woman who wanted motherhood and art, too.''

I. A. GUTSELL.
DOLL PRODUCING BLANK.

No. 503,316.   Patented Aug. 15, 1893.

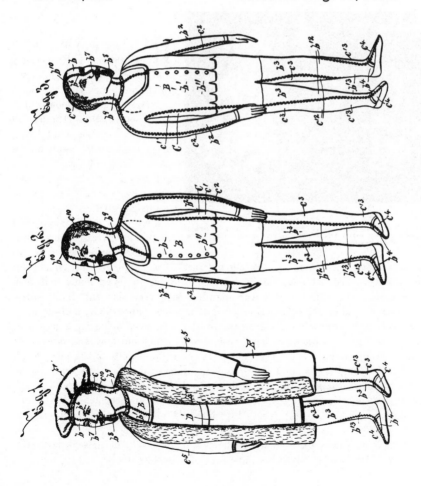

Chapter XVI

RAG DOLLS

(Walker, Gutsell, Newell, Kruse, Steiff, Poupée en Chiffon)

Courtesy of Elizabeth Hooper

Two china head dolls with rag bodies. One, in original plaid dress, circa 1840. The other circa 1899. One stockinet doll circa 1900.

RAG dolls date back to the eighth and ninth century and have endured right down to the present. Old rag dolls, now treasured heirlooms, once made some little girl happy in a simple New England home, or in a pioneers' cabin of the west. The indestructible **rag** doll was a very American doll, and never became over popular in Europe.

Made in many sizes and shapes, and dressed in a variation of costumes, rag dolls all had some points in common . . . rather flat faces, stiff hands of cloth, or old kid gloves, and turned out toes. Many had shoe buttons for eyes, many had wool embroidered eyes. Many faces were painted with vegetable and fruit juices. Hair was of wool or hemp, of string, even of wisps of human hair, and often, it, too, was merely painted on. Garments and bonnets were made from scraps of calico, from an old sweater or coat, from India prints and sprigged muslin, or even homespun linen. These rag dolls were the beloved dolls of the new world, found later in old trunks and attics, and mentioned time and time again in the stories of colonial days. There is a shapeless rag doll, called, 'Bungwell Putt', now in the collection of the Deerfield Memorial Hall, at Deerfield, Mass. This doll was cherished for eighty years by Clarissa Field of Northfield, Mass., who was born blind.

Ingenious American mothers made unique rag dolls in those early days, many of which have survived the hardships of a settlers life.

In 1909, in Munich, Germany, Bertha Kaulitz created a doll very representative of a child, with considerable individuality and animation of facial expression. She endowed miniature ladies and gentlemen with a charm that was very much in keeping with their costumes. The heads of these dolls were modeled by the Munich sculptor, Paul Vogelsanger but the faces were painted by Bertha Kaulitz.* Joseph Wackerle, well known as the Nymphenburg potter and designer, also worked on dolls, which were introduced to the public by the equally well known German firm of Tietz. By 1910 the Kaulitz dolls had encouraged other artists to try their hand at doll making. (Kathe Kruse was already at work on her to-be-famous dolls).

Lotte B. Pritzel, also of Munich, originated a technique in wax modeling, and created a doll that was more suited for adults, as a work of art, than as something for child play. Lotte Pritzel was the first artist to introduce the doll known as the Kultur Doll. This doll, which appeared in 1914, was in a class by itself, plastic and unbendable. Modeled in colored wax, the Pritzel doll was baroque in the sense of the odd, the corrupt, and the bizarre. Dressed in the richest and most delicate of materials, with real jewels on the fingers and toes, the hair sometimes of fine gold threads or wire, these dolls were very exotic.

Dolls made by Erna Pinner were in baroque spirit, also, healthy but not luxurious. Reduced to elemental shapes, rather than to the bizarre, they were flexible, with flat faces of painted material. The Pritzel and the Pinner dolls could be seen only in private collections, and in studios. Very, very few, if any, are in America. Prior to the Nazi regime in Germany, these dolls were on exhibition at the Palais Stourdza, Baden-Baden, and in the Galleries of Friedman and Weber in Berlin.

The Kathe Kruse doll, originated by Frau Professor Kruse, is the work of a real artist. Every bit of this doll is made of ordinary muslin, sewed by hand and stuffed with cotton. Like the French, ''Poupée en chiffon,'' it belongs to the rag doll family. Frau Kruse had first made dolls with potato heads for her own children, and it was five years before she offered her famous Kathe Kruse dolls to the public, circa 1914.

The head of the Kruse dolls was dipped in chemicals. One outstanding feature is the shell-like ears. Frau Kruse believed that every toy should have an educational end in view. These dolls were marvelously life-like. Molded from the artist's own children, they show a profound understanding of the child mind. Unbreakable and washable, the Kruse dolls have a sympathetic individuality that makes them most desirable as character dolls. There is a charming variation in each type, an expressiveness in mood and pose. The skeleton of this doll is the secret of its life like appearance, for its steel frame is wound with many thicknesses of soft cloth. The arms, legs, body and head can be turned or twisted into any position, and the doll will ''stay put.'' Washable and unbreakable, charming and life-like, these dolls present in a realistic manner many characteristics of the child.

Rag dolls, or Poupée en chiffon, appeared in France in 1914, the creation of Mme. Lazarski who believed that a child was impressed by simplicity, and

---

* Marion instead of Bertha was found in one reference but Bertha Kaulitz seems to be the correct name.

elementary things. Mlle. Fiszerowna, who worked in the same studio, revealed further originality by the use of rounds of blue and rose, for eyes and cheeks, appliqued. Hair was made of thread, cotton, wool, fur and silk, sometimes stitched, sometimes embroidered. Japanese and negro dolls were very popular. The Japanese were already beginning to compete in the doll industry and were making European looking dolls which made them serious rivals of the Germans.

Many of the designers of this period were well known. For those collectors who have been fortunate to preserve this type of doll, here is a guide to a few of the French artists who made them.

Mlle. Desaubliaux	—Work very French in feeling.
Mme. Roig	—Doll friendly in type.
Mme. d'Eichthal	—Bebe and Doll. Same size. Showed good health
Mme. Manson	—Dolls inspired by des Contes de Perrault.
Mlle. Verita	—Dolls known as toddling babies, little girls, roguish boys. Charming.
Mme. Dhomont	—Clown dolls.
Mlle. Duvall	—Dolls with smiling expressions.
Mlle. Lloyd	—Dolls with sweet faces.
Mlle. Rozmann	—Very realistic dolls.

Mme. de Laumont was the founder of the *French Toy League (La Ligue du Jouet Français)* which devoted itself to helping unemployed women and in providing toys for the children and this group was soon followed by others. *La Federation du Jouet Français (The Federation of French Toys)* which was sponsored by Mme. Sautter. La Francia, whose Bretonne dolls were very popular, was founded by Mme. d'Eichthal and *Les Veuves de la Guerre. (The Widows of the War)* by Mme. Pierre.

Monsieur Botta made the doll for Francia, a doll of elegance, good taste and high standards. Simple and pure in form, this doll was modeled after the form of a five year old child, everything typical of the age being included, as well as everything about the shape of the body. These were the Poupeé en Chiffon, as the Rag Doll of France, circa 1914.

In 1918 in America, Marks Brothers of Boston, advertised a fine rag doll.

There is, of course, a close relationship between the rag doll and other dolls whose bodies were often stuffed but whose heads were of bisque or composition.

Two types or groups of rag dolls were popular at this era, ones with sewing on face and head, and others without sewing, with no neck and no nose. Dolls without stitching depended upon a pattern, and the cut because there were no definite features to follow and, naturally, the effect was quite rudimentary. The coloring or tints made the dolls seem much earlier than they were, and only the modern dress broke the illusion.

Outside of the costumes the shapes of the heads differed greatly, according to and denoting the manufacturer. There were bumps on some heads, and some cheeks were often more round than others. The limbs were supple which delighted the children. Some of the dolls looked innocent and somewhat resembled the Kate Greenaway's. But these dolls were all French, amusing, or character dolls.

A long letter from Merrythought Ltd., of Dale End, Iron Bridge, England, in answer to an inquiry about the story of English dolls, had considerable to say about the rag doll, and its influence on subsequent later English dolls. To quote:

"Perhaps the o n l y types of Dolls which were commercially made in England before August 1914, were the types which can be called 'Rag Dolls.' These rag types would be the printed doll and the Golliwog. The printed doll was a very simple type where the body, clothes, and head were all printed in as few separate parts as possible and then sewn up and stuffed with any suitable

Courtesy Velvalee Dickinson
Kathe Kruse Dolls

materials such as old rags, sawdust, etc. It is doubtful however if the printing was done in the British Isles at all but actually done on the Continent and sent over here in sheet form to be either made up and sold as a doll, or sold as a sheet for people to cut out and sew up for themselves. The Golliwog was actually sold as a made up doll and in a small way manufactured in this country. Commercially no other types of dolls were actually manufactured in England. By this I mean the 'straight' doll as of course the Golliwog must be put into another category, as a character doll. There were one or two other 'Golliwog' or 'character' types commercially made, but not to any appreciable extent in England and prior to the outbreak of the war in 1914."

"The war changed the circumstances of doll supplies in this country. August and September were the two biggest months for the deliveries in bulk to the wholesale and distributive trades of the Christmas season types of toys from the Continent, which practically meant Germany. The main supplies of toys which came from Germany and enemy countries were cut off. Further, as we realized that England was not going to be invaded and that practically speaking 'business was as usual' would be carried on and also that it was just as essential and perhaps even more essential that the children should have an adequate supply of toys, something had to be done about these supplies. Some, of course could be got from the United States of America, and some from France, but such supplies were completely inadequate so that the Toy Distributing, the large Stores, began to interest people with manufacturing ability and resources to take up the manufacture of dolls and other toys. The War also brought about the all fabric doll, apart from an increase in the Printed Rag and Golliwog types.

"One of the first soft fabric type of doll was developed by the Entertainment World. Some actresses made soft dolls for their own children out of their worn out skin coloured tights. Showing bare legs, i. e. uncovered legs, was taboo on the English stage in those years, and the fashion of not wearing skin coloured tights had not come in, so there was a supply of skin coloured stockinette in worn out tights. The doll made by this group was most ingenious. The legs, body and head were of one piece, and sometimes even the arms. Stuffed with kapok, which became a universal substitute for feathers and down during the war, this doll was a splendid example of the rag or fabric type.

"The head and face were quite unique and were formed as follows:

"A calico pad filled with flock was cut behind that part of the stockinette which was to be the face and a thin layer of kapok to form the head size was inserted, and then a pink mercerized cord tied around to form the neck made the division between body and head. A pellet formed the nose and chin, or even a dry pea beneath the stockinette and in front of the calico pad. A number of hand stitches, embroidery style, formed the mouth. The pellets forced the stockinette out to show a nose and chin while the stitches would draw the material in to form the mouth and shape the cheeks. In the earliest dolls of this type the eyes were made with little discs of cloth, or old fashioned shoe buttons. Subsequently the common glass eye as used for ordinary animals was used to form these doll's eyes. This glass eye had a black pupil with the back of coloured blue glass. This eye, formed on a malleable wire, of iron, was pushed through the stockinette and the calico pad, and secured by twisting in the back. Mohair served as the wig material. Toes and fingers were represented by cotton stitches. Hands at first were just 'ball' shaped, being formed by the mercerized cord tied about the wrist but the feet were made by an ingenious method of pattern cutting.

"Eventually a firm set up to make these dolls commercially as they had met with such favor by the children. I believe the name of this firm was the Tar Toy Co., but it went out of business December, 1918. This Stockinette doll was the forerunner of most of the fabric dolls now made in England.

"I made this Stockinette doll in enormous quantities starting in June, 1919. Quite elaborate dressing styles were introduced as well as some extraordinarily good wigs, these wigs being made from what is known as drawn off mohair which was permanently curled by steam, hand woven in such a way as wigs for humans are woven and then fitted on to the doll. By January 1920 I had developed this type of Stockinette Doll with several important innovations and improvements. A papier maché mask behind the face formed the face better and dispensed with the pellets. A few months later I improved on the papier maché by actually pressing the face on the doll, by using buckram dampened temporarily to break down its stiffness and pressing a mask out of the buckram. This pressing innovation resulted in a natural looking face and dispensed with stitches to form the mouth. The eyes were fitted correctly from the back. For a number of years I made as many as 700 to 800 of these dolls every working day of the year.

"A further development of this Cuddly Doll, as it was known, was that the arms and legs were made of velveteen and only the head and body were of stockinette. From this doll many adaptations by other makers resulted. Personally I went on innovating and inventing until I evolved one of the most popular types of English dolls—the Fabric Jointed Doll, which comprised a movable head, arms and legs. This doll was made possible by the pressed head of the Cuddly. The Luton Hat Press was the machine I applied for making the modern fabric head in felt and other materials. While still continuing to use kapok for the stuffing, the improvement of technique and pattern in the doll shape, permitted the doll to stand and the limbs to move although the doll remained very light in weight. This is the history of the Rag or Fabric Doll.

"No doubt you know of and have seen the Lenci Dolls. At one time they were quite popular in England, from 1920 up to five or six years ago. They were the most artistic fabric dolls that have ever been produced and they ranged in price from a few shillings to as much as £15/-/- each. Lenci, I understand is an Italian word meaning 'rags.' They were made by an Italian firm in Turino, Italy, called Scavini. I am not quite certain of the facts but I understand these dolls were developed originally as follows:

"The wives of artists called up to serve in the war had to find means of supplementing their allowances and they started to make fabric dolls. Naturally as the war went on one or two of their husbands returned to them, invalided by wounds, so that artistic talent, both male and female, was available in modelling shapes and designing dresses etc. From this beginning I understand developed what were at one time the most artistic dolls ever produced."

Yours truly,
C. J. Rindley."

Courtesy Mrs. Elsie Clark
Krug
Lenci Dolls.

This story from England is most illuminating and especially is it interesting for its notations on the Lenci dolls. Other stories exist about these dolls. One is that Mme. Lenci created the doll and so, it was named for her. This seems to be generally accepted, along with the additional data that Mme. Lenci makes the dolls at Turin, Italy, in a factory that employed, before the war, several hundred workers. Mme. Lenci also has a collection of historical costume designs which undoubtedly aid her in dressing her dolls so charmingly. These dolls are known all over the world. Not only are they renowned for their loveliness, but for the very skillful way in which the felt is utilized to fashion the entire doll, and the charming way it is costumed.

Dolls from Mexico are often "rag" dolls, and represent adults with an astonishing amount of personality, accomplished by means of a few deft stitches and a bit of paint. A Peter Pan Rag Doll is quite a favorite with Mexican children.

Raggedy Ann and Raggedy Andy, authentic replicas of the story book characters, have been very popular in America, and are again coming into the limelight. With their wool yarn hair, their shoe button eyes and their 'I love you Heart,' they are lovable and delightful favorites of the children. Through the kindness of William C. Erskine and Howard L. Cox of New York City, the story of Raggedy Ann, Raggedy Andy and their creator, Johnny Gruelle, was obtained.

Courtesy Claire Fawcett
A Lenci Doll

"A Brief History of Raggedy Ann

With the release of the first Raggedy Ann motion picture, produced by Max Fleischer and distributed by Paramount, millions of Americans will meet an old friend in a new medium. As a result many of our friends are already asking for a brief history of Raggedy Ann which we are please to present in this first issue of the *Raggedy Ann Reporter*.

"Johnny Gruelle began his work as an artist with one of the smaller Indianapolis papers shortly after the turn of the century."

"He came by his talent naturally. His father was a well known landscape and portrait painter and a member of the Hoosier group, and his younger brother, Justin, became a skillful painter of portraits and an expert illustrator.

"During the winter of 1917-18, Johnny, quite by accident, stumbled upon the inspiration that was to make him famous. He was in the attic hunting for something and came across a dilapidated old rag doll tucked down in one of the several barrels in which a wide variety of odds and ends were stored. He took the doll downstairs and his mother, who was visiting him at the time, told him the story of how this old rag doll had been made for her when she was a little girl, and Johnny decided to name the smiling old doll 'Raggedy Ann.' Raggedy Ann was renovated and her features painted on like new and she immediately became the pride and joy of Johnny's daughter, Marcella.

"Johnny was so impressed with the story of Raggedy Ann as his mother told it that he sat right down and wrote the first Raggedy Ann book and illustrated it. The first Raggedy Ann Book was published in 1918. The first edition was sold in two months' time and this particular title has sold more than 150 editions averaging 5,000 books to the edition. Subsequently in the period 1918-1940 millions of books based on Raggedy Ann have been sold to the American public, and with each passing year sales figures mount until at the present time Raggedy Ann has passed the records of "Alice in Wonderland" and other children's classics. It can well be said that Raggedy Ann is perhaps America's leading folk tale.

"The public response was so good that Johnny devoted most of his time to the writing and illustrating of books for children.

"Johnny Gruelle died in January 1938 leaving a large accumulation of unpublished manuscripts and illustrations that he had done over a six year period."

In 1939 Mrs. Johnny Gruelle formed a partnership and the new Raggedy Ann book appeared. For twenty-two years the American children have loved and played with these dolls and the motion picture based on the dolls and their story book adventures will be the first two-reel film produced in full color and animation. It looks as if Raggedy Ann and Raggedy Andy will find renewed popularity with the children of another generation and that their future looms up as "Bright and glowing."

Raggedy Ann and Raggedy Andy created by Johnny Gruelle.

For fifteen years the "Cream of Wheat" Rastus Rag Doll has been in existence. This doll comes ready to be sewn and stuffed and may be obtained through the company for a very minimum sum. It represents a smiling colored chef and is "reproduced through the courtesy 'Cream of Wheat' corporation registered United States Patent Office."

A little poem on The Children's Page of the *Christian Science Monitor*, November 25, 1940, gives a good picture of a modern rag doll.

"MY RAG DOLL

Today a rag doll came to stay with me—
a rag doll gay and saucy as can be!
Her yellow hair could really not be better:
(it's made of wool from Aunt Louisa's sweater!)
She's wide awake I fully realize
by looking in her shiny button-eyes;
and not in rags at all—but smartly dressed
in scraps left over from my Sunday-best.
I like her hair, her eyes, her modish style,
but best of all I like her happy smile!

—JANNIS PARKER."

Rastus

The Cream of Wheat Company's Rag Doll

Chapter XVII

A FEW OF THE ARTISTS
THAT MAKE DOLLS

Ravca, *Bruyère, Heizer, Ackley, Jury,*
Chase, Hall, Keys, Kriger,
Diecks, Baughna   Miller, Snyder

Courtesy Mrs. Daniel Hampton

A French Doll sold for the Benefit
of the French Red Cross.

THE facial expression of the modern doll is not limited to a mere smile as was often true of those of the pre-World War period. The doll of today can, and does, express a range of emotions revealing joy, eagerness, vivacious pensure, even pouting. It is much more likely to be a true representation of an individual, or a mood, than just an object "as pretty as a doll."

Across the Atlantic, in Dublin, Ireland, a young Irish artist, Violet M. Powell, has made Irish peasant dolls. A year on the Island of Aran, where the quaint fisher folk dwell, convinced her that these simple native people would make excellent subjects. The result was figurines made of clay. The idea gradually evolved into the making of dolls, the story of which was told in *Avocations* for March 1939 under the title *"Irish Folk Dolls."*

The heads of the dolls, modeled from life, are reproduced in papier maché and are then hand painted. All the clothes are handmade by the Islanders themselves. Careful study of the costumes has made for accuracy of detail. This is the first time that dolls of this kind have been made in Ireland, and the costumes of the Aran Islands, the most primitive in the country, had not been copied in miniature before Violet M. Powell decided to do so. Now, there are eleven types, from the grandmother down to the baby. Many of the larger dolls look like oil paintings for the facial expressions are typically Irish, and very life-like. An old fisherman is particularly good, with a far away look in

Collection Esther G. Veno.

Irish Folk Dolls from the Aran Islands, County Galway, Ireland by Violet M. Powell.

his eyes. His sweater is hand made, and his jacket is of Irish homespun, called a "bauneen." Little old ladies have hand crocheted shawls, and plaid scarfs for their heads. Aran mothers are often very superstitious so the little boy dolls wear dresses like their sisters, lest the "wee folk" steal them before they are old enough to care for themselves. The cow-hide shoes, which are made and worn by the natives, are called "Pampooties." They are kept pliable by being soaked in water over night. The home spun, hand woven, belt which the dolls, as well as the peasant folk wear, is called "Cris," and is one of the earliest known forms of weaving.

Often it is the personality behind the doll that is as interesting as the specimen itself. To know something about the artists who create the dolls and why the doll was chosen as a medium for artistic expression holds a dual interest for the collector.

For example there is the story of the dolls made by Madame Nicholas Khrabroff or rather how Madame Khrabroff came to make her dolls. Irina Khrabroff was kind enough to tell her mother's story.

Courtesy Esther G. Veno.

Dolls of the Aran Islands by Violet M. Powell.

Courtesy Mme. Nicholas Khrabroff
and Irina Khrabroff
Russian Dolls in Boyar Costume

In 1916 Madame Khrabroff and her husband, General Nicholas Khrabroff of the Russian Army, came to the United States to purchase ammunition, and supervise its production for the Russian government. In 1919, after a tragic trip to Siberia where General Khrabroff joined the Kolchak government a few weeks before it was defeated by the Bolshevik forces, Mme. Khrabroff and her husband settled in a little town in Vermont.

Here Madame Khrabroff, who had always liked to make and design hats and dresses, and found handiwork fascinating, quite accidentally became interested in fashioning some dolls and dressing them. The first of these Russian dolls was made for the big War Benefit of the Allies which was held in New York in 1916-1917. The doll was donated and Madame Khrabroff dressed it in a beautiful Russian Boyar costume, exactly like a costume she had made for her daughter Irina.

Irina Khrabroff sold chances for the doll and it raised more than $400 for the Russian cause.

Some time later Madame Khrabroff, wishing to express her gratitude to one who had helped a friend in Russia conceived the idea of dressing a pair of dolls in Boyar costume and presenting them as her expression of thanks. These dolls were so successful and were received with so much enthusiasm that the idea became a tradition and other dolls resulted, some fifteen in number, representing besides the Boyars, Russian peasants, of Great and White Russia and Ukrainia, Tartars of Crimea and of Karan, Finns, Circassians, Mongolians, and several pairs of different little nationalities of Russia, all wonderful examples of authentic costuming, made according to minute drawings in color from the anthropological models in the Russian National Museum at Moscow. On several occasions these dolls were duplicated and donated to some charitable affair where they were auctioned off and brought in considerable funds. One Russian peasant and his sister were so well liked that their faces and clothes later became patterns and, through a national magazine, were sold to subscribers who liked to make up their own dolls.

Most of Madame Khrabroffs dolls are, to-day, to be found in the Museum at Chazy, New York about fourteen miles north of Plattsburgh in Clinton County. This museum, which belongs to Mrs. Alice T. Miner, is open to the public. A few fortunate persons also possess the dolls in their private collections.

And still others perhaps bought the patterns and made Tania and Vanya, the Russian twins who look as if they just stepped out of some little village in Russia in the heart of the vast steppes and endless forests.

In ancient Rome, pantomime dances, sometimes accompanied by music, were very popular. Later the ballet, as it is now known, was produced in Italy, often in connection with an opera. The earliest form of the modern ballet was the interpretation of a dramatic plot, by means of the dance, with music, and sometimes with singing. The Kings of France were very fond of this theatrical form. Catherine d'Medici spent great sums of money on the ballet, with the sole purpose of diverting the minds of her sons from the affairs of state. Cardinal Richelieu, too, used the ballet to aid his political ambitions.

Authentic and beautifully exotic Russian Ballet Dolls are being created exclusively, after designs from the original Russian Ballet, by Andreef Saroff, in his studio at St. Louis, Mo. These dolls, all hand made, and wired to stand in the dance positions, are mounted on a wooden base. They are not only very colorful and artistic, but also very helpful in the educational field of music and the ballet. Andreef Saroff brings his knowledge of the stage and of costume designing to his dolls. Well known operatic representations are revealed in dolls representing:

Petrouchka, after the designs by
  Alexander Benois
Prince Igor, after the designs of
  Nicholas Roerich
Scheherazade, after the designs of
  Leon Bakst
Le Cog d'Or, after the designs of
  N. Goutcharova

and many others. The Saroff dolls include African figurines, based on extensive research on tribal customs, religious dolls that faithfully reproduce the ecclesiastical costumes and historical accuracy of such personages as His Holiness, the Pope of Rome, and monastic Padre dolls. The latest series is called 'Rulers of the World' and includes the leaders of various nations in the headlines of the newspapers today. As artistic creations these dolls earn their place, along with the creations of other artists, who are helping to improve the world of dolls by their contributions to it.

Courtesy Saroff

A Gypsy Dancer from the Ballet Petrouchka.

**M. Bernard Ravca with a pair of life like peasant dolls.
French in origin and spirit.**

John T. Lowe, former-ly of Cologne, Germany, contributes this interest-ing bit of information "There are many coun-tries in the world where it is customary to give a lady flowers, jewelry, and other priceless objects as gifts, but in Russia, it used to be the proper thing, to give a lady a doll. And so in Russian households, it was not at all strange to find many, and beautiful, dolls, not necessarily in cabinets, but on the divans and the chairs. Even the demi-mondaine women had dolls, usually expensive ones."

The colorful costuming of these Russian dolls may be traced perhaps, to the gilt and the tinsel of the well known Russian Vyatka toys. The peas-ants in remote districts found, through color and rhythm, a way to introduce beauty into their simple lives. From sand, water and brown clay they fashioned dolls which were brilliant in color, and had considerable artistic feeling. There is surely a definitely different touch in the Russian dolls that make them of double interest to the collector.

Quite a different type of doll, but one also of artistic workmanship is being created by Bernard Ravca, formerly of Paris, France, and now of New York City. Once a painter in silks, and beautiful Spanish shawls, Bernard Ravca now specializes in making dolls representing the old wrinkled peasants of the different provinces of France. "Poupeés Vieux et Vieilles—Poupeés Paysannes de toutes les Provinces de France et de L'Etranger. Poupeés pour Museés et Creations Artistiques. Entiérèment faites á la main" is the way the dolls are described. M. Ravca has won several awards for his dolls, among which was the Medaille d'Argent in the Exposition Internationale Paris 1937, the first prize in a competition of forty two nations for the 'nicest dolls'. The dolls that won this award were life size.

At that time M. Ravca, alone in the art of doll making, lived in the Montmartre, Paris, along with many other artists who began their careers in the shadow of the Église de Sacré Coeur.

From his studio window lay the vista of Paris, like in the opera Louise, the towers and spires and chimney pots. From this point of vantage, M. Ravca carried on his deep research into the costumes of all nations, but with special attention to those of the French provinces. Traveling through Alsace-Lorraine and Normandy, from Brittany to Bordeaux, he watched and studied, not only the costumes but the lines in the many types of peasant faces. At first he made young, rosy cheeked dolls representing more than twenty five provinces of France. Then one day an Englishman came to the studio and wanted an old man, and an old woman doll. And so began the now famous old people dolls, every line, every wrinkle of a mature face carefully studied and perfected.

To do this M. Ravca became a sculptor in cotton and achieved the realistic facial expressions by sewing in here and there, and so obtaining the contours and deep lines necessary. A silk stocking stretched over the head, and painted spun wool, for fine soft hair, marked the finishing touches for the head. This alone took five hours of concentrated work to say nothing of the hours and hours of previous research, or the hours to follow in costuming. In Paris, a group of Russian women dressed the dolls, according to the directions of their creator.

"Ensemble" is one of M. Ravca's latest creations, a man and a woman grown old together, with faces sculptured from white bread, or bread crumbs. "In texture," Mrs. Elsie Clark Krug observes, "the bread resembles wax or ivory for, by some method known only to himself, M. Ravca has molded the bread into a permanent plastic and has made it his medium for art." The faithful old couple, seated side by side, the woman placidly sewing, the man with a twinkle in his eye, seems to be telling her a joke from the newspaper which he holds in his hands. Both are very, very true to life. The bodies may be of ordinary material, cotton or straw stuffed, but the faces are very exquisitely molded, to exact color shading. They represent a newer and higher art for the doll maker, not only that of portraying people, realistically, but in letting the doll suggest, and even tell the story, itself. "Why a character doll" asks Bernard Ravca, "If there is no character in the face?" And surely the characteristic things about these dolls is that they do duplicate human expressions so very well.

Courtesy of
Muriel Atkins
Bruyère

**Heirloom Portrait
Dolls**

Courtesy Bernard Ravca
A Pair of Old French Peasants.

When the organ grinder doll, made before the recent German invasion of Paris, turns the crank of his genuine Swiss music box, and the strains of the Marseillaise come forth, doll collectors will pause to think of another Paris, and be grateful that, in America, there is a doll maker who can continue to perpetuate the France that once stood for 'Liberté-Égalité-Fraternité'.

Because of prevailing conditions in Europe, the American doll collector must look more and more to the American artists for distinctive dolls. This is not as discouraging a factor as it may seem to be. Many individuals are making fine contributions to the world of dolls and although it is utterly impossible to mention them all, a few will be discussed, some who have told their own story, and others who are already recognized for their splendid artistic achievements.

First on the list comes Mrs. Paul Tulane Bruyère (Muriel Atkins) of New Haven, Conn. who won the Grand Award in the Chicago Antiques and Hobby Exposition in the fall of 1939 for her 'heirloom', or, 'Portrait dolls'. Mrs. Bruyère is a portrait painter and was formerly a pupil of Howard Chandler Christy. As a child she used to make her own dolls, and years later while she was assisting in the University of Chicago Settlement House, she really began to make dolls seriously. Her first 'live' doll she modeled from a living person for her own daughter, Peggy. She began to make doll-likenesses of her own family, and then of famous people, in fiction, and in life. These dolls stand from ten to twenty inches in height, and although their bodies are cloth stuffed, their hands, feet and heads are modeled of clay and fired into a hard bisque before the doll is dressed. Mrs. Bruyère estimates that she has made well over 192 dolls of various descriptions. In copying pictures of living children, Mrs. Bruyere prefers to use the profile rather than the full face, although she must have both the full face picture and the profile to study, for mothers are the most difficult to please, as all portrait painters know only too well. Modestly, Mrs. Bruyere has this to say about her work:

"It is dangerous for me to start on the subject of dolls for I scarcely know where to begin . . . I have made dolls from the time I was five . . . nor where to end, because I love doing it so much. I have made over 200 dolls and no one has so much as sewed a button or hook or eye on the clothes. I even make the wigs on most of the dolls myself. The heads are modelled as likenesses before they are fired, the hands and feet too, absolutely permanent.

"The result is a nice, lifelike texture ready for the final water color painting. The bodies can be stiffened with wire so the dolls may be placed in certain positions suited to the character they represent.

"The portrait dolls are copied from whatever photograph or daguerreotype the owner may submit. These are the 'Heirloom-Portrait Dolls' made for people who want to perpetuate the memory of persons in their family in the three dimensions.

"I received my student training at the Woman's Art School, Cooper Union, and at the Art Studio League, in New York City, and studied portrait painting under Mr. Jack Buehr later in Chicago.

"My favorite doll is one of my mother. Many people like the one I did of "The Blue Boy". I make up the molds for all my dolls myself, and such dolls as Alice in Wonderland, the Little Children of 1836, Kate Greenaway and others meet with popular favor. I also do a line for the gift shops, types copied from my own or other daguerreotypes, or from story book characters. All my dolls are hand made and signed.

Muriel Atkins Bruyère"

An Egyptian Queen. A Copy of King Tuts mother-in-law.

So through such fine artistic efforts, the doll collector is able to perpetuate the memory of loved ones, in these original 'heirloom' dolls.

One of the most outstanding of all the artists in the American doll world, is Dorothy Wendell Heizer of Essex Falls, New Jersey, whose dolls are also made for the collectors, and not for children, are wonders of artistic ability, perfect in detail even to their painted and shellacked finger nails. In a letter written in April, 1939 this famous doll creator had this modest bit to say of her work:

"There is hardly anything I can tell you about dolls for I am not a collector. I am a maker only of my own particular type of doll

Collection Janet P. Johl

Melanie Johl, as a child, from an old family portrait. By Muriel Atkins Bruyère.

which really can hardly be called a doll at all. In fact
I prefer to label it portrait figures. My aim is to reproduce in miniature as much of the illusion of reality
as possible. The matter of reduced scale of course
presents many problems as to the materials to be used.
Each figure that I do I try to make as perfect as I can
in accuracy of detail and in general effect. This means
a great deal of time and labor and accounts for my
prices which are out of the doll category. It has taken
me many years to evolve the complicated methods of
construction I use. I am always finding new ways to
do things and discarding old ways. As I make every

Collection
Mrs. Greville Bathe

**One of a group called
"The Colonial Dames"**

Courtesy Olive O. Jury

"Art Dolls" from Famous Paintings.

part of each of my figures, my work presents much variety, though there are parts of it that are exceedingly tedious."

"I have lately done chiefly portraits either of present day people or of the Kings and Queens of History. It is always easier to work from a painted portrait of a queen than from the photograph of a living person, for photographs can be quite deceptive. Then, too, there is the matter of comparison with the real person in a contemporary portrait . . . . Dorothy W. Heizer."

Mrs. Samuel Yellin, of Wynnewood, Penn. who has some very beautiful Heizer dolls in her extensive doll collection, considers these dolls the finest made, and in this opinion, she is not alone. In fact it is fairly well agreed that these miniature portraits are distinguished, not as toys, but rather as museum pieces which represent the heights in artistry. Mrs. Yellin has won six blue ribbons in exhibiting six of her Heizer dolls. Among the dolls in her collection are George and Martha Washington, small but perfect in detail, Henry VIII, a Dutch Lady, an exquisite ethereal Madonna in blue, and three figures representing ladies of the Gay Nineties. It takes great ingenuity to make these dolls and a tremendous amount of research. Every bit of the figure is made to scale. Mrs. Heizer is a true artist, who first makes her sketch, then shapes the skeleton upon which will be built the body and face, and to which will be applied the flesh. After the figure is molded, much time is spent on the costuming which must be absolutely authentic from the hair arrangement to the tiniest jewel or bead design. It is the attention to the minutest detail that makes for the perfection in the Heizer figures, a single figure may take a month to complete but, when it is finished, it is a little masterpiece.

When a mother and a daughter combine their artistic talents, there is sure to be an interesting story behind. A few summers ago, Telka Ackley after completing a course at the Students Art League, went to the little fishing village

of Port Clyde, Me. with her family, with the idea of doing some landscapes. Her mother, Edith Flack Ackley, who is known for her books, "*Dolls to Make for Fun and Profit*", and "*Paper Dolls, Their History and How to Make Them*", was busy with her own project of doll making and so did not notice the thick, heavy fog which rolled in from the sea, and enveloped the little village. It was impossible to see outside, and after several days of inactivity, Telka Ackley decided to pass her time painting a subject other than a landscape, and she chose her mother's dolls, as models for still life, water coloring painting. She completed three paintings before the fog rolled away and she could devote herself to the native scenery.

A little while later the family moved down to Rockport, Me., and Telka Ackley decided to paint a few more dolls, and so on

Courtesy Frederick A. Stokes
EDITH FLACK ACKLEY
And one of her handmade dolls.

rainy days at Rockport, she did three more paintings. Almost before she realized it, her work was being exhibited in a local shop, along with Edith Ackley's dolls . . . a mother and daughter exhibition . . . revealing a charm and an individuality all their own. The pictures were seen by a lady connected with the Tricker Gallery in New York City and she asked Telka Ackley to put on a 'one man show' down in the city, which received good reviews. When the combined exhibition of the *American Water Color Society* and the *New York Water Color Club* open-

ed in February, 1939, one painting was entitled 'Still Life with a Doll.'

Now the dolls which Edith Flack Ackley makes may also have paintings to go with them, in soft colorful water colors, or deep rich red, coral and old blue. They are at Velvalee Dickinson's in New York City.

Mrs. Ackley has designed dolls for magazines and started hundreds of women and girls making dolls themselves so that it may truthfully be said that American women— and women outside of America—are once again making charming original cloth dolls for their children, at home.

Another artist collector is Olive O. Jury, an Art Supervisor, at Shamokin, Penn., who makes up famous paintings from her dolls. In this fashion she stages the works of great artists and makes the doll of value to the art instructor. With over 600 dolls in her own collection, Olive Jury has plenty of material with which she can work.

An exhibition of a group of "Characterettes", sculptured and costumed by Mrs. Grace Carpenter Banzhaf of Winter Haven, Florida and Green Farms, Conn. was of special

Courtesy Velvalee Dickinson
Rhadames from the opera Aida. By Mrs. Grace Carpenter Banzhaf

interest to music lovers, for the figures were based on various operas. In the group were Tristan and Isolde, in harmonious color combinations perfect to the minutest detail, with Isolde particularly lovely in a fuchsia colored cape lined with blue. Aida and Rhadames, from Aida, were garbed in their Egyptian costumes, Rhadames wearing a metallic collar.

Mrs. Banzhaf made her first characterette, "Ann of Cleves", as a project for a course in costume designing. She found the modeling so fascinating that she continued until the group was finished including Henry the VIII and all of his six wives. All these figures, twelve inches high, were copied from the Holbein paintings, and dressed authentically.

Courtesy Katherine Walbridge.

The Artist with a group of her own doll creations.

The completed group created considerable interest, especially at Rollins College where Mrs. Banzhaf is the chaperon at Lucy Cross Hall, and an exhibition was immediately planned. With this in view, Mrs. Banzhaf set to work to model more of her 'characterettes', and chose the field of the opera, and the works of Shakespeare as her inspiration. Over a period of two months she completed fourteen more dolls, all beautifully proportioned, made of wire armature, stuffed with cotton, and covered with satin, with the face, the hands and the feet molded from permoclay, painted, after it is set. Each figure was truly a gem. The exhibition opened at Rollins College in January 1938 and was so popular it ran until June. In February 1939 the figures were displayed in a well known book shop on Park Ave., New York City. During the winter of 1939 Mrs. Banzhaf continued to study sculptury with the result that she is now able to produce, in her 'characterettes' likenesses from old miniatures and daguerreotypes. One couple, the great grandparents of the artist, are beautifully rendered, and costumed, even to the tiny old cameo necklace. These dolls, too, may be seen at Velvalee Dickinson's, who was kind enough to help furnish the story of their origin.

Perhaps one of the youngest artists engaged in making dolls is sixteen year old Katherine Walbridge of Van Nuys, Cal., who became interested in designing, and in the history of costumes. In the summer of 1937, she began to experiment with materials. While engaged in this pursuit, she finally hit upon the idea of making heads from papier-maché. For several years she had been doll-minded, showing special favor to the Lenci type, the Ravca French stockinette, and dolls of all races that were correctly proportioned, with good facial expressions and attractive costumes.

Katherine models the head, the neck and shoulders of her dolls in one piece and covers it all with stocking material. Features and facial expressions are painted on and real hair serves for the wig. The bodies are built up over a wire framework. Costumes are carefully copied from such sources as the National Geographic Magazine and from publications on costumes. If possible, the materials used come from the country the doll represents. The embroidery is copied to scale, and the dolls include young, and old members. The head and body usually take from four to six hours to make, the clothes from five to fifteen hours, shoes and boots are made from leather of different colors.

Katherine's mother writes that when her daughter was a little girl of ten years she used to gather dried kelp, a sea weed, from the beach and make dolls from it. The kelp had a bulb two or three inches in diameter at the lower end of the stem with short roots attached. When dried, the roots formed the hair, and the features were put on the bulbs with pastel pencils.

Miss Dewees Cochran, American sculptor and painter, lived ten years in Europe, painting, studying and later on lecturing on Art History. She came back to the United States to face 'Facts', with the firm belief that if she originated something American, vision and enterprise would do the rest for her. Thrown completely on her own, in 1934, she set to work to prove her theory.

"Her first inspirations were two completely fantastic rag dolls which she named "Topsy" and "Turvy". They had very much modeled noses and

mouths and appliqued eyes, could stand on
their heads, do the splits and completely
live up to their names. The New York
buyers of the best shops could not resist
them but warned Miss Cochran that there
would not be a very great sale for them
since they would only fall into the hands
of grown-ups. America had become so
psychology conscious that children were
no longer allowed to play with fantastic
toys which might distort their minds. The
faces of "Topsy" and "Turvy" were not
exactly human."

Courtesy of Dewees Cochran

The Dewees Cochran Portrait Doll

"Reality" was demanded. It gave
birth to "The Idea." Why not a doll,
an actual portrait of the child who plays with it? This was before the
Shirley Temple doll. Of course dolls had always been made down through the
ages to resemble important personages but this should be made possible for
everyone to possess of themselves, or someone in the family. It should be constructed of durable materials and made practical as a toy as well as valuable
as an heirloom. She originated the name "*Portrait Doll*"".

Miss Cochran brought her idea to New York City in 1935, and found it met
with enthusiasm. When she returned to her home, she found a telegram for
five orders of 'Portrait Dolls', among them the two little Irving Berlin children.

At this point she did not know of what material she was going to make
the dolls but she rushed back to New York from her Bucks County studio, made
sketches of her young clients, and had the good fortune to be told of a soft light
wood that could be carved very easily. This was used for these first somewhat
crude examples. After the first Christmas rush Miss Cochran was not content
with this material and needed leisure from the exacting business of doll making
to do some research work on compositions that could be turned out in hand
molds. This was made possible by no other than the fantastic "Topsy" and
"Turvy" whose mechanism she had patented and at this point sold to one of
the New York doll firms. They intended to apply the novel manner of joints
to a naturalistic rag doll. She was also designer at this firm for three months.
This made possible the necessary research for work on the hand-made Portrait Doll, and inspired by the keen interest which the doll had aroused, she
began at once to work hard on the idea. Because of her study of physiognomy,
while in Europe, she decided to work out a series of basic types of American
children. After very thorough study and concentrated effort, she achieved
her now famous Portrait Dolls, a portrait head first modeled in plasteline as in
sculpture, and then followed by a plaster cast of a lightweight and durable
composition of which the doll is molded. Wigs of real hair to match that of the
child are woven in the method of real wigs and toupeés. The workmanship
and time required to make these dolls, to say nothing of the skill, made the
price prohibitive for many interested persons. A commercialized version of

the portrait doll developed from the four basic physiognomy types was produced by the Effanbee Doll Co., in New York City, and were introduced as an Easter Feature in 1939 by a leading Fifth Ave. store. Dewees Cochran has been working, during 1940, on a new idea in portrait figurines and small portrait heads, as well as water color portraits called "environment portraits." These newest dolls are scheduled for exhibition in the near future.

For the child who loves to play with a doll house, and the dolls scaled to proper size, another artist has done helpful and interesting work. The "True Family Real People Dolls" are little dolls made to scale, one inch to the foot, and flexible, so that they may be placed in any position that a person might assume. Made of rubber, these dolls are sanitary and can be bathed. The heads are of molded rubber, hand painted, and of various distinctive types. The creator Marjorie True (Gregg) writes "I hope both as toys that children may play with, and as material for artistic creative work my own dolls will some day be important." These little dolls are entirely American made.

Needle Sculpture is a most unique form of work which Mrs. Gilda Snyder of New York City has employed artistically and successfully. Mrs. Snyder starts with a bunch of cotton. Then she dabs on tiny layers for features and gets the most remarkable likenesses of prominent persons. Mrs. Snyder uses darning thread as if it were plastic material, building up, stitch by stitch. A small core, or bunch of thread, serves as the starting point for the head. When this core has become about as big as a half dollar, Mrs. Snyder adds extra stitches, working back and forth until the features are formed to her satisfaction. Besides modeling public characters, she has done life-like faces of American Indians, gypsies, Ubangi Africans, Chinese and such personages of world importance as President Roosevelt, the late Mr. Chamberlain and the Duchess of Windsor, as well as the dictators.

Mrs. Louise Chase, a member of an old aristocratic Southern family, descending from Lord Lovat Fraser of Scotland, began to fashion dolls of historic interest about ten years ago. Before she made her dolls she had started a show garden of azaleas, which developed into one of the loveliest small gardens in the south. However, when her health failed she was forced to give up working in her garden, and being the type of person who is unhappy when her hands are idle, she turned her thoughts to dolls, which she had always loved and of which she had a small collection.

Memories of childhood dolls made of grass and hickory nuts spurred her on, and in August 1938 she began her "Worthwhile Dolls." The first pair were Hill Billies fashioned after some characters on the old Fraser plantation. Mrs. Chase makes all her own patterns for the doll bodies, also the clothes. At first the dolls were displayed in the garden as an added attraction to the many visitors whose love of azaleas takes them yearly to the mid-south. But family and friends insisted that the dolls belonged outside as well as in the garden, and so they have become items for the collector who is interested in period dolls, and in story book characters.

Up in New England, at Wareham, Mass., to be exact, Mrs. Edith Savary Hall, as a Public School Supervisor of Art, made marionettes and puppets for fifteen years. Add to this a good deal of curiosity about people, and, especially

Courtesy Mrs. Louise Chase.
Historical Dolls.

Courtesy Mrs. Edith Savary Hall.
Elizabeth Gorham.

early American people, and the beginning of the Savary Dolls is told. These dolls, made of cloth, developed from school work, and the efforts of a doll minded artist to make an accurate representation of the characters and fashions of a given period. No two of these dolls are alike. The heads and faces are hand modeled from old portraits, prints, miniatures and daguerreotypes. The costumes are exact from the smallest detail of underwear to the last bit of ribbon on a hat. Each doll is named for the character represented. Rich in early Americana, New England has been a fertile field for Mrs. Hall, and her dolls do not belong in the toy class. Whole families of Savary dolls have been made and exhibited for museums and class-rooms. The small "children" dolls are about five inches, the adults range from two to twelve inches.

"I never intended to make anything but American dolls," writes Mrs. Hall, "but with the demand I have made a few

others like David Copperfield, Mr. Micawber and Queen Victoria as a little girl.''
In period the Savary dolls date from 1500 to 1895 and include many familiar
historical names.

Many individuals are interested in presenting to the doll collector just such
historical dolls, particularly dealing with the story of the growth of America.
Mrs. D. H. Keys, of Norfolk, Va., has created a Pocahontas doll and others
pertaining to the history around Jamestown and Williamsburg. Mrs. Keys
makes the dolls herself and in the Pocahontas doll she has followed the wood
cuts from Bruce's *"History of the Colonial Period."* The result is a little
doll dressed in corn colored kid skin with fringed skirt, moccasins and bead
trimming. Mrs. Keys has also made Captain John Smith, John Rolfe, Pocahontas after her marriage to John Rolfe, and many other interesting personages belonging to the settlement of Virginia.

Mrs. Lawrence Krieger of Hastings-on-Hudson has a set of dolls which she
has made representing the First Ladies of the United States which she right-
fully calls "White House Ladies." Copying in exact detail the costumes which
these First Ladies have worn, as displayed in the Smithsonian Institute, at
Washington, D. C., the dolls, which are all hand made and hand painted, are
fine specimens for period costume study, as well as historical interest.

White House Ladies created by Mrs. Lulu Krieger.

Mrs. Greville Bathe of Philadelphia has made a series of splendid dolls, which she calls her "Colonial Dames." With them as a medium she portrays the story of the first settlements, giving credit and attention, perhaps for the first time, to the gallant women who followed their men from many old lands, to the new world across a strange sea, and helped to build this great and enduring country. Mrs. Bathe studied Edward Warwick's "*Early American Costume*," and Elizabeth McClellan's "*Historic Dress in America*" so that her little dolls, eleven inches in height, are correct in every detail of dress, and each accessory is carefully worked out and historically as accurate as a painstaking effort can assure. The dolls begin with the founding of the Colonies in Virginia in 1607 and go up to the settlement in Georgia in 1737. With truly adult faces, these foremothers of America are representative of the courage and determination that all the early colonists had in common. Mrs. Bathe has also made other historical dolls for her collection including Daniel Boone and the Marquise de Lafayette.

Courtesy Mrs. Florence Baughman
"Florida Crackers"

Mrs. R. J. Gardiner has made a group of dolls representing the wives of the Governors of Ohio, dating from 1887 to the present, each doll dressed in an authentic model of the inauguration gown worn by the first lady of Ohio. Mrs. Gardiner received fine co-operation from several of the wives of the governors. The first doll she dressed was Mrs. Joseph Foraker who contributed a piece of jet and gold trimming which had been used on the inaugural gown of 1887. The last doll Mrs. Gardiner has completed is Mrs. Bricker, the wife of the last governor.

Mrs. Florence Baughman of St. Petersburg, Fla., has produced a pair of unique dolls, the heads of which are made of electric light bulbs, covered with papier maché and molded. The pair depict an old man and old woman, typical of the Florida Crackers, and dressed accordingly, the woman's underskirt made of a flour bag, which reads, "Bread is the Staff of Life."

Margaret Zimmerman of Lock Haven, Penn., makes two kinds of dolls, one a popular type, ten inches in height from pressed paper. The faces are wee masks made over a carved head so that they may be easily duplicated. These are mostly of famous, or notorious persons, with clothes designed to further the likeness rather than to reveal detail of costume. Thus a militant figure may wear uniform and shiny boots, but the costume will have no pockets or extras. The other kind of dolls are made to order, or are just characters which Mrs. Zimmerman fancies. The heads are of composition. Such touches as eye lashes and fingernails are not forgotten. Every costume is authentic and detailed to scale. Mrs. Zimmerman who studied commercial illustration began to make crude little doll portraits for dinner parties, during the early depression years. Dolls, for doll houses followed, and gradually a mere hobby became a profession that is not only profitable, but most pleasant labor.

Grace Stanley Miller of Long Beach, Cal., recently displayed her dolls at the Los Angeles Museum. They represent characters from books, as well as costumed people from foreign lands. All her life Grace Miller has painted, modeled, and cut patterns. Each doll head is modeled, and the ideas and designs, the methods and ways of making these dolls, are all her own. Each head is different, some are of plaster, some of clay, others of papier maché or of a composition material, and no models are used except her own ideas. Every stitch is done by hand, and the finest materials are employed. Water color paintings accompany the dolls, for painting is Miss Miller's real profession and the dolls have served her as a secondary interest, and another means of expressing herself, artistically.

Courtesy Grace Stanley Miller
Dolls displayed at the Los Angeles Museum by Grace Stanley Miller

Frances Elinor Diecks of Cohoes, N. Y., is another costume designer who has become a doll creator, making the doll in its entirety. She takes her characters from the world of drama and has done doll likenesses of Cornelia Otis Skinner, in "Romance," Jean Muir in the "Taming of the Shrew," and Helen Hayes in "Victoria Regina." She has also concentrated on the stars partaking in the Mohawk Drama Festival. In addition Miss Diecks has done Louisa Alcott's "Little Women," and many other book personages and people of historic or stage fame. The bulletin of the *National Doll and Toy Collectors Club* described Miss Diecks work. To quote:

"The dolls are cut from patterns made from paper, the bodies stuffed solid with cotton, no wires or foundations used, rayon is used for the body and pure silk for the face, yarn for the hair. Features are hand stitched and hand painted as well as all clothing which is perfect in every detail. Miss Diecks' first attempt was a life size doll which she dressed in her father's clothing and which

Courtesy Frances

"Little Women" dolls inspired

Courtesy Ideal Novelty
and Toy Co.

Judy Garland in
"The Wizard of Oz."

"scared her mother" every time she passed it.
sprung from her desire for making historical
School of Fine and Applied Arts, and because of her interest in the Mohawk
Drama Festival Plays at Union College, Schenectady, N. Y."

Two sisters in London make the Pixy Dolls which are found in Bermuda,
in two sizes, and with most winsome little faces. Well known to collectors are
the English dolls by Norah Wellingston. It is utterly impossible to mention
all the artistic people engaged in the fascinating work of doll making. Suffice to say that only a very few have been mentioned. And last, but far
from least, are the lovely creations of Walt Disney who will never be forgotten as the artist who has brought new beauty to old stories, and created

Courtesy Ideal Novelty
& Toy Co.

Gaby

Courtesy
Ideal Novelty & .Toy
Co.

King Little

dolls to match his exquisite motion picture films. Following the Snow White Doll and the little dwarfs, has come Pinnochio and his friends, Stromboli the puppeteer, the Blue Fairy and although an animal, the ever present conscience, Jiminy Cricket. Max Fleischer, also of the cinema world, has contributed King Little and Gaby from Gulliver's Travels.

Courtesy
Ideal Novelty & Toy Co.

Walt Disney's Pinnochio

Courtesy Ideal Novelty & Toys Co.

Shirley Temple

Courtesy of Ideal Novelty & Toy Co.

Mortimer Snerd

Chapter XVIII

CRÈCHE and
FASHION DOLLS

*(The Nativity Scene, Other Religious Dolls, European Fashion
Exponents, The Modern Fashion Doll)*

Nativity Scene from the collection of
Verai de Ferré Fagen

WITH Christianity came the telling of the beautiful story of the birth of Jesus, through the medium of the Passion Plays, the Mystery and Miracle Dramas, art, music and the doll. Just as the mythological gods and goddesses were represented in small figures, so the crèche developed in Europe, after the birth of Jesus, and reproductions of that holy night in Bethlehem became popular, not only in the church, but in the home.

The crèche dolls were, however, originally church property, carved and painted by artists of the time, who, through their study of the paintings of the great masters, brought spiritual beauty of expression to the faces of the crèche figures, and grace and sensitivity to the hands. Not infrequently the figures were portraits of prominent persons, or individuals to whom the artist was indebted. People wishing to atone for a sin, large or small, often would fashion a doll for the church. Sometimes the figure represented characters of biblical times, again it might be in the image of a saint, or even an angel. The church used these dolls for special religious occasions, and the earliest examples are finely wrought and well made throughout, and very often large. Later on the figures diminished in size. But the style of adorning the churches with dolls, to denote certain religious characters, seems to be nothing more than a tradition today.

205

Many an ancient church in Europe has its crèche, and many homes, of all classes of people, have miniature representations of the Nativity scene. In the colder countries the stable is usually thatched, and white to simulate snow and icicles. In the warmer climes, the crèche scene is in the open air, with mountains and trees, for its setting.

It is not exactly known when the crèche actually started. Collectors have never been able to determine the exact origin. Sermons delivered about the year 400 by St. John Chrysostom and St. Gregory Thaumaturgus, refer to the existence of a crib with figures of the Holy family. But it is said that the puppet-crib existed prior to 400. Some authorities attribute the creche idea to St. Francis of Assisi (1181-1226). It is all more or less suppositional.

Ancient Venice showed ecclesiastical dolls at the annual fair on Assumption Day. The Italian Presepio, or in native dialect, Presepe, the nativity group comprising doll figures in the manger, was mentioned in notarial records, of the fifteenth century in Naples, and the custom of exhibiting them in convents and houses is found still earlier. Whether the Italian, "presepio," the French "crèche" the Spanish "nacimientos," the Mexican "Posadas," or the German "krippe," these figures all represent the Holy Child, with Mary and Joseph, the Three Kings, the Sheperds, the Angels, the lowly stable and the farm animals. That the crèche doll served as a symbol is fairly well evidenced, and to the student of these figures, the large size of the hands is of especial interest.

The figure of the Virgin, another type of religious doll, also appeared in the churches and it is an established fact that the marionettes or Little Marys, as they were called in the Middle Ages, served to illustrate religious stories.

These early Presepio, then, may be said to be a translation, in detail, of the biblical narrative of the birth of Jesus. In addition, today, they serve to teach the student something of the fine examples of early workmanship, and peasant costuming. The doll figures, many of them jointed, had heads of carved wood, and later of terra cotta and papier mache. It is said that those coming from southern Italy were of lemon wood and brittle faience. Those from northern Italy were, like the ones from Oberammergau, of composition. Those from Spain were mostly of terra cotta, as were the German. Many of the heads were modeled of wax. Often the bodies were of rags to make them pliable. All were true representations of the cultural background of the people of their region.

Two famous modelers were Guiseppe Sammartino (1720-1793) and a follower of his, Guiseppe Gori, whose specialty was the figures of orientals and nobles. In 1760 Charles III of Bourbon, King of Naples, prepared a Presepio, himself, and his Queen cut up her own luxurious garments to dress the dolls. The best talent of the day was employed in the construction of the figures and the results are now housed in the historical museum near Naples, one of the most exquisite Nativity groups in existence. There are 500 figures of people, and 20 of animals, all made of finely carved wood and wax. The shepherds are modeled from life, the peasants of the time serving as the inspiration. The royal figures were dressed in rich brocades in the style of the period. It is said that when the Queen of Naples fled from Sicily she took the presepio with her.

In the church of Ara Coela, on the Altar of Heaven, the Franciscan Church of Rome, there is the Blessed, or Jeweled Bambino, representing the Infant Jesus, and supposed to have been carved from a tree that grew on the Mt. of Olives, by a Franciscan monk who died before the work was completed. Carvers, not skilled workmen, evidently finished the infant, for the image is crudely done. His wooden curls are very rigid, and there is little, if any, facial expression. This Bambino wears a jeweled crown of real and imitation jewels, silken garments, and has feet of gold. He was crowned in the Vatican on May 2, 1891. A semi-religious Italian Lenten doll, dressed in black, is often hung from upper windows during the Lenten season.

Some years ago, in the Rice collection in New York City, there was a Christ Child doll of papier maché, which had been brought from the European continent. It was similar to the little Bambinos found in Italian churches. What happened to this particular doll is unknown. It may possibly have found its way into a museum. Garbed in embroidered robes and decorated with gold spangled lace, the Bambinos were lovely to see, life size, with real hair and a halo of gold encircling their baby heads. It was believed that they had a healing quality, if touched, and sick babies were brought to them to be cured.

The Bambino doll also served another purpose. It was given to a mother upon the birth of a child as a compliment, and was also placed in the church before the statute of the Blessed Virgin Mary as a token of Thanksgiving. The beauty of the Bambino doll depended upon the wealth and rank of the family to whom the baby was born, and in aristocratic families the doll was usually wrapped in costly fabrics, trimmed with real lace, and studded with real jewels.

Dolls in ecclesiastical costumes, accurate to the minutest detail, appeared in the eighteenth century. Models of the habits worn in the Nativity groups at Christmas time also served to teach the children the history of the church. It has been rumored that in Baltimore, Md. a doll called 'La Infantila' occupies a room in solitary grandeur, reclining on a canopied bed of solid silver and possessing supernatural powers of healing, and performing miracles.

The German 'Krippe' figures differed from the Italian, in that they were less artistic and more like toys. Those from Nürenberg were of wood, and as early as 1744 were in popular usage for the crib. The idea of the 'krippe' appealed to the religious people of south Germany, and in the hands of the people the figures revealed a more simple art, but not so much artistry. It was the Germans who added new figures to the Nativity scene. German men and women carved and modeled and painted the figures for the church, and for the home. As the demand for the crèche figures increased, the fine craftsmanship lessened, despite the efforts of the church to bring back the spiritual expression to the faces. As time went on only a very few sincere artists remained to carry on the tradition.

Prior to the present war, and perhaps in spite of it, the small village of
Oberammergau, in the Tyrol remained the sole place which faithfully presented
a 'Passion Play' every ten years, and carved the small figures to represent the
story of the birth and life of Jesus Christ. One of the rare sets of Nativity dolls
in the United States has been given by Mrs. Gustine Courson Weaver to the
Historical Collection of North Texas State Teacher's College at Denton, Texas.
In 1922, while on a visit to Oberammergau to see the Passion Play, Mrs. Weaver
became interested in the part that dolls have had in religion. As a guest in

Courtesy of Mrs. Velvalee Dickinson

A very fine pair of Crèche Dolls.

Louise Lang Bold's home, she saw original dolls that had been used by the priests in the fourteenth and fifteenth centuries to teach the story of Christ. Mr. Bold, who was a skilled wood carver, made for Mrs. Weaver an exact copy of some of the groups, including the little Christus, Mary, Joseph, the shepherds and even two of the grazing sheep. The Cleveland Museum of Art has also acquired a Nativity group from Oberammergau but Mrs. Weaver is undoubtedly one of the few persons who have been fortunate to have had contact with those who personally enact the immortal story, as well as carve the religious dolls. The Thayer Collection at the University of Kansas fills two glass cabinets with one hundred little Italian presipio figures. This collection was formerly in the home of Prince Massimo of Rome and has been exhibited at Castle San 'Angelo. Another similar collection may be found at the Bavarian National Museum, Munich, Germany. In most of the outstanding museums of Europe beautiful crèche dolls are to be found. Occasionally single figures are discovered hidden away in antique shops, and are generally very high priced.

Mrs. Virginia Woodin has two antique crèche dolls from Mexico City representing Mary and St. Joseph, and dating the eighteenth century. Mrs. Velvalee Dickinson has two fine examples. Mrs. Grete Dreifuss, formerly of Freiburg, Germany, reports an exceptionally beautiful Madonna with child which she saw in the cloister at St. Ulrich in 1922. This figure seemed to be of French origin, and the hands, small and with pointed fingers, and the tiny feet, were more like those of a French dancer than of a religious figure. The priest in charge also believed that the figure was French in feeling. Mrs. John B. Yerkes of Bryn Mawr, Penn. has a collection of crèche dolls between 300-400 years old. Mrs. Earle E. Andrews of Winchester, Mass. also has a splendid crèche doll.

Many of the modern artists have begun to make ecclesiastical dolls. Andreef Saroff, of St. Louis, Mo. does a group that includes the dignitaries of the Roman Catholic Church, and also includes such early Bible characters as Moses. A southern company in New Orleans puts out twelve different orders of Catholic nun dolls. Modern artists also have attempted crèche figures in a more decorative mood, perhaps, than a religious one.

There are several collections of nun dolls, presenting a striking picture in black and white. For the collector who desires to represent biblical and church figures through the medium of the doll, the path is wide open for even such historic persons as Pere Marquette and Pere Charlevoix are obtainable. How much can be taught of matters religious through the medium of the doll is revealed in an article from *The Lutheran Boys and Girls Magazine* entitled 'Biblical Dolls'. To quote in part:

Courtesy of Toy Creations

A Little Sister Doll

REBECCA

"In the city of Nahor, in Mesopotamia, lived a man named Bethuel who had a very fair and lovely daughter, Rebecca. At evening time, she was accustomed to go to a certain well at the outskirts of the city to draw water, as did all the women of those days. This particular evening, when she had filled her pitcher by the well, a manservant came running up to her. He said, "Let me, I pray thee, drink a little water from thy pitcher." Rebecca replied politely, "Drink, my lord," and she hastened to let down her pitcher a second time, and gave him to drink. Then she noticed that his camels were thirsty, too, so she offered to draw water for them. The man was more than pleased at her generosity for he had come to Nahor with a very special purpose. He had been sent by Abraham who dwelt in Canaan to find a wife for his son in Mesopotamia, the country from which Abraham had originally come. The servant, traveling with the camels, had come to the well at the outskirts of the city, and had stopped there, entreating God to guide him toward a proper wife for his master's son, a damsel who when asked for a drink of water, would give generously not only to man, but to his beasts, also. Rebecca, who was as good as she was fair, came to the well and granted his wish. So the manservant knew that God had guided him to Rebecca and when he returned to Canaan, Rebecca was with him. She became the wife of Abraham's son, Isaac, and he loved her dearly.

The doll, Rebecca, stands for all the loveliness that belonged to that other fair Rebecca as she stood by the well. Her costume of rich velvet, of a deep blue hue, is embroidered in soft shades of green, gold and red, at the cuffs and the neck. Her belt of white is also embroidered. Her long full white homespun scarf is deeply fringed in colors, and bound about her head by a simple narrow blue silk band. The features of this doll are oriental. Her eyes and hair are dark, her lips red and full. Travelers in the Near East find living Rebeccas today. To the doll collector this Rebecca is most symbolic of a famous old Biblical story which all the world knows as "Rebecca at the Well.""

JOSEPH AND HIS MANY-COLORED COAT

Perhaps one reason why the story of Joseph is an old favorite is because, despite many hardships and unfair treatment, Joseph managed to rise above the circumstances and become a successful man.

His father Israel loved Joseph very much and he made him a fine coat of many different colors, and Joseph's brothers disliked him even more.

One night Joseph had a dream. In the dream, which was symbolized by sheaves in the field, the older brothers all obeyed Joseph.

*   *   *   *   *

After many years, his brothers, in want, came to him for help, not knowing who he was, and only after he tested them did Joseph reveal his identity. So his dream came true—that he would rule over his own brethren.

The doll representing the story of Joseph wears a fine coat of many colors, trimmed and bound at the hem, neck, cuff and front edge with striped colorful material. About the waist is a wide band of homespun material, knotted once. Joseph wears a neat white turban. Like most people native to the Orient, or Near Eastern countries, his complexion is dark and his hair and eyes a deep brown. His moustache, which is large, covers his full red lips. His features are very much those of the people who still live in the part of the world he represents. Looking at the doll one is carried back to those old Biblical stories, that still hold the interest of the world."

It would indeed be interesting to devote more space to a comprehensive study of the religiously significant dolls, with particular emphasis on their evolutionary history. The custom of presenting the Nativity story still survives, especially in Catholic countries, a custom that contains too much of interest to hope to include it all in one small chapter.

The fact that these dolls led people from the religious world, directly to the world of fashion is an astonishing, but an absolute fact. A doll of Venice, Italy, attired in the 'toilette of the year', was exhibited at each Ascension Day at the 'Merceria' for the style edification of noble Venetian ladies.

Jerusalem Pair, made by Refugees in Greece.

Therefore, it is possible that the Fashion Doll originated in Italy, when Venice ruled as the Queen of the Adriatic. Milan, Padua and Venice were fashion centres and London, Berlin and Madrid vied with each other, and with the other cities, for a share in the fashion honors, but it was always Paris that won the first place, and France led the world in creating new and ingenious styles, and employing designers and skillful workers. As there were no fashion magazines, nor daily newspapers carrying descriptive and pictorial advertisements, the people had to see the styles, instead of reading about them, and so the artistic, and clever French designers created the Fashion Dolls, little creatures of crude body, but correct in every detail of costume and craftsmanship. Clothed in costly materials, in exquisite taste, they found their way around the world as the heralds and ambassadeurs of all that was chic. French fashions were ruling the world in those early days, and have continued to do so down to the present, with Hollywood, Cal., the only competitor for the place of honor today.

As early as 1391 in France, the records reveal, the royal expense account showed that a goodly sum had been spent to send one of these Fashion Dolls to England. One hundred years later another doll was sent to the Queen of Spain, and still later, another went to the Duchess of Bavaria. In France, during the sixteenth century, dolls made of wax, wood and a composition of sawdust, straw and oxblood, were sold as trinkets, but were more often used as figurines, costumed in the most beautiful gowns. These dolls were also used in Italy at this same period. As printing had not come into general use, often the doll held a crown in one hand, to indicate that the style was for court usage. History notes that in 1600 Henri IV, King of France, wrote to Marie de Medici that he had learned that she desired patterns for a dress and accordingly was sending her a model doll. A French writer claims that the custom of dressing dolls, or figures, originated in the Hotel Rambouillet, with a figure called 'La Grande Pandora', which was exhibited in full dress at each change of the current fashions. A smaller doll, 'La Petite Pandora', garbed in the most polite of fine under garments, also appeared at this time.

Serving all through the sixteenth century as models, these fashion dolls were valued more for their lovely costumes than for their own beauty. They were not given as gifts, except to reveal to a lady a general idea of how she would look in a certain costume. They were highly valued all through this period for their display of style, and were found in castles and palaces. Costly dolls were often more easily admitted to the court of the King, than were individuals. Elegant only in dress, the dolls themselves were very primitive, carved of wood and poorly painted, with bodies, legs and arms made of stuffed pads held together with ribbons. The notorious hairdresser Legros exhibited dolls coiffed with forty various styles, showing his latest ideas of hair dressing. Doll coiffeurs followed Dame Fashion, piled high in intricate manner, or in dangling curls, either short in back, or one on each side of the head. The same type of head dress is found in china head dolls, and in papier maché.

As early as 1493, Anna of Brittany sent to Queen Isabella of Castille, a 'large poupée' probably to show the fine fashions in vogue at the French court. When Maximilian entered Augsburg, in 1504, the little daughter of the Syndic Pentinger addressed him in Latin verse. Maximilian was so pleased that he later sent the child the finest and most costly doll he could find.

In 1772, one doll, in court dress, was sent to the Ladies of the Bed Chamber of Queen Caroline. Madame de Sevigné wrote from Paris, to her daughter, Madame de Grignan, who lived outside the city that she was having a doll sent out to her. This casual mention indicates that the gift of a doll was a common procedure. In the court of Louis XVI Fashion Dolls were very popular. A life sized doll was dressed in the latest Versailles style, and called 'La Poupée de la Rue St. Honoré'. Replicas sent to England, to Italy, Spain and the French archives, claim that Catherine de Medici had sixteen of these dolls dressed in mourning after the death of her husband, the King.

Even in times of war, when the ports of England were closed, a large alabaster doll, four feet high, and termed 'la grand courier de la mode' was permitted passage. In the War of the First Empire the ports were closed to dolls, and English women, badly dressed, blamed William Pitt for their lack of suitable fashionable attire.

In the seventeenth century these Fashion Dolls were very costly, and several thousand dollars paid for a superb gift to royalty, was not unusual. At this period, the French excelled in the manufacture and dressing of the Fashion Dolls which served as publicity agents to reveal to the world the supremacy of French styles. Hundreds of these dolls journeyed all over Europe, dressed in the loveliest of clothes, without question the forerunners of the present day mannequins, which display styles in the windows of dress shops and fine department stores in great cities, all over the world. Many of these dolls, garbed in the finest of laces, and the richest of silks, landed at Dover, England. Mrs. Stewart Campbell of Bristol, R. I. reports a pair of wax mannequin dolls, circa 1720. This pair consists of a very grand lady, and her blackamoor flunkey in scarlet livery.

The English sent dolls to the continent to show how ladies should dress. Several of these dolls, with a variety of costumes made in London, were sent to the Czarina of Russia to show her the English fashions of the moment. Many of these dolls originated in the Netherlands and were known as 'Flanders Babies'. It was this type of doll that ultimately found its way, as a plaything, into the nurseries. When the Pilgrims arrived in the new world, these dolls were already well known in England, and on the continent. One type was called the Bartholomew Baby because the doll was sold at the Bartholomew Fair.

It is certainly possible that such a doll could have been brought to the shores of America, at an early date. Mention is found of Fashion Dolls, or Fashion Babies, as they were often called, and an advertisement in a New

England Weekly Journal told of the latest fashion babies arrived from abroad, and on display at the home of a 'mantua maker'. There was a small fee of a shilling or two for the privilege of seeing the dolls.

The first toy shop in Boston was in business by 1783, and among the fascinating novelties, there was occasionally a French or English Fashion Doll, which was usually too expensive to be classed as a toy. In New York City, about 1757, two mantua makers advertised 'Fashion Babies' as 'Just arrived from The Kingdom of Ireland.' Even the Quakers of Philadelphia had their fashion babies, dressed in exact replica of the Quaker dress.

Mrs. Imogene Anderson of Greenwich, Conn. who has the famous doll named 'Anstiss Derby'' in her collection, was good enough to send this data on the doll, which came from France, to Salem, in 1826. The doll's dress, and her coiffeur were copied for the first ball of young Martha Derby, the grand daughter of Elias Hasket Derby, who was a powerful figure in the Salem-East India trade. "Anstiss" has beautiful brown eyes and is very aristocratic looking. She has white kid arms, and wears a gown of blue satin trimmed with silver braid. Her elaborate hair dress is entwined with pink roses and silver ribbon.

When the House of Valois reigned in France, a beautiful doll was made wearing a richly embroidered gown of green satin, stitched in gold and silver thread. The doll was of carved wood, twenty seven inches high, and was supported on a crinoline like stand of cane which held out the skirts. The legs either dangled or were non existent. There were few or no underclothes, a great contrast to the dolls of Victoria's era when layers and layers of embroidered petticoats were shown on dolls for the first time. In the Musée Carnavalet in Paris, there were fine lady dolls of the time of Louis XV, eight inches high with well modeled heads, neck and arms of wax decolleté, as was the fashion, with a wicker cage to keep the hooped skirts in place. The wigs on these dolls have disappeared with age, but the chic little tricorne hats remain.

Through rudimentary in composition these early dolls, with their fixed shiny stare and painted curls, gave the effect of a most unnatural symmetry. Far more attention was given to the costume than to the doll. Like the French lady, the doll stood for beauty and taste in dress and in the second half of the eighteenth century, choice dolls could be found at the shop of Sieur Juhil, Rue St. Denis, along with playthings from England. Dolls could also be purchased from Rauxle Fils, in the Rue des Petits Leons, and always this doll played the role of the arbiter of Parisian

Courtesy Mrs. Imogene Anderson

'Antiss Derby,' French fashion doll of 1826.

elegance whether in the sixteenth, the seventeenth, the eighteenth or the nineteenth century. However it is to be noted that, in England, Queen Victoria set
the fashions for her era.

At the Metropolitan Art Museum in New York City there are thirty one
dolls dressed in the costumes worn over the last eight hundred years. This
group is known as "A Fashion Study of Long Ago."

Mrs. Earle E. Andrews, of Winchester, Mass. has a lovely French fashion
doll with real hair done in a beautiful French roll. The doll wears a white
taffeta gown draped into a graceful train and trimmed with red ruffles. Her
high heeled red kid shoes have little gold buttons and she has a handsome
ermine scarf with muff to match. Red crystal earrings complete her very chic
costume, and a peep beneath the skirt reveals exquisitely made underthings
with hand embroidered scallops, fine tucks and lace ruffles. She is a splendid
example of a fine French Fashion Doll.

The elegant lady doll of the 1870-1890 'Golden Age of Dolls' period, must
have been influenced by the older Fashion Dolls. Gentleman and small boy dolls
were not exceptional, for good dress in men was considered of importance. The
mannequins of to-day, the inanimate ones, owe their being to the doll of an
earlier period.

Mrs. Florence Sutro Esberg of New York City has some very interesting
wax fashion models displaying gowns up to 1921. It was from just such little
figures that fashionable and notable women of history selected their wardrobes.
Other mannequins in the Esberg collection, not antiques, are wax models, the
earliest dressed in the fashion of 1908. Mrs. Esberg bought the dolls over a
period of years when she was in Paris and her last one is 1923. Two years ago,
when in Paris, she was no longer able to locate the woman who had made these
dolls for her. Mrs. Samuel Yellin of Wynnewood, Penn. has a nice group of
this type of doll. Mrs. Arthur Goldsmith of Narbeth, Penn. has fashion manne-
quinns in her collection.

In April, 1939, *The Christian Science Monitor,* of Boston, Mass. had an
article entitled "Rubber Maidens with Fashion Careers" which revealed the
fact that the Fashion Dolls are once again very much in vogue. To quote:

"After a century and a half of disuse, dolls are appearing to show off the
dresses, coats and suits of Milady's wardrobe . . . miniature mannequins ranging

Collection of Mrs. Arthur S. Goldsmith.

A Group of Fashion Dolls

Collection Mrs. Angelina Comport.

**Figurines, of modern make, which are reminiscent of
Fashion models of another day.**

from 15 to 36 inches tall are making their appearance . . . a famous New York artist sculpts these diminutive maidens out of hard rubber while it is still in a malleable state like wet clay, rouges their lips, curls their silk, thread hair, and casts that sophisticated look over their eyes.''

These dolls are the creation of Margit Nilsen of New York City and they grace many a window display. The newest doll, by this talented artist, is called Deb-U Doll. She is made of unbreakable life-like Lasticoid, with a real human hair wig, and even nail polish and lipstick carefully matched. This doll is designed for fashion minded girls in their teens, and for doll minded adults as well as doll loving youngsters. Articulated to stand or sit, Deb-U Doll has fourteen different wardrobes and there are constant additions, so that she keeps pace with the styles. Her 'Kid-Sister' has four wardrobes. Margit Nilsen also makes a 'Glitter Girl', with complete up to the minute costumes and a series of costume dolls which include White House Ladies, Betsy Ross, A Puritan and other dolls depicting fashions of dolls from early Byzantine, Grecian and Roman days, through the Empire and Colonial periods right to the very modern bride of 1941.

So the Fashion Doll is again serving its original purpose as an advertising and publicity agent, this time representing the styles that America is producing. On October 4, 1940, in *The Christian Science Monitor* the following article appeared:

'ROYAL' DOLLS AID REFUGEES

Special to The Christian Science Monitor

MONTREAL—Two little visitors will arrive in Montreal Oct. 8 on a tour which will take them to every large Canadian city from coast to coast. They are France and Marianne, two dolls presented to the Princesses Elizabeth and Margaret Rose by the children of France in 1938.

During their stay here they hope to augment relief funds of the Canadian National Committee on Refugees under whose sponsorship they are touring Canada.

Courtesy of the Margit Nilsen Studios
Deb-U Doll and her Kid Sister

The little French demoiselles came to Canada from their royal home in England upon the invitation of the Committee. Under the chairmanship of Senator Cairine Wilson, the Committee approached Queen Elizabeth, asking for the loan of the dolls and their famous wardrobe to show in a series of exhibits in Canada. The money raised is to aid in the work being carried on among needy refugees. The Queen's gracious consent was expressed in the prompt arrival of the dolls and their trousseaux.

The dolls and their famous collection of hats, dresses, lingerie, furs, gloves, stockings, shoes, and parasols, all designed by celebrated French couturiers, have been drawing crowds of interested adults as well as thousands of children for the past three weeks in Ottawa.

France, a blonde, and Marianne, a brunette, both standing three feet high, will undergo several changes of costume during their stay in Montreal. They will be surrounded by one of the most complete collections of feminine wearing apparel ever assembled at one time. There will be six fur coats, two ermine evening wraps, several dozen gowns and pairs of shoes, piles of lingerie and accessories to go with each costume. Trunks, dressing cases and hat boxes belonging to the dolls, each with its owner's initials will be included in the exhibit."

Here, as in other days, the Fashion Doll serves as a propagandist.

ADDENDA.

The eastern collectors seem to differ with the western collectors regarding doll restoration. As a rule the eastern collectors want to keep the doll looking old. If an arm or a leg is missing, they want only to match the old, worn one. On aged and yellow garments, the plea is usually 'Please do not wash'.

The dividing point on these two schools seems to be through Kansas. The western collector wants the doll to appear new and lovely. If parts have to be made over, the old ones are refinished to match the new. The shade is toned down a bit, but there is no 'antiquing'. One western collector remarked "I do not want my dolls to look as if they have been in a smoke house for fifty years". The old materials are matched as nearly as possible. The old garments serve merely as the patterns from which new clothes are made. Mrs. Clear comments, "Personally if the dolls are for museums, I would not mind them looking as if they came from King Tut's tomb. But for a private home, I like them fresh and clean. When they were young and beautiful, they *were* fresh and clean. If we have our way, we strive to make them look as they once did". Mrs. Izole Dorgan also feels that a doll in poor condition is in no respect representative of its original self, or the period to which it belongs. More and more collectors seem to be leaning to this point of view and a number of doll hospitals are concentrating on the restoration of the antique dolls.

It is quite important for the collector to study the types of arms and legs that appear on dolls, for often the style of limbs or hands gives a clue to the age of the body. China legs offer a variety of shapes and colors. For instance the ribbed stocking leg, with a lace top high heeled boot appears in the same period as the bulbous pattern, and is assuredly more humanly proportioned. The bulbous legs are almost grotesque, if they are interesting, and whether their originator thought them beautiful, or was merely being humorous, no one really knows.

Chapter XIX

THE MATERIALS FROM
WHICH DOLLS ARE MADE

"Sugar and spice, and everything nice,
Thats what little girls are made of."

Courtesy Mrs. Elsie Clark Krug.

Leather Dolls Made in Morocco.

BUT not dolls! No indeed, although there
are delicious edible dolls,
too. Dolls are made from
every conceivable material, and climate and clime
have as much to do with
the stuff from which a
doll is fashioned, as the
clothing, worn by mankind, varies from the land
of the Eskimo to the jungles of India. In ancient days there were jointed dolls made of wood, alabaster,
bone and ivory, marble and perhaps a few of leather, linen, papyrus and wax.
Wood has always been such a durable, and such a workable material, that many
dolls have been fashioned from it, and yet it is almost safe to add that as many
more dolls are fashioned from a variety of materials, a credit to man's ingenuity
and inventiveness, and to his ability to make things from whatever may be at
hand.

There is a well known fairy tale about a Ginger Bread Boy who was shaped
in dough, and then baked in the oven until he looked just like a real little boy.
There are cooky dolls, current eyed dough dolls, chocolate babies, even dolls
made of dried prunes. Every child knows about edible dolls; most children
have enjoyed them. From 1780-1800 dough, combined with papier maché,
pressed into a form, and then hardened, was used to model dolls, the papier
maché being covered with the dough.

218

Primitive dolls may have been made from a bit of bone wrapped in a rag or a leaf, or not wrapped at all.

Doll Talk had an interesting article entitled "They're Made Of—P. S." which gave the following materials from which dolls are made:

"Aluminum and Brass.
Butter (as used for modeling figures in the Choni Festival in Tibet).
Candy and Sugar. Maple Sugar Men. Parrafin Gum
Cane.
Chamois. (under leather)
Crepe Paper (Twisted and quite apart from Paper Dolls)
Fish. A Starfish Doll. A Lobster Doll
Fungus.
Georgette (under silk for especially fine faces)
Horse Hair. (Mexican tiny dolls in horse hair baskets)
Orris Root. (Dolls formed of twisted strands)
Potato. (Heads carved, dried and then painted)
Rice. (Smallest doll, carved from a grain of rice. Rice paste and pulp models
        exquisitely with a texture as fine as wax)
Soap. (Usually used for statues and figurines)
Spanish Moss. Makes witchy looking creatures."

To this may be added silver, sponge, amber, shells, rags, pipe cleaners, beads, cocoanuts, bisque, rubber, china, porcelain, yarn, straw, wood, wax, cornhusks, corn cobs, rubber nipples, clothespins, kelp, pine combs, papier maché, nuts, roots, (of trees) palm fibre, cork, raffia, sealing wax, gutta percha, stockinet, even *dead* fleas and beetles dressed as dancing girls. The list could be stretched out even more but this should suffice to reveal the fact that the composition of the doll is varied, and indicative of its place of origin and the imagination of its creator.

In Trinidad, seed and shell dolls are dressed in silk. In Granada dolls are made from Orris Root. A typically Bermudian doll is one made from several strange materials—banana leaves and screw pine and a nut for a face. This doll is made by the natives and no two dolls are ever quite alike in appearance. They are about eight to ten inches high and their handwoven shawls are caught together with a bunch of real flowers, dried. The doll also boasts a little verse which comes with her and which reads:

> *"I come from Bermuda*
> *The Isles of Sunshine*
> *I'm dressed in banana*
> *And native screw pine."*

From the West Indies come dolls fashioned from banana leaves, screw pine, shells and nuts. They are of native workmanship, handmade and no two are exactly alike. Bouquets of dried flowers or seeds decorate hand woven hats. Sponge dolls from Nassau speak of the large sea-sponge industry there, just as leather dolls from Morocco give a glimpse into a place famous for its leather. A very unusual doll is made from the root of the cotton wood tree by the Indians in New Mexico, the Katchina doll already mentioned for its religious significance. Bead dolls, with a rabbit foot for luck, are made by the Zunis. Lustrous red and white shell dolls come from Brittany. In the eighteenth century, shell dolls came from Normandy, and these dolls wore tulle dresses, embroidered with the shells, in a variety of colors. Shell dolls also come from Florida. From Greenland come dolls of carved wood with clothes of fur, and bead trimmed cape. In the National Museum at Copenhagen, Denmark is a doll with a real bird's head, but dressed as a woman of Greenland.

Beeswax serves in Peru to model dolls representative of the life of the peons. Dolls from Mexico are made of sugar and pastry, of straw and of rags. One doll called "charro" is a glorified cowboy with silver buttons on his tight trousers and a wide brimmed sombrero. Some of the queerest dolls in the world come from the Mexican valley of Cuernavaca. They are called 'Queen of the Needle'. The eye of the needle used, is almost invisible, and the tiniest of clothes are embroidered in excellent detail. Dressed fleas also come from Mexico, and have found a place in the world of dolls. Other tiny dolls from Mexico, made by the Indians there, are done on a framework of wire, about three quarters of an inch, and are wound with silk. Their perfect detail is seen with a magnifying glass. Perhaps the smallest dolls in the world live in a house that measures one half an inch. Inside this house, or shell husk, is a rice kernel carved into a

Courtesy Mrs. Daniel Hampton.

A Hindu Seer from Calcutta and an old plantation boss from Johannesburg, Africa.

boy and a girl. Mrs. S. Camille Tenney has these dolls in her collection. It is also said that there is a doll so tiny that it sits on the head of a common pin, and must be looked at through a magnifying glass.

Mrs. Tenney also has a Japanese Royal Family group encased in a pearl shell no bigger than a walnut, and a carved ivory junk housing a family of nine. On the other hand, Mrs. Mary Lewis has, in her collection, a doll which wears the same size shoe as a six year old child. This doll has no markings whatever. Such large dolls were made years ago in Germany but, because of their size have been off the market for some time.

Silver decked dolls are

given as wedding gifts in India, and in Australia the natives make dolls of wax and cane. Mrs. Lenore Mason of Des Moines, Iowa, reports some interesting dolls. One made of tobacco with a painted face, a tobacco skirt, placed over brown crepe paper and then scalloped, a cigarette serving as a feather in the dolls hat. A doll from the Pitcairn Islands is carved of soft wood, resembling balsa wood, with a dress made from the bark of a bread fruit tree. A native man from the Fiji Islands has a lei of whale teeth around his neck. The whale's tooth is very sacred to the native and is given to the chiefs of the various Koros. A Brazilian doll has quill finger nails, and a basket of fruit upon her head.

Lillian L. Stupp of University City, Mo., reports a British Soudanese witch doctor doll, crudely carved of wood and dressed in beads and leather thongs. Dolls from Eastern Equatorial Africa, by the Masai are carved from teak, cedar, ebony and mahogany wood, and modeled after the natives of the tribe.

Mrs. Daniel Hampton of Colorado Springs, Colo., reports several dolls of decidedly interesting material. One is an old plantation boss doll from Johannesburg, modeled from a soft black gum, from a tree resembling rubber. It was soft when it reached America but is now quite hard and brittle. Another from Suva is made from cotton, wrapped in a leaf of tobacco and draped in a sort of sarong. A Hindu seer, molded entirely out of tobacco, with a bird of paradise in his turban, is remarkably well executed. From Abyssinia is a doll, straight and shapeless, made of wood, with a gourd shaped gadget on his round head. A lady from Maracaibo, Venezuela, is made from sea shells taken and molded into shape, with a bit of gum and sand holding head, arms and waist. Each part of the doll's features and elaborate costume is an oddly shaped tiny, sea shell. The oldest doll in Mrs. Hampton's foreign group is an old man from the islands off the coast of Greece, twenty-nine inches tall, his head is of a material that resembles a heavy starched paper and his facial expression is old, wrinkled, but jolly. He is believed to be over two hundred years old and was obtained from an old rug-dealer who owned him and did not want to part with him. The body of this doll is cloth over a wire frame. Mrs. Hampton also has some chubby, black South American Negro dolls, made of satin, with real finger nails, carefully attached and

Courtesy Olive O. Jury

Dusky Delia, carved from a solid piece of coal.

resembling claws. The girls who make these dolls let their fingernails grow and then cut them off about one thirty second of an inch in length, oil and soak them until they are pliable, and then work them into the tips of the dolls fingers, and glue them on.

Mrs. Lulu Kriger writes of a native African doll made from a piece of black rag, and rows of green and red beads that came from a Zulu Kraal in the Valley of a Thousand Hills, in the Natal Province.

From the middle anthracite region of Shamokin, Penn. comes "Dusky Delia" a coal black lady indeed. Carved by an old gentleman, a former underground worker in the mines, Dusky Delia required over 200 hours of labor to be cut without disaster from a solid piece of coal, and many more hours of polish-

Courtesy of
Mrs. Florence Baughman
"Button Doll" wearing a dress made from 4200 buttons.

ing. She stands twelve inches high and is undoubtedly one of the strangest dolls in the world, in fact collectors believe she is the only one of her kind in existence.

It requires days and months of hunting, even in a region that has enough coal for another hundred years, to find one chunk of coal hard enough to hand carve. Like jade, one mistake will ruin the entire piece of work. The miner who carved "Dusky Delia" holds classes in coal carving in which his pupils have produced fraternal emblems, ash trays, crosses and small ornamental hearts, all carved.

Olin Gillespie, Chairman of the Goodwill Industries sent some interesting data on the kelp dolls created by Mrs. Marion Reton of San Diego during the last thirty five years. Kelp, which grows on the floor of the ocean, and was once very easily obtained, must be gathered from the beach, where it is tossed by the tide, and cured for almost two years. While working with the kelp in fashioning the dolls, it is necessary to keep it damp, in order to mold it into the desired shape. The finished product is then tied and dried. This sea-material has been used to make a number of dolls of varied types. Mr. Gillespie owns a pair of Kelp Dolls which he obtained over thirty years ago.

Mrs. Florence Baughman of St. Petersburg, Florida, is a most ingenious person. Besides collecting dolls and possessing some fine, unusual specimens, she also has collected buttons. Some time during the past year she decided to combine the two hobbies and so she created what she calls her "Button Doll."

The doll is twenty-two inches tall, of German make, and she is clothed in a dress which Mrs. Baughman made after many weeks of steady work from 4200 antique buttons, some of which date back to 1775. The dress weighs 8 pounds.

In St. Cloud there are many members of the G. A. R. or their widows and families, and the elderly ladies were eager to help Mrs. Baughman locate the old buttons. That is how one button happens to have been on a uniform that was worn on the battleship *Maine,* and another from the suit of a veteran who died in the Philippines.

"In no other town," writes Mrs. Baughman, "could I have had such aid. There are old buttons from railroad men's coats worn in the days of wood-burning locomotives; there are Italian, English and German buttons; buttons made of brass, glass and copper and many are decorated with jewels in varied colors."

Some of these buttons are small, others measure as large as two inches in diameter. It would be impossible to tell all the kinds of buttons that adorn the gown but it took four months to finish it as well as the hat which is also covered with more buttons. Many of the buttons used are over 100 years old.

It is certainly safe to say that there is probably not another Button Doll in existence, and credit goes to Florence Baughman for the original idea, and the patience to carry it out so well.

The Indians undoubtedly taught the white capped Pilgrim children how to make cornhusk dolls, and these dolls were still being made by New England children during the Civil War period. Now the cornhusk and corn shuck dolls also come from the mountains of the Carolinas and Kentucky, as do dolls of hickory nuts. Other typically 'American' dolls are the nut dolls from the Ozark mountains, and those carved from oak balls. Clay pipe dolls from Massachusetts and turkey wish bone dolls from Vermont are typical, the latter having been taught their present maker by her grandmother. The children in the Vermont of an earlier period could not go to the store to buy a doll, and so made them from turkey wish bones.

Another type was a home made answer to a child's plea for a doll. This was a Spool Doll, a clever little bit of handicraft, with a large spool for the body and half of another large spool for the head. Four ordinary size spools served for arms and legs, and bobbin spools made the hands.

In 1903 James W. French patented a process for hardening egg shells to make the heads of dolls, and created dolls from every kind of egg known, from those of the hunting bird to one of an ostrich. These egg shell dolls were not at all well received until the World War broke out, when the German doll supply was cut off. Then the government granted the patent on the grounds that waste material was being utilized. Thus the Merry Widow doll head, was originally laid by a bantam hen, and President Wilson appeared on a duck egg. These dolls were difficult to break for the eggs were specially treated. It would be interesting to know if any of them exist today in private collections.

When is an apple not an apple, might well be the question asked of Mrs. J. Howard Smith of Wenatchee, Wash. The answer would be, when it is carved, treated, mummified, and put away for some weeks, and then prepared for an everlasting life as a doll, instead of being hastily consumed as a delectable fruit, as nature intended.

Mrs. Smith claims that she just stumbled on the idea of making these dolls. At harvest time, one year, she was standing by a chute in the apple orchard, keeping the boxes moving down the "daily" to the waiting truck. Between loads there is a breathing spell for the man at the top of the chute, and the "shower downer," so Mrs. Smith sat down in the shade to rest, with "Davie," the man on top. He took out his jack knife and peeled an apple to eat. While Mrs. Smith was peeling an apple for herself, she became so engrossed in conversation that she forgot to eat it and absent-mindedly carved a face on it. About the time the face was finished, work was beginning again, so she put the apple in a crotch of a tree and forgot all about it. About two weeks later when she returned to help pick up the bags and ladders, there was the apple, shriveled up, and "looking exactly like an old Siwash."

Let Mrs. Smith tell the rest of the story herself: "The center had begun to rot badly but it was so lifelike and so comical that I brought it in and showed it to several people. Then I carved another, and several more, before I could find a way to preserve them. Now the dolls are everlasting. One made six years ago is as firm and unchangeable as on the day it was finished. I use baby lima beans for eyes, and shredded paper for stuffing as moisture does not affect it. Mostly I purchase feathers by the pound, commercially, but often I pay the neighboring youngsters when they bring me any kind of feathers, from Aunt Emma's pet guinea hen to those of a majestic eagle, shot, or a chicken hawk. I use both the claws and the feathers, for they make excellent imitations of the coveted bear claws which the Indians use as a badge of honor. Because I have lived near the Kiana Indians and am familiar with their customs, I chose to portray them in my dolls. They are a wonderful tribe, religious and kind, and with a sixth sense that enables them to size a person up at a glance."

"In short, after an apple is peeled, while still a little green, the face is carved and the core removed. The apple is then put through a curing process similar to what a taxidermist uses, then dried. This takes considerable time as they cannot be hurried. When dry they stand in large cans for future use. Each face is carved alike and yet each takes on its own individual appearance in the drying process. A wire through the head and body furnishes a spinal column, for an apple cannot be sewed or tied. Hands are of plaster of paris. I am working now on a formula that will make the apple impervious to mice and ants and yet safe for a child to taste."

And so, the very American Applatchee Doll.

New York is the home of the indestructible rag doll, and the papier maché, in America. At one time a boon doggle doll appeared with arms, legs and body of frayed hair, made by the unemployed. Soft dolls have come into vogue during the last fifty years, and now rank among the most popular toys even if in the past they have not proven to be the most durable. Sheep's wool, washed and dried, is used to stuff these dolls, also the sound parts of old garments and kapok. Wool and stranded cotton make excellent hair and glass serves for eyes. The Betsy Holt dolls of today are made from Turkish towels. Stockings also make interesting dolls. One called Old Dinah is made of an ordinary soap shaker for a body, and a black stocking stretched over for a face. The features are applied in cotton. Many of these home made Mammy Dolls appear as utility dolls, as for instance a doll labeled, "I'se in the Kitchen, Honey," which is made of dish towels and dish cloths, a dish mop for a head and black duster for a skirt. Other utility dolls serve as perfume bottles, telephone covers, pencil sharpeners, dinner bells, sewing cases, flower vases, garden ties, and holders of tools, and tea "cosies." Many of the Tea Cosies are Russian. There are also nested Russian dolls, of wood, called Malrishea, and these are made so that one doll fits within the other, graduating in size. These dolls are dec-

A Korean Fisherman

orated by the peasants, and often represent a fairy tale or old story. Small children like them because, like blocks, they can be played with alone, or as a group.

Mrs. Frances Krieger, has a full ballet of thirty dancing figures, one and one half inches high, made of wire wound with silk and wool, with tiny rosebuds on the skirts. Mrs. S. Camille Tenney has wool dolls from France, carried by the French soldiers, in the World War, for good luck on the battlefield.

From the Island of Formosa comes a Taiwan doll, a crude figure made of native like reeds painted brown, and dressed of woven textile fibre with a skirt of grass or fibers.

Little girls in Korea, or Chosen, make their own dolls from a bit of bamboo stem cut about five inches long. Into the top they put long grass, which is salted to make it soft. It is then arranged like the hair on a woman's head. The doll has no face but sometimes a little white powder is pasted in its place. The bamboo stick is then dressed in clothes, like those worn by the women, and sometimes a decorative hair pin is thrust into the coiffeur.

Doll Talk reports that a family craft of India is the making of the Jhandoo Dancing Dolls. The story of these dolls is interesting reading. To quote:

"Madhamie sat at her bench-like table patiently gluing the bright metallic paper in formal designs onto cloth. Such intriguing cloth it was. Not silk or damask but crisp evenly woven cotton and dyed in their native factories. Only in the Mother land would they mix such a glowing magenta, such a luminous citron tone yellow, green brighter than the hill side after a summer shower and purple blue, deep, mysterious and yet vivid. Lovingly she spaced and glued and pressed the tinsel tape and longed for the day when she could lay the pleats and press them in as Sister Magda did. For too all this splendor was to dress the dancer dolls that father made. He had learned when a lad to fasten the leg sticks firmly into a pretty base. The arm stick crossed and bound, the little balls for head and body holding all together. This was an ancient art their family had known for many generations. Father would visit, argue vehemently on politics or peace the while his fingers deftly wrapped around and 'round this little clay-like body with strips of linen, smooth as skin itself when finished.

Madhamie always loved to see him tweak the bit which was to be a nose, always identical with all the other noses of pinched linen, yet apparently so easily, carelessly, he did it all.

Another day the painting was done with black stick ink. Father held the brush of camel hair as lightly as a wand, first the eyes straight at the bottom curved on top with a beady ball in the center; the brows curving like winging birds away up in the blue, caste mark, a bow shaped mouth, mustachios on the man and painted hair.

Mother now strings the fragile beads that glow like temple gold in the blue gourd bowl. She makes them into bracelets, ear and nose rings, chains for throat and brow.

Fingers of blood red stiffened hemp make the hands. The bodice and sleeves are wrapped around, more tinsel paper added, the pleated skirts which the sisters have made so lovingly, the scarfs and shawls, the conventional little hat worn just so by the man for hundreds of years.''

In whimsical humor are dolls, modernistic in feeling, made from scraps of metal, of tin, aluminum and copper. The metal is cut with a heavy shears and then bent into the shape desired. This idea originated in the movie studio workshop floors and it is said that one actress in Hollywood designs the dolls as a hobby. Fantasy and humor are seen in the artistic pipe cleaner figures shown recently at the Pendleton Galleries in New York City. These were twisted with ingenuity, and, painted in bright colors, looked very much like a chenille fabric.

There is no end to what one can do with materials in an effort to fashion dolls, and doll construction is becoming a real project in many of the schools. Although not made "from sugar and spice," dolls, made from anything and everything, are "very, very nice." ADDENDA

Courtesy Fannie Sowter

Two Unusual Plaster Dolls

Mrs. Walker also contributes an interesting story about Sonnenburg porcelain. It was customary in Germany to give a doll and cradle to newly wedded persons, as a symbol of their future responsibilities, and the doll chosen was a lovely smooth Parian type with hair and net, glazed. The church authorities criticized this doll as being too worldly in appearance, especially when adorned with net

an attitude of the church. She also adds data about doll heads of beautiful French bisque, circa 1850, with exquisite eyes and lovely faces, heads sold separately, with holes in the shoulder for attachment to the body."

From *Mrs. Katherine Deane Fry, Claremont, N. H.,* comes a rare and most unusual group of dolls. A large Jumeau lady is seated holding a baby doll, a Jumeau about forty-five years old. Standing by is a Toddler, also a Jumeau with beautiful porcelain hands and the precious face of a two-year old. However, this doll is about sixty years old and the Lady, which Mrs. Fry terms a 'dressmaker doll' is thirty inches tall and over seventy-five years old." Three dolls in one photograph, representing three periods of the beautiful French Jumeau's.

Courtesy Katherine Deane Fry

Three Jumeau Dolls of different Periods

Chapter XX

CHINESE DOLLS

*(The Wedding Procession—The Eighth Immortals—
Typical Chinese Dolls)*

Courtesy
Elsie Clark Krug

A Chinese Family

A VAST country in eastern Asia, with a long official name, Chung-Hua-Min-Kuo, and a mixture of many peoples due to the invasion of outside races, and the intermingling with tribes within the great country, is the Republic of China. Ancient writers used to speak of the Chinese as the people of the land of Seres, and during different periods in the past centuries, the country has been known as Sin, Sinae, Chin and, lastly, as China. Travelers, like the adventurous Marco Polo, brought back stories of exquisite porcelain work, of lovely flowers, of strange writing, of curious animals, and beautiful and petite women. They described a race of people with saffron colored skin, black slanting eyes and shining black hair. It was not long before the people in the Western world knew China both as "The Flowery Kingdom," and as "The Land of the Dragon." Chinese culture and art were old when the western hemisphere was very young, and Chinese dolls give an insight into the high ideals of design and craftsmanship, and of the artistic skill that belongs only to China.

Fashions in dress have only changed recently in China, and not completely. In its main characteristics, the dress is unchanged, and has been the same for many centuries, falling under the set of laws which governs the styles and the conduct of the Chinese people all their lives. Garments of silk and velvet were handed down from parent to child, and ancient dolls served to instruct the children rather than to amuse them. The tilt up doll is probably the oldest kind of doll in China and has religious significance. On the seventh day of the New Year there is another symbolic doll, called an "honor-doll" and it represents the gods of happiness, rank, wealth and longevity. These dolls, dressed in multi colored garments, are hung on the doors of houses as omens of good luck. Dolls in Chinese costume are significant of ancient Chinese culture.

227

**Chinese Wedding
Procession**

To the Chinese, the Lotus flower, used decoratively in so much of their art and costumes, is the emblem of Life. The roots of this flower grow in the mud, and so represent the physical body, or the lower aspects of man. The leaves come up through the water, striving for more light and growth, or aspiration. So they represent the beginnings of the search of the mind for something higher and more spiritual. The blossom, lying on the water with the sun coming down upon it, represents the very spirit, or soul, itself . . . the real man. Another flower, famed in legend and symbolism in China, is the peony, called the King of Flowers. It is the national blossom, the floral emblem of spring and an omen of good fortune, thus the flower of wealth and honor. The peony is used as a favorite art design in the Chinese Wedding Procession.

There are forty-two figures in this procession, including the bride, who, accompanied by lantern bearers and musicians, journeys from her home to that of the bridegroom. As red is the Chinese color of hope and happiness, the wedding sedan is scarlet, gaily embroidered with peonies. Even the groom wears a red peony as his boutonnière. If the bride's family is rich, eight men will carry her gaily decked palaquin. The lanterns are painted with the Chinese ideograph signifying "prosperity." The musicians are indispensable, for with their cymbals, their trumpets and horns they give notice to the entire neighborhood that the marriage contract is to be consummated. Also by din of their noise they chase any evil spirits away and make for a joyous atmosphere. Preceding

Courtesy Mrs. John C. Albright
Chinese Wax Dolls

the chair is a single attendant. He carries the visiting cards, delivers messages and takes care of any emergency. He is the Chinese best man—serving the bride. The bride sits in state in her sedan chair, going alone to meet her fate. Her gown is of bright scarlet satin, heavily embroidered, and her cap is of pearls. The bridegroom, who will be waiting for her, wears a deep red satin robe with high boots and a turban.

Mrs. John C. Albright of Tulsa, Okla., has a pair of Chinese dolls, of papier maché and wax. The hands and feet, and paper wrapped bodies, are of composition, and the heads are of wax. The maiden has her hands in her kimona sleeve, indicating that she has just been married. She is dressed in the customary red, but the groom is in white.

In times of peace, it is not at all uncommon to see wedding processions in the streets of China, with scarlet boxes containing the brides' trousseau. However a much more common sight to-day, in war stricken China, is the funeral procession. The red box is carried on bamboo poles and it contains a black coffin. Musicians accompany the procession but there are no gay lanterns. The Chinese widow covers her face with a veil to signify, no matter how young she is, that she will not marry again. Often the chief mourners are dressed in clothes cut from sacking to tell the world of their sorrow and humility. A Chinese mourner doll, so garbed, is indeed a literal interpretation of the biblical, 'sack cloth and ashes.'

Both of these ancient customs, the wedding and the funeral processions, are to be found in tiny dolls, in reality, little clay figures, painted. Generally speaking, the Chinese doll is represented by a figure with straight, black hair, slanting black eyes, saffron skin, long tapering arms with long pointed fingers, and long legs. Both arms and legs are loosely jointed. That dolls express the individual, or the nation, is easily proven by the Chinese dolls which represent various classes in the numerous provinces, from the Manchu doll, twenty inches high with feet of natural size proportions, wearing three inch wooden heels on bespangled slippers, with toes resembling the dragons head, to the very old dolls, with tiny deformed feet like those of most Chinese women, up to recent years.

Typical of the upper middle class, for example, is a doll family from Taoting-Fu, made by girls and women in an industrial school. The gentleman in this family wears the Chinese dress, a pajama like suit, and slippers, a costume which is as comfortable as it is dignified. In this doll family from Taoting-Fu, the gentleman is evidently a merchant for his round cap and slippers indicate that he is not a poor man. However he does not possess great wealth for the soles of his tiny slippers are not whitened. His wife wears a simple black skirt and a silk blouse, and the two children are dressed in printed and colorful cotton material, in a style similar to that of their parents. The little girl has straight black hair, braided, and tied with a bit of red ribbon. The little boy has a tuft of hair on the very top of his head, but otherwise he is shaven. The mother's hair is dressed in the simple fashion of married women, drawn into an oval knot and held with a gold pin. She wears an embroidered fillet on her forehead. This particular group of dolls seems most representative of happy family life in China, in normal times, for the father has a merry twinkle in his hand painted, almond shaped eyes, and the mother, the patient kindly expression so often seen in Chinese women.

Chinese Jointed Dolls, not difficult to obtain, offer an interesting contrast in facial appearance as well as costume. They are splendid examples of the fine modeling and coloring, the perfection of detail seen in Chinese Dolls. Clothed in silk trousers, with loose jackets, elaborately embroidered with gold and silver to carry out a flower or dragon design, these dolls are most decorative. The jackets, or outer tunics, fall down to the ankles, practically covering the trousers beneath and when edged with fur, denote the wealth of the gentleman or lady. The lapel of the jacket folds over on the right side and fits very closely to the neck. The sleeves are so wide and long that they serve as pockets. When a Chinese person receives a gift, he never says he "puts it into his pocket", but rather, "into his sleeve."

White cloth stockings are worn under tiny shoes of silk, highly embroidered in designs of birds and flowers. The soles of the shoes are painted white to denote the rank of the wearer. These dolls have graceful, slender arms, with long fingernails. Their beaded headdress is very elegant, their faces beautifully painted and the hair on their wigs is made of black silk thread.

In China it is customary for each person to dress according to class, so the costume the individual wears has been decided for him hundreds of years before his birth. The outstanding gilt pieces worn on the ear, with curious characters, read 'long life, happiness, many children'. They are facsimiles of those found on the caps of the Emperors. Chinese dolls, carefully handled and lovingly cared for, like the old costumes, are handed down from generation to generation. The costumes vary with the different provinces. For instance in Souchow a narrow skirt of blue and a loose wadded jacket, under which is a brocaded jacket, is worn. Cloth soled shoes, and a band of black velvet across the forehead, complete the costume.

A Manchu Nobleman will wear an inverted wash bowl shaped hat and an embroidered chest protector. In Pekin tiny feet wear embroidered shoes and trousers trimmed with bands of rich embroidered material. Artifical flowers and gold ornaments, or large ear rings, are worn by the ladies.

The Pekinese servant however wears dark blue, and her feet are of natural size. When winter comes it grows bitter cold with each succeeding blustery day, and the people appear to grow enormously stout. Instead of burning fires to keep warm, they put on more and more thickly padded garments, sometimes wearing as many as three coats of cotton fastened up on one side by frogs of cord. Chinese people, from this locality ask, 'Is it a two coat day'?, or, 'Is it a three coat day?', instead of, 'Is it cold?'

The poorer people, living in the south, often belong to the farming and coolie class, and they wear simple blue cotton jackets and trousers, and huge hats of bamboo to keep off the sun and the rain. The farmer wears a bamboo raincoat, and is barefoot for his work in the muddy rice fields. His crude pitchfork is homemade from small trees bent into the needed shape.

One of the loveliest of Chinese dolls is the dancing girl, a beautiful example of the exquisite workmanship seen in Chinese dolls. Her tiny gracefully poised hands and feet, her delicate features make her a veritable work of art. It is a little difficult to determine if this doll is a dancing girl, or a male actor, wearing a mask replica of a beautiful girl, to hide masculine features. All Chinese people love the theatre, where the plays are mostly historical, repeating the wise sayings of the ancient sages. They delight in music, too, that is strange and weird to western, untrained ears. This 'dancing girl' is a splendid example of the elaborate costume and head dress worn for performances at which there are no stage settings, or scenery, save for a few benches. Bamboo poles serve as a background. The imagination of the audience does the rest. The "Dolls of the Theatre" have been used for many years to portray scenes in classic dramas and may be posed in a number of positions. Some of these dolls may be seen at the *Mission Inn*, in Riverside, California. Serving as actors, these ancient theatre dolls, which are in a way closely related to puppets, preceded the dolls now known as the Chinese Theatre character dolls.

The Chinese piano dancers, or spinet dolls, are made of paper, sticks and rice paste. They are gaily dressed and often hideous in their masks. When placed on the piano, or radio, the vibrations of the instrument on the edge of their skirts, make these tiny figures dance about.

Perhaps the most interesting of all Chinese dolls are the figures representing the Eight Immortals, or the Pa Hsien. These legendary beings of the Taoist sect are said to have lived at various times and obtained immortality. They are well known to students of China and are depicted on porcelain ware, in ivory and bone and in enamel jewelry, as well as in dolls of silk, and rayon. Taken individually each one of the Pa Hsien is of interest.

"THE EIGHT IMMORTALS"

"The Pa Hsien or Eight Immortals are legendary beings said to be immortal. Each has a characteristic significance which is given in detail as follows:

Lee Tee Kwai was instructed by Lao Tse the founder of Taoism himself, who used to summon him to interviews in the celestial spheres. To do this, his spirit had to leave his body, which he instructed to the care of his disciple. On one occasion the disciple was summoned away, and when the disembodied spirit returned, the body was gone. Lee Tee Kwai, therefore, took refuge in the body of a lame beggar, in whose shape he continues his existence. He supports himself on a crutch or staff. His emblem is the Pilgrim's gourd, and he holds a staff in his hand.

Lan Tsai Ho is of uncertain sex, but generally considered a female. She carries a flower basket, her usual emblem, from which she dispenses the good things of life.

Courtesy Eleanor Bumgardner
A splendid group of Chinese Dolls

Tsaou Kwo Kiu is said to be the son of Tsaou Pin, a military commander who died A. D. 999. He is represented as wearing a court head dress and his emblem is a pair of castinets. He is worshipped by scholars.

Chang Ho Laou flourished towards the end of the 7th century. He was a great necromancer, and used to be accompanied by a white mule which carried him immense distances, and when not required, was folded up and put away. The Emperor Ming Hwang summoned him to his Court, but he refused to go. He is represented with a bamboo tube, a kind of musical instrument used by the Taoists, and two rods with which to beat it. The latter are carried in the tube.

Han Seang Tsze is a Great Nephew of the statesman Han Yu, who lived 768/824 A. D. He was a pupil of Leu Tung Pin, by whom he was carried to the fabulous peachtree of the Genii, but fell from the branches. He is represented by a flute and is worshipped as the God of the Musicians.

Han Chung Lee is said to have lived in the Chow Dynasty which lasted 1122 B. C. to 249 B. C. He obtained the elixir of Immortality. He is generally represented as a fat man and holds in his hand a fan, with which he is said to revive the souls of the dead.

Leu Tung Pin was born in 755 A. D. While a magistrate of the District of Tehwha, he is said to have encountered Han Chung Le from whom he learned the mysteries of alchemy, and of the Elixir of immortality. He was exposed to a series of ten temptations, and having overcome them, was invested with a sword of. supernatural power, with which he traversed the Empire, slaying dragons, and ridding the earth of divers kinds of evils for upwards of four hundred years. His emblem is a sword.

Ho Seen Ko was the daughter of Ho Tai, of Eseng Cheng, near Canton. She used to indulge in solitary wanderings among the hills, and rejecting the ordinary food of mortals, ate powdered mother of pearl, which was supposed to produce Immortality. She was summoned to the Court of the Empress Wu (690/705) but on her way disappeared. She carried in her hand a Lotus flower, which is her emblem. She is supposed to appear when China is in great danger.

These Eight Immortals are also used as good luck pieces by the Chinese. Chinese Doctor Dolls belong to an early period when modesty reigned. Another doll known as 'Faithful Ssu', or the 'Tomb Doll', is in the likeness of a lovely Chinese lady who escaped being buried in the tomb of King Wu by having a doll carved in her image and buried in her place. Thus, because the doll saved the life of a lovely lady, the Tomb Dolls are now symbols of good luck and are found carved in jade and in wood.

The 'Chinese Girl from Puebla' or, the 'Chinese Poblana' is an interesting doll found in Mexico. The story goes that a merchant from Puebla bought a Chinese girl as a slave. She was, in reality, a princess. To pass the long hours in captivity, she made exquisite Chinese dresses, and medallions of ivory, which she sewed on the garments. The eagle of Mexico was done in gorgeous patterns. The doll, representing the princess, wears a full red skirt, scintillating with sequins and a gaily embroidered blouse. To top off the whole legend, and complete both costume and story she wears a Mexican rebosa.

Never a big industry in China, the doll has been manufactured on a commercial basis at Kiangsi, which is a porcelain manufacturing centre. These dolls are scantily dressed, and the favorite is a baby with a patch of black hair on the top of its head, lying down or crawling on the floor with a napkin in front of its chest. These dolls are rarely larger than five inches, although there were some larger ones manufactured for adult usage, as porcelain pillows.

Clay dolls from Wusih were also popular with Chinese children a few years ago, and in these clay dolls the Chinese displayed their innate artistic talents. Made of sticky clay, available only in the vicinity of Shihshan, a hill outside the city of Wusih, these dolls were made in sets showing scenes from popular Chinese operas, plays or fairy tales. Baked in the sun, the clay was then polished, and hand painted and the doll placed in a glass case. Clay dolls of inferior quality were produced in various patterns, some for adults and others exclusively for the children. However, unless there is a renaissance very soon in China, these clay dolls may exist for only a brief time, and then pass into oblivion.

In this brief discussion of Chinese dolls, and Chinese symbolism, as expressed through the medium of the doll, it is easy to see that China is a land of tradition and ancient culture. It is regrettable that it is no longer easy to obtain genuine Chinese dolls that typify so well the many peoples living in that country.

Collection Janet P. Johl

A Clown, a Baby and a Scotch Lassie. A Dutch Girl and St. Nicholas. A Modern China head doll, an American Clothespin Farmer and a Tyrolean peasant girl.

Chapter XXI

JAPANESE DOLLS

(Hina Ningyo—Hina Matsuri—Musha Ningyo
—Gosho Ningyo and others)

Collection Janet P. Johl.

Dairi-bina or Court Dolls. Top row: Emperor and Empress. Middle row: Historic set Empress Jingo with her Prime Minister and infant son. Bottom Row: Furisode Ningyo (Kimona Dolls.)

JAPANESE and Chinese dolls differ as much as the people of almost any two countries. In Japan the doll is used to promote patriotism and except for a few of the better known kimona, or Furisode dolls, children use the little figures, not as playthings but as symbols. The study of the Japanese doll leads into by paths of fable and legend, religion, historic deeds, and courageous characters all bound up in the ancestor worship of the country.

The very primitive Japanese doll was made from a shaved willow stick, with a string, or shavings for hair, and paper clothes. Many of the first dolls represented gods of the country, mythological beings, demi-gods, or evil and beneficent dieties of certain religious ceremonies and plays. These early and authentic Japanese dolls were made with absolute fidelity to nature, a fact that shocked conventional persons. But the dolls for export and world consumption to-day lack any manifestation of sex.

According to one authority, the Japanese doll is of three dimensions, showing front, back, side and top. A book of pictures by Moronobu Hishikawa, in the second year of the Tenna Era (1683) entitled *Ehon Omakura* or *Great Pillow Picture Book* has a picture with two dolls dancing as puppets. In the seventh year of the Meiwa Era (1770) in a book called *Ehon Yamato Shikei*, or *'Illustrated Book of Japanese Poetry'* there is mention of the Osaka Puppet dolls. Under the picture are the words ''Pretty as dolls look, what sort of hearts they have, who knows? Osaka dolls are fair of face, but otherwise not.'' These dolls were supplied with heads from Kyoto and dresses from Osaka.

Japanese dolls were first made of paper for amusement purposes, then they became the token of parental affection in order to protect children from disease. The highest development for the Japanese doll came after the Tokugawa family founded the Shogunae in Yedo (the ancient name for Tokyo) at the beginning of the seventeenth century. Through the succeeding 300 years of peace, the art of doll-making progressed, and began to take on ceremonial interest which was the prevailing taste of the period. Festival figures perhaps better define the dolls of this era, for they are admired for what they symbolize, rather than for their beauty. In Japan everyone loves miniature images, so the dolls representing the ancient gods, and Mikados, met with favor.

There are a great many kinds of Japanese dolls, in fact some 300, and it is only possible to mention a very few. The materials from which the dolls were made are also numerous. Bamboo, for centuries an art craft in the long history of Japan, has not deteriorated with the years, but has improved. Fine bamboo dolls still come from Beppu, in Kyushu, and from the vicinity around Okayama. Other dolls made of wood, were covered with paste in varied colors, others were of papier maché, for the use of cardboard also seems to have been known for a very long time. Still other dolls were cast in a mold, from a mixture of sawdust and paste, or made from the roots of the willow tree. It is assumed that the first doll was molded from paper, and then covered with colored paper. This doll was called Harinuki Ningyo. The clay doll, Fushimo Ningyo, of Kyoto, is perhaps the oldest type. In old Yedo (Tokyo) doll heads were supplied for the bodies and these were called Gatten Kubi, or 'head that fits'. Around Yokkaichi are found the famous dolls of Banko faience.

An article in the *Japan Mail and Times* for October, 1939, published in Tokyo, and furnished by Mrs. Ione Perkins of South Pasedena, Cal., had this to say about two doll makers:

''Doll making is an art handed down from Father to son and Mr. Okamoto is the fourth generation to take to the profession, the first Okamoto having begun in the Tokugawa era. The art developed from the making of the 'Noh' masks and Buddhists images. These were made back in the Kamakura era and it was not until the Tokugawa, that doll making was actually started.''

''Gyokusui Okamoto and Goyo Hirata make dolls of carved wood, which are painted from time to time with a certain type of paint called 'gofun'. This paint is made from shells which are first powdered and then mixed with a liquid to form a sort of paste. According to the two doll makers the painting is the most difficult part of the process. The features are cut in the wood, and after the painting, the eyes, mouth and nose seem to have a sort of rounded, run over effect and this must be corrected with a knife, by again making the sharper edges, corners and indentations needed for the proper finished effect. The eyes are then filled in with glass and the doll dressed. Before it is sent forth into the world, the clothing is painted with 'gofun', and stiffened. Many of these dolls are very beautiful depicting the characters of Japanese legend and the Kabuki.''

Japanese dolls divide into three distinct classes of the people.

(1) Chubby cheeked dolls of the peasant type that lack any great beauty.
(2) Samurai family—Dolls that are beautiful and distinctive in costumes.
(3) Royal group.

In poor families a child carries a doll on its back, the size of the doll being increased until the child is strong enough to bear the burden of a baby sister or brother.

The Hina Ningyo, or China Sama, has become universally popular in Japan and typifies the Japanese dolls with which the world is familiar, the word, 'hina', meaning miniature, or small. These tiny dolls are of ancient origin and are referred to in the Genji Monogatari, a masterpiece of Japanese literature written by Lady Murasaki Shikibu more than 900 years ago.

Few nations have as many delightful festivals as Japan, and the Hina Matsuri, the Feast of the Dolls, which comes during the month of the Peach Blossoms, and so is known as the 'Momono-Sekku', or Peach Blossom Festival, is one of the loveliest. It falls on March 3rd when it is tradition for Japanese parents to pray to the gods for the protection of their babies, and for the happiness of their little daughters in celebrating the Hina-Matsuri. No where else in the world, are there happier children than the children of Japan nor children better versed in the arts of courtesy and respect.

The *San Francisco Chronicle,* in a reprint in '*Doll Talk*' describes the festival as follows.

"A doll collection is started after the arrival of the first daughter in each family. On the first doll festival after a girl baby's birth, it is customary for relatives to present the child with a doll. The collection thus formed at that early age is increased yearly, until the girl, grown to womanhood, takes her dolls with her to her husband's home, a valued asset to her trousseau.

"Instances are not lacking in which tens of thousands of yen were spent by mushroom millionaires and other rich, fond parents in making up a complete set of dolls in honor of a new born daughter. From year to year additional dolls are added, many of them representing historical characters or scenes from

Courtesy Mrs. Frances Krieger

A Japanese Lady Doll

famous plays. These are supplemented with many tiny accessories, such as tea sets and toy animals, and, as the collection is carefully packed away following each annual festival, it grows in the course of years into a truly impressive display.

"First on the list of dolls come daidibina, or a couple in ancient court dress, representing the Emperor and Empress. They are designed to instill patriotism into the youngsters. Then come retainers and musicians, court guards and petty officials. These, together with musical instruments, court carts and household utensils in miniature, all represent the aristocratic life of Japan.

"The custom of the Doll Festival is said by some writers to have originated as early as during the dynasty of Emperor Sujin, which lasted from 97 to 30 B. C., although some other writers assign it to a much later date. This custom is mentioned in ancient literature, and there is no doubt as to its antiquity."

Little Japanese girls pay their due respects to their dolls, dressed in crisp new kimonas and bright ribbons. Then they entertain their parents and friends with story telling, music and refreshments, which consist of colored mochi cakes and a bit of shirazake, daintily served on doll dishes no bigger than a fairy would use, and in bowls as small as thimbles. With grave dignity the little girls kotow, or bow, to welcome their guests and wait upon them courteously, showing them the precious court dolls, arranged on shelves like steps, with the Emperor and Empress enthroned on the very top in elaborate costumes, and the other dolls arranged beneath according to their rank. Through the Doll Festival, the little girls learn the charming manners and hospitality for which Japan is so well known.

The court dolls, or dairi-bina, cannot be bought at ordinary toy shops for they are the work of skilled craftsmen who model the tiny hands and feet perfectly, and fashion the elaborate costumes. The Emperor and Empress, squatting stiffly, wear robes used for the Ascension to the Throne, or, an Imperial Wedding. In his right hand, the Mikado holds a sceptre. On his head is an odd styled crown, looking like an inverted bowl with a knob, to which is attached silken cords of purple tied beneath his royal chin. A long black quill rises from the back of the hat. In his left hand, he carries a long curved sword.

The Empress is lovely in a red and white kimono highly embroidered and designed to represent the sacred Mountain Fujiyama at sunrise. She wears a gorgeous head dress of gold filigree from which dangle golden flowers and silken cords. In her dainty hands she holds a folding fan.

Below the Royal Pair are the court nobles behind whom are small standing screens. Then come the court ladies. On the third shelf below the singers and musicians. The fourth shelf has the military and civil dignitary, between whom are lacquer boxes containing suitable offerings. Then comes a fifth shelf for the male servants, kneeling between a miniature cherry and orange tree, in bloom. In the real Imperial Palace in Kyoto, where the Emperor is crowned, the orange and the peach tree have a place at the entrance of the Coronation Hall. So fruited trees have their place at the Hina Matsuri. The lower shelves contain furnishings and other articles such as mirrors, swords, ceremonial wine vessels, dishes and cakes of rice and beans.

Some of the collections for this festival, possessed by Japanese families, are treasures of high artistic value, each successive generation having added new dolls. Japanese historical and traditional dolls are only shown during the time of the Doll Festival for the Girls, and the equally interesting Festival for the Boys. The other dolls found during the remainder of the year are played with and not cherished, and many of them find their way into the foreign market or are purchased by tourists in Japan. These are mostly the long sleeved kimona doll, the Furisode Ningyo, a smiling bald headed boy with a tuft of black hair on the top of his white pate, and a dainty little girl with short, fringed black hair. Both dolls have fragile bodies made of paper and bamboo and muslin, and break easily.

The Musha Ningyo, or, Boys Festival is the big celebration for the boys and the Warrior Doll is the favorite, gorgeously accoutered in brocade and metallic paper, with helmets and swords and glittering little eyes in masque like faces and often with wooden hands. This festival occurs on May 5th, the month of the iris flower, or shobu, symbolic of the sword, the "soul of the samurai." Tradition informs us that this celebration had its origin in honor of a devoted patriot, the Chinese poet Kutsugen who was known as the "best boy in the world." Around the festival is a wealth of symbolism and reminders of the past. The dolls displayed are in reality, historical sets with figures of warriors in full armor, bearing shobu swords, banners, bow and arrows, spears, and occasionally mounted on horses.

The cult of Bushido plays a cardinal part in this festival, for Bushido is the name applied to an old code of chivalry, and the cult is closely allied to ancestor worship. Every May the figures of these famous knightly persons are brought out for exhibition and the boys listen eagerly to the stories about them, knowing that the Bushi never really die.

It is hard to realize that this festival is intended to be more chivalrous than militaristic, and that the lesson is to teach the youth of Japan how to be healthy and loyal, as the Girls' Festival teaches good manners, hospitality and dignity. Without the doll, both of these festivals would be non existent.

From "*Doll Talk*" comes this additional data of doll ceremonials:

"An old Shinto purification feast seems to be the genesis for this holiday, on which occasion whole families went down into the river to bathe. Specially cut towels in human shape were supplied by the priests, upon which the bather blotted out his yearly sins. These paper doll towels were then given over to the boys of the family, transferred sins and all, to ceremoniously throw away into the water!"

The hairdressing of the Japanese women is indeed a true work of art and requires so much care that when the women go to sleep at night, they use a little block of wood beneath their heads upon which their hair may rest, safe from any danger of disarrangement.

A most interesting doll is a little lady, with five different wigs, who comes in a tiny wooden box, with a glass top. Japanese women have such an individual and pretty way of dressing their shiny black hair, in high stiff coils, and the hair dress is so varied in arrangement and decoration, it is splendid to have a doll that illustrates the meaning of the coiffeurs.

There are five styles of hair arrangement for this doll, and it is possible for her to wear them.

(1) *Okkapa*. This is worn by little girls from five to seven years, and is similar to a long straight bob, except for one roll on top of the head which is set off by three yellow flowers in the front.

(2) *Momoware*. This is for girls between ten and fifteen years. The bob is gone except for a long strand of hair, in back, which is looped up at the neck

with a red ribbon. The yellow flowers are at the back, and the roll on top of the head is decorated with red ribbon drawn through it.

(3) *Soku-hatsu*. This follows the European style somewhat and is worn by students and women of all classes. It is a simple arrangement, with a braided roll on the top of the head and a single ornament of ribbon or gold cording.

(4) *Shimada*. For girls from sixteen to twenty years. This is more ornate with two rolls on top of the head, the one smaller than the other, and a loop at the neck. A silver, flat comb is beneath the larger roll and between the two rolls is a ruffle of ribbon. A silver ornament is thrust in at the side.

(5) *Maru-Wage*. This is worn by married women of almost all classes. It has two rolls and two pins thrust through the rolls. A touch of a gold ornament at the front and a bit of ribbon, lavender, completes this headdress which is more simple than the Soku-Hatsu.

Sometimes the head dress of a young girl represents a pigeon about to make a flight, with a red ribbon in front and large pins at the back. Wigs, decorated with flowers, are for small girls, and young girls before their marriage; wigs with combs are for married women.

There are many other kinds of dolls in Japan that hold interest besides the ones mentioned. There are the Satsuma Standing dolls made of paper and the wooden puppet dolls. Each district in Japan is noted for its particular type of doll. The city of Nara is very famous historically and is the home of many of Japan's art treasures. The Nara doll is a carved wooden figure, painted in colors. Then there is the Gosho Ningyo, a fat bodied little doll with a round head used for decorative purposes, and therefore not so well known abroad. Of course during the season of festivals lovely dolls appear, such as the Fuji

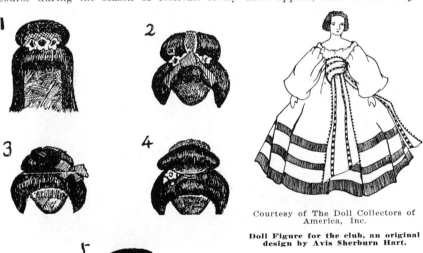

Courtesy of The Doll Collectors of America, Inc.

Doll Figure for the club, an original design by Avis Sherburn Hart.

Collection Janet P. Johl

Five wigs which come with a little Japanese doll
(1) Okkapa. (2) Momoware. (3) Soku-hatsu. (4) Shimada. (5) Maru-Wage.

Musume, or Wistaria Maiden. These dolls are very popular with the girls of Japan for they are 'ready to make', and the set includes the doll body with parts of the costume, the hair ornaments etc. and the 'elder sisters' may be seen during the Cherry Blossom Festival crowding around the store counters buying the 'Fuji Musume', to take home and make. Another modern doll that is popular, especially with students, is a sort of rag doll, with a body and head of cloth stuffed with cotton. 'Botchan' is the name of the brother doll, and 'Musume', the sister. He carries a potted plant and his kimona is of boy material, while Musume has a tiny parasol. Instead of being posed stiffly on their small round stands, they are in a very life like walking position, with a naturalness which the students seem to appreciate.

The more modern Japanese dolls are of porcelain, rubber, celluloid, composition, and other materials, in imitation of foreign dolls, which although made in Japan, are not truly Japanese. Yet some Japanese doll makers fortunately do persist in creating dolls that typify the beautiful island. Mrs. Ione Perkins, who formerly resided in Japan and now is in South Pasedena, California reports several interesting dolls of this kind such as ''a Bon Odori dancer, dressed in appropriate kimona with nagajiban showing at the lower edge and with hat and samison; a peasant from the Yamaguchi district carved of wood with a basket on her back and a tenugui, or towel, on her head; a mountain girl, wood carrier, of textile material; Kago carriers, two men dolls with a kago swung on a pole between them and a pine tree and wayside marker behind them, the whole giving the effect of a scene from a 'Noh' play. Two other men doll, from Hakata, are of wood painted in colors with egg shaped heads and egg shaped bodies, standing like totem poles; A Gifu girl gathering twigs, and a Gifu woman with nursing baby in her arms, seated on a tree stump.''

People have written volumes about the dolls of Japan. It is needless to add that this culling is but the merest glimpse into a world which the doll collector should study to obtain a keen insight, and deeper knowledge, of the origin of the doll.

Courtesy Mme. Alexander

The Dionne Quintuplet Dolls with their Nurse.

The famous Dionne Quintuplets, from babyhood and onward, are made by Mme. Alexander of New York City.

Chapter XXII

Courtesy Helen Siebold Walter
The Courtship of Myles Standish.
Capt. Myles Standish, John Alden, Priscilla Mullins and Elder Brewster.

NOSTALGIA

(Dolls Commemorating Persons or Events)

DURING the Civil War, dolls served as a means of getting news from one district to another, and precious articles were conveyed inside the body of the doll. There are stories of how the heads of dolls were utilized to conceal quinine and calomel. It was almost impossible for the Southern soldiers to obtain these vital drugs. The doll heads, whether of composition, or of china, were fastened to the body by means of tapes, so that it was a very simple matter to remove the head, fill it with the drug, and then replace it. When a little girl went to visit a soldier she seemed only an innocent child, fondly clasping her doll in her arms. No one thought to stop a little child to question her. There is a doll in the Confederate Museum in Richmond, Va. called, 'Nina', whose sweet look does not bespeak her exciting life. It is said that she belonged to the niece of General Patton and that she actually made several trips through the Northern lines, carried by her little mistress, her head filled with drugs. In one of these Civil War dolls, the story goes, cotton seeds were hidden, and so the cotton raised during the war was the result of a doll's ingenuity in transporting the seed, secretly, or was it the ingenuity of the doll owner?

There are many commemorative dolls. There is, for example, the Dixie doll around which Frances Parkinson Keyes wove her story "The Dixie Doll".

There is Rose Percy, a Civil War Doll Belle, now at the American Red Cross Headquarters, at Washington, D. C. There is a doll known as 'Polly Sumner', sometimes called the Boston Tea Party doll because she is said to have come to America on the famous ship that carried the tea.

There were dolls commemorating the Spanish American War, dolls that looked like Admiral Simpson, in full navy uniform with gold stripes and little brass buttons, carrying a pewter sword, and with a pewter star on the left coat sleeve. There were Theodore Roosevelt as a Rough Rider, Admiral Dewey, Schley, Hobson and many others. There was Captain Kidd, the pirate, and there were the Polar Expedition dolls, simulating Cook and Peary. There was even Uncle Sam with a bisque head, and long white hair and goatee, hooked nose and a broad grin, wearing red and white striped trousers, a blue vest with stars upon it, a blue cutaway coat, a red bow tie and a high hat.

The Spanish American dolls were evidently of German make, with the usual lovely bisque heads, some even with bisque hair. "The older character dolls" comments Miss Eva Page Daly of Albany, N. Y. "Put to sleep many of the more modern ones. There was, for example, a complete set of the Gibson dolls . . . Mr. and Mrs. Charles Dana Gibson, her two sisters, one brother and the Grandmother and Grandfather, with gray hair. Mrs. Gibson came from the southern family of Langhorne to which Lady Astor also belongs." Mrs. Emma C. Clear feels that "The Gibson girls—and the Floradora girls—were made in Germany." She has this to say "I have only seen two of the real Gibson girls in the last years, the ones with the jointed bodies and tight little waists. This is sometimes called the 'pregnant' doll, because the little abdomen is rounded out just right. This doll was in vogue before the straight front corset and gave a regular hour glass effect, with high full bust. One of these dolls is in the Cutter collection. They came undressed, as all fine jointed dolls of those days did. I did not know of the Spanish American War group, but there were similar ones of the World War."

Miss Daly agrees that "there is no question about the Gibson dolls being of German origin. The woman from whom I obtained them told me her uncle worked in a toy factory in Germany, and sent a complete set to her and to her sister."

The Floradora doll, also of German make, was fairly common during the period when the famous sextette was flourishing. Sometimes one finds a paper label on the kid body, or the name stamped, or impressed, in the bisque head. These were very often second grade dolls and may have been made by the house of Armand Marseille, a German manufacturer who was still producing dolls up to the time of the present war. The pompadour style of wig seemed to make the pretty bisque face look different. Moustache gentlemen of bisque with or without caps, make good companion pieces to the smaller 'gay nineties' lady dolls.

Godey dolls also intrigue the collector. This is usually a doll, with hair parted in the middle, and curls up and down, and across the back of the head. Another type has hair combed, so that the ears show, and is the older of the two. These dolls are dressed in costumes taken from the designs of the 'Godey Lady Books'—Fashion of 1850-1885. These books also carried directions for knitted dolls, which have become very difficult to find and are fine examples of the early home made American dolls.

Courtesy Mrs. Elsie Clark Krug

George Washington and Martha Washington.
A Confederate Couple

Sarah Josepha Hale, named for the Mrs. Hale of Godey's Fashion Book, a lovely 32 inch doll, with a China head that dates her in the 1865 period, is the Foundation Doll of the *National Doll and Toy Collectors Club, Inc.*

Sarah wears a "solferino watered silk" or garnet moire taffeta gown, with a fine lawn undersleeve and collar, and a black lace shawl bedecked with tiny velvet bows. Her bonnet is the same color as her dress, covered with black lace and trimmed with velvet violets and forget-me-nots. This costume, a faithful replica of the style worn in Sarah Hale's day, was made by Mrs. Lulu Kriger of Paterson, N. J. Mrs. Kriger also fashioned Sarah's other dress, a three tiered, lavender sprayed dimity, with each tiny ruffle bound with lavender satin. A simple bodice, in the off shoulder style, shows Sarah's lovely white shoulders. For cool weather, there is a coat of heavy sage green satin lined with nile green, leaving no doubt in the minds of present day stylists that the ladies of yore liked their colors. A well fitted bodice allows the coat to fall gracefully over the whale bone, hoop skirt.

Mrs. Greville Bathe, of Philadelphia, Penna., made for Sarah Hale a horse hair trunk with brass buttons, to house the splendid wardrobe. Mrs. Bathe also made all of Sarah's underthings, including a pair of "stays" and numerous petticoats, finely stitched.

All in all, Sarah Hale is a splendid character, commemorating the memory of her namesake, the first woman editor, of a period when it was considered a disgrace for a woman to work outside her home, and representing today a group of persons who believe that a doll is more than a toy.

Mrs. Peggy Zere the Secretary of the *National Doll and Toy Collector's Club* tells of a doll in her collection called "Teddy's Nig." Mrs. Zere writes: "This doll was introduced by Theodore Roosevelt about 1906 and found its way into the editorial rooms of the old New York World of which my Dad was the Art Director. Stories and pictures were gotten out around the doll. Several attempts were made to make this a popular doll, but commercially it never did go as children were afraid to play with it. Here is a brief description. Teddy's Nig is about twelve inches high and made of a stockinet material, fur hair, shoe button eyes, brass rings in nose, ears, bracelets and anklets. He wears a little fur apron and bright ceremonial beads. The failure to promote this funny looking doll at the time was my gain and I am happy to say that it is the only doll like it any place. My Dad brought Teddy's Nig home to me as I was a young child, and I have had it all this time. It was the first doll of my collection, of course, an African doll originated by Theodore Roosevelt after one of his expeditions.''

Marie De Sylva, of Los Angeles, has two old dolls known as the "Bartlett Dolls.'' They were discovered in an old vault by F. C. McGiff, of Santa Barbara, in his home and had been handed down from his mother, Mary B. McGiff, who was the daughter of Joseph Bartlett, son of Josiah Bartlett, one of the signers of the Declaration of Independence. According to Mr. McGiff the dolls came from Paris in 1776. Don de Costa who knew of Miss De Sylva's doll collection prevailed upon Mr. McGiff to allow her to add them to her collection. One is very odd, its legs, arms and hands are made of thin pieces of wood, and the head is somewhat like a wooden top with the features painted on in bright colors. What looks like a cap is in reality human hair wound around several times. The other is also made of wood, with a cloth body and feet, also brightly painted and in its original clothes.

Many dolls, treasured in private collections are historical reminders of early American days. There is, for example, a doll which once belonged to Annie Hancock, wife of John Hancock, signer of the Declaration of Independence, in the collection of Mrs. S. Camille Tenney of New Haven, Conn. It has kid hands and feet, and blue eyes set in a china face.

Mrs. J. Madison Taylor of Philadelphia, Pa., owns a doll called "Miss Flora McFlimsey of Madison Square,'' which was bought by her mother at the Sanctuary Fair in Philadelphia, in 1863. It has the entire wardrobe of a lady of that period. Mrs. Daniel Hampton of Colorado Springs tells of a doll 181 years old which belonged to the grandmother of General Ulysses S. Grant. It is a wooden doll in its original clothing. The woman from whom Mrs. Hampton obtained the doll was a Mrs. Dr. Gerald B. Webb, the grand daughter of Mrs. Jefferson Davis of the Confederacy, and quite naturally she was connected with the notable Civil War personalities. She died two years ago. She owned just a few old dolls and was generous enough to give this particular one to Mrs. Hampton, who in turn, expects to pass it on someday to the local "Colorado College Museum'' in honor of her father, an early day educator in the town. Mrs. Hampton also tells of a covered wagon doll in her collection with a wooden head and sawdust body more than 100 years old.

"The covered wagon doll is a honey, a primitive daughter of the soil. The head and shoulders are of wood, the body, made of hand woven cotton stuff that looks like a flour sack, is stuffed with sawdust. In the spring of 1832 a man, woman, and 2 year old daughter traveling in a covered wagon between Ohio and Missouri, stopped at a trading center for supplies. The merchant had this doll, which attracted the child's attention but the parents were too poor to consider purchasing it.

"After taking leave, the little girl cried lustily. The kind hearted merchant ran down the road and gave the doll to the child. That child died in Colorado Springs in 1932, at the age of 102 years. Her name was Mrs. Henrietta Richards and the doll came to me the following year through her grand daughter, Della Blackwell. It is in perfect condition save for a few moth holes, and generally faded clothes, which are the original ones."

Courtesy Mrs. Daniel Hampton

The Covered Wagon Doll and the General Grant Doll

Mrs. William Harvey of Cortland, New York tells of an old doll commemorating Abraham Lincoln, and she believes that there were never more than two like it. Grace Woodworth, of Colorado Springs, Colo., tells of an Abraham Lincoln doll in her collection which was sold in Philadelphia at a Benefit Fair during the Civil War and named for the President. It was bought for a little boy named Henry Pratt and later given to his niece who resides at Colorado Springs, and who gave the doll to Miss Woodworth. The doll is dressed in replica of the original clothes. An excellent modern Abraham Lincoln, with very exacting facial figures, may be found in a doll which Mrs. Elsie Clark Krug describes as "Lincoln as a mature man," his face not too deeply lined with tragedy, colored in oils by hand, and his costume the usual old fashioned long frock coat.

From Grace Woodworth of Colorado Springs, Colo., comes the story of a doll that survived the flood, unharmed. The waters came on swiftly; raging waters that soon covered the land, uprooting trees, bridges and houses. After the angry tide had subsided, the people came out to search and dig for their belongings and the doll was found, covered with mud and soaking wet. She was ultimately taken to an antique dealer, who dried her clothes, and cleaned her nicely, and she turned out to be a lovely blonde lady, with the gold lustre name of MABLE upon her chest. How she survived is a mystery and where her home was originally, is equally mysterious. She just floated along on the raging stream until the good earth caught her and held her fast in its arms. At any rate she did not remain long with the antique dealer but found her way into Miss Woodworth's collection.

Down at the Palace of Dolls at St. Petersburg, Florida is a doll which a mother gave to her little girl on Christmas Day, 1866. This doll, named Mary Almina, has a fine china head and very interesting arms of wood. The owner of the doll, Mrs. Jennie Paine, is now seventy three years old and lives with her mother, who is ninety three years old, in Florida. Mrs. Paine gave the doll to Mrs. Florence Baughman for her doll collection, and wrote a long poem to Mary Almina of which a very small part is given:

"I could not close her china eyes nor comb her china hair,
    She might be French or German but I really didn't care
I loved her very dearly, I shall love her for all time,
    She is most beautiful to me, this dear old doll of mine.

I know you think her funny, and old-fashioned as can be
    But not a thing in dolly land looks half so good to me,
And I would like old Santa Claus, this Christmas Day to know
    That I *have* the doll he gave me, OVER SIXTY YEARS AGO."
                                                —JENNIE PAINE.

Mrs. Baughman also has a beautiful German bisque doll dressed in white taffeta trimmed in old black lace, with fan, and hat trimmed of genuine ostrich feathers to commemorate the gorgeous Lillian Russell.

The Ann McGuffy dolls came out in 1937 to commemorate the 100th anniversary of the famous Primer. These are but a few examples of the many, many dolls that represent people and events.

The most famous royal dolls are undoubtedly those which belonged to Queen Victoria, some one hundred and thirty two little wooden creatures ranging from three to nine inches in height. They would probably be scoffed upon by any modern child accustomed to a more elaborate doll, but they were cherished by the little Princess and are now tenderly preserved in London's *Kensington Museum*. It must be admitted that they are not objects of beauty, with their stolid little Dutch faces. Victoria dressed the dolls to represent "theatrical personages" and "court ladies," and posed them accordingly. This may account for the popularity of the small wooden jointed doll. "Every country made its own dolls," says the introduction to the *Picture Book of Dolls and Dolls' House* of the *Victoria and Museum* of London "But it is worth mentioning that in England the eighteenth century, wooden, Dutch

Courtesy Mrs. Florence Baughman

Mary Almina

dolls, known as 'Flanders Babies,' were very popular." Victoria played with these unattractive little wooden creatures all through her lonely childhood. Droll little dolls, they were, with carved wooden joints, hair parted, small sharp noses, dabs of bright paint upon their round cheeks, broad placid foreheads and tiny yellow combs in their hair, which was mostly painted a coal black, but sometimes had gray curls. The little Princess dressed about thirty of these dolls herself with accuracy, precision and with great detail. The costumes were designed after those worn by the ladies of the court, or by the actors and actresses of a popular play. To make the dolls seem more lifelike they were inserted loosely into holes in a wooden board, so that they could be maneuvered to strike various attitudes. When she was fourteen years old, Victoria put her dolls away in a trunk and gave her attention to more queenly duties. Today the wooden Pomona dolls from London, homely little wooden figures, with round painted faces are very similar in size and general style to those of Victoria's childhood. Today, too, Victoria herself is represented in the world of dolls, in a remarkable likeness of the great Queen in her old age.

During the World War the English toy factories supplied rag dolls, china and wax headed dolls, the latter started by the Suffragettes. There were dolls that simulated Tommy Atkins and Scottish Kilts dolls that became very popular for a short while. With a more terrible war being fought today, the English Royal family is being perpetuated in life like dolls. How difficult it is for these dolls to reach our shores, is told in a cryptic and stirring letter to doll collectors, written by Mrs. Elsie Clark Krug, October 11, 1940.

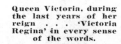

Queen Victoria, during the last years of her reign . . . 'Victoria Regina' in every sense of the words.

Courtesy Mrs. Elsie Clark Krug

Abraham and Mary Todd Lincoln: The Great Emancipator is shown in his middle years dressed in his usual, old-fashioned frock coat, over his shoulders a hand-woven shawl. Mary Todd stands beside him in a characteristic attitude—her dress of purple velvet a faithful copy of the original preserved in the Smithsonian Institution. Both heads are sculptured, in remarkable likenesses.

Mahogany Clock: Hand-made reproduction of an old Simon Willard clock. Dial is authentic copy of original. Keeps perfect time.

White House Ladies by Mrs. Lulu Kriger.

Marie Monroe 1817-1825, Louise Johnson Adams, 1825-1829, Emeily Donelson 1829-1836, Sarah Yorke Jackson, 1829-1837.

White House Ladies by Mrs. Lulu Kriger.

Sarah Angelina Van Buren 1837-1841, Jane Irwin Findlay, 1841, Julia Gardiner Tyler, 1844-1845, Sarah Childress Polk, 1845-1849.

White House Ladies by Mrs. Lulu Kriger.

Betty Taylor Dandridge 1849-1850, Abigail Powers Fillmore, 1850-1853, Jane Appelton Pierce, 1853-1857, Harriet Lane Johnson, 1857-1861, Mary Todd Lincoln, 1861-1865.

White House Ladies by Mrs. Lulu Kriger.

Mary Johnson Patterson (1865-1869), Lucy Webb Hayes, (1877-1881), Lucretia Rudolph Garfield (1881), Mary Arthur McElroy (1881-1885).

Courtesy Elizabeth Hooper

King George VI and Queen Elizabeth
His reign began Friday, December 11, 1936.

"There'll always be an England" the refugee children sing and so pray we from the bottom of our hearts. Under the fury of bombers, the terror of fire and crashing walls, are the English workers at Liberty's still able to make dolls? Yes, they are, for the reputation of the shop for endurance and stability must be maintained; and the selling of the dolls in America (not many are selling in London now) helps to create part of that precious "credit" by which the heavy British purchases in our country can be maintained. Nevertheless, it had been a long time since any dolls had arrived and I was anxious about them. Then when the tide on the English Channel was at the full, and invasion seemed imminent, a ship got into port. On her were some precious dolls. They had not had an easy time over. They left England on a ship which was damaged by a torpedo, which was helped back into port and needed repairs so badly that the cargo was transferred to another vessel.

Courtesy Elizabeth Hooper

Mary, Queen of Scots

**Archbishop and
Chorister**

Courtesy
Elizabeth Hooper

Royal Princesses and Prince

Courtesy
Mrs. Velvalee Dickinson

**The old spinning
wheel.   N a n c y
Hanks, mother of
Abraham Lincoln
with   two   early
American Ladies.**

Courtesy Eliza-
Hooper

Once again the dolls set out and the second time came safely along in convoy. It was on Saturday, September 21, that the dolls were delivered to us and we felt as if we were receiving doll refugees from a perilous trip. To have been made in England in the recent anxious months, to have suffered a direct hit on the ocean, to have come safely across the water at last, to have reached us while London is under attack day and night makes them very precious to us.

"The English dolls represent the King and Queen and the important members of their court in their most splendid regalia. Significant as they seemed at the time of the coronation, how much more significant they seem now. A king and queen who have had

Courtesy Elizabeth Hooper
John Bull and Stanley Baldwin

Buckingham Palace bombed over their heads and have walked undismayed among the poorest homeless of their people, sticking it out, smiling under the most fearful ordeal to which human nerves have ever been exposed—what a heroic tragic page of history it is!"

The complete list of these English dolls includes the following:

King George VI in royal purple.
Queen Elizabeth in royal purple.
Queen Mary in gold color and lace.
Yeoman of the Guard in Tudor dress.
Knight of the Garter in white and blue velvet.
Lord Chief Justice in scarlet.
Lord Chancellor of the House of Lords in black and gold.
Speaker of the House of Commons in black and gold.
Ambassador in blue and gold braid.
Earl Marshal with baton.
John Bull in red, white and blue.
Princess Elizabeth.
Princess Margaret Rose.
Princess Royal (Mary, the King's sister).
Archbishop of Canterbury.
Archbishop of York.
The Peer—Viscount.
The Peeress—Viscountess.
The King's Guard.
The Chorister of the Chapel Royal.

Chapter XXIV

THE EDUCATIONAL VALUE OF THE DOLL

*"And Like a Mothering Child With Toys
Anticipates a Woman's Joys"*

Courtesy Mrs. Velvalee Dickinson

**An International Group of Dolls live together
harmoniously**

IT does not seem to make any difference what the clime or what the race, it is an established fact that dolls are loved and cherished the world over. They always have been, and they always will be. The child of all times, and of all peoples, is alike in instinct, giving its pulsing life to the doll, and the doll, in turn, furnishes the stimulus, and helps to bring into play the various emotions which aid in developing a sense of devotion, of authority and responsibility.

Benjamin Franklin had this to say about the influence of toys in forming the character of children. "To love playthings well as a child, to lead an adventurous and noble life as a youth, and to settle, when the time arrives, into a green and smiling age, is to be a good artist in life and deserve well of yourself and your neighbors."

The earliest stirrings of the play instinct corresponds to man's most elementary faculties, and through the doll, the child ministers to one of the deepest of human desires, that of an escape from life itself, into the land of make-believe.

*Sappho. "Dream of Childhood."

"When I was a little girl," says Grace Storey Putnam, "I loved my dolls. They were alive for me. Long years afterward I realized what a deep imprint such early emotions made upon the impressionable brain of a child. When I was only eight years old I knew that I wanted to be an artist, to paint and draw and form images. I made dolls at this age out of scraps of cloth, and paper dolls which I drew first on paper and then tinted with water colors. This was the beginning of the doll motif that was to play so vital a role in my life. In this child's play are the first basic trends of life . . . trends that either form new characteristics or help to develop inherent ones. The imagination and idealization natural in my play with dolls was a very *creative* thing."

Mrs. Mary E. Lewis, the founder and president of the *National Doll and Toy Collectors Club,* believes that no little girl should ever be told she is too old to play with dolls. She claims that when a doll has ceased to be a boon companion, it should not be thrown away, but should gain a place as a guide and tutor, aiding studies in costume design and dress making, in infant hygiene, geography and history.

Small wonder that the psychologist considers it a bit distressing that the modern parent sometimes seems to forget the value behind the doll, which, from time immemorial, has held its place in the development of man's culture. It is gratifying, that through the ardent doll collectors, old dolls have been taken down from their dusty and moldy seclusion, and to them have been added the colorful foreign doll, or the more modern regional, or historical, doll, all bespeaking certain periods and phases in the story of man. This exceedingly rich psychogenetic field, which until quite lately has been sadly neglected, is again coming to the fore, for educators and hobbyists are growing conscious of the remarkable social influence of the doll, which opens wider horizons of national and international understanding. It is not only that the colors and costumes of foreign dolls make the prosaic study of history and geography interesting, but the ethnological and archaeological research as to the origin of the doll, and its kinship to the human race, make the collecting of old and unusual dolls a fascinating study. The greatness of a civilization is measured by its artistic achievements, so dolls, are far more than sentimental mementos. To the connoisseur, they are valuable records of another day and age.

Dolls belong to the field of art, the spontaneous expression of the human spirit. Combined with the economic world, the doll, through the Middle Ages, and the Renaissance, revealed the exquisite workmanship of the period, in an

era when toymaking was not a separate industry as it is today, but rather the result of a master artist's leisure hour. Down through the ages, the dolls march, historically playing the role of propagandist as well as plaything.

It is possible to go on ad infinitum, citing where the doll serves, especially as it is an easily established fact that the doll is a veritable laboratory of visual education.

Down in Texas there is a lady who is known as ''The Dean of Texas Story Tellers'' and also as ''The Texas Doll Lady''. She is Gustine Courson Weaver who for many years has made collecting one of her chief interests.

For a time she concentrated on Early American Glassware, then on Children's (early) Books, then Prints of Children of Yesteryear. She had over one hundred pieces of glassware, over 2000 items in her juveniles, and over 400 prints.

That not being enough she also had collected, all this time, dolls, until she possessed over 400.

The longer she collected dolls the more certain she became that the doll was of value, not only to the youth of today but to the youth of tomorrow. With this knowledge, Mrs. Weaver began a scholarly research, with the ideal in mind to make, out of her expenditure of time and strength and money, some worthwhile service to the field of education. Having spent seven years in the Orient, each of those years being a bidden guest to not one home, but many homes each season of ''The Doll Festival'', she became more and more convinced that there was an illusive basic ideology which undergirded the thought world, which found eloquent expression through the diversified uses of dolls.

At the end of her collecting, (some four years ago) she decided to make a gift of her different collections, to one of the Texas Colleges, near the Manse where she presides as ''Mistress''. Since North Texas State Teachers College at Denton has a department which appealed to her, in its ''Historical State Museum'', she turned a deaf ear to other centers which invited her to place her treasures with them. On the campus of this college, therefore, housed in fireproof buildings, handsomely exhibited in padlocked glass cases, one may see her collections, and the one most popular is her old and rare dolls, each with a romantic history, represents over fifty nationalities, and over 400 dolls.

Dolls also inspired Mrs. Weaver to creative work in other fields, and she fashioned a doll made of cotton even to its wig and its jewelry. One doll led to others and eleven pairs of cotton dolls were used by the Committee of World Friendship Among Children as an international traveling exhibition.

They have become Esperanto Dolls who speak a universal language. Mrs. Weaver has written a delightful story ''Santa's Cotton Doll Farm'' picturing the farm where the cotton dolls grow, and also an operetta, ''The Cotton Doll Farm'', the music written by another Texas woman, Belle Biard Gober, and the illustrations by Kitty Beth Edwards. Mrs. Weaver's contributions to the doll world are constant reminders of the bond of world fellowship.

There can be no doubt of the Pedagogical influence of the doll. Back in 1907, dolls were first used in schools to aid in teaching the costumes and customs of foreign lands. The idea spread through the country, and ever since.

Chapter XXIII

AMERICAN REGIONAL DOLLS
FOREIGN DOLLS

(Negro, Indian, Hill Billies, Puppets, Penn. Dutch,
Hawaii, Philippines)

Amish Mother and children in typical Amish farm wagon.

A MERICA has been called, by, at least, one well known writer, 'The Melting Pot', and it is this truism which has built up our great nation. One of the most interesting things about traveling throughout the United States is the great diversification, not only of the scene, but of the people, who live in various sections. It is this regional America which has been offering so much material to artists and authors in the past few years, and which is now beginning to be represented in the doll world.

In July, 1939, an article appeared in the *Lutheran Boys and Girls Magazine*, entitled, "Dolls from the Land of Cotton", which gave a glimpse into a phase of life in the south which is of considerable interest, and which certain dolls portray very well.

"To anyone who has been in the South, or has read about it, there is always brought to mind the picture of gnarled old trees in gray Spanish moss hanging from the branches in long streamers, swaying in the warm soft breeze. There is the vision of Negro children playing happily in the dirt before small, squat cabins from which a single strand of smoke may be coming from a thin stovepipe chimney. The Negro is indeed a part of the southern scene, and through Negro dolls one may develop a pictorial corner of America. First it is interesting to look briefly into the sad history of this race of happy people.

The first Negroes, or slaves, to arrive in North America were brought to Jamestown, Virginia, by a Dutch man of war in 1619, a few months prior to the landing of the Pilgrims from the **Mayflower** at Plymouth, Massachusetts. These twenty Negroes paved the way for many more of their race who followed them to these shores in quick succession, coming from Africa.

256

The Mammy, the Washwoman and the Chicken Fancier

**Mr. Palmetto and a Carolina Plantation
Worker**

The Convict and the Preacher

Collection Janet P. Johl.

During a period when Jamestown and its vicinity flourished, due to the tobacco crop, a plant which the Indians showed the white man how to use, and which Sir Walter Raleigh brought to England to introduce to Great Britain, the Negroes were imported to help with the work in the fields. Besides the tobacco, indigo, cotton and rice were also cultivated successfully, until toward the end of the eighteenth century when the industry declined. At just this time, however, Eli Whitney perfected his cotton gin and the whole picture of the South changed. Cotton was grown as never before in America. More and more Negroes were brought from Africa, because they were able to stand the hot sun which beat down upon the cottonfields, and soon slavery was firmly established.

This went on for a number of years, and the story of the Civil War which ultimately freed the slaves, some four million of them by 1865, is too well known to bear repetition in an article on Negro dolls. It is enough to say that most of these people had only known work from their earliest childhood, being born on the

Two phases in the life of the cotton picker. Sitting on the full bale at the end of a day's work, the boy forgets his cares as he strums his banjo. The old negro is picking from the cotton plant and filling his bag.

plantations which many of them never left. Living in small cabins and receiving their food as the result of their labor, these free people had to learn how to live like other men. To earn their way was a great problem to men and women who had never known the taste of freedom. With each succeeding year, however, more educational opportunities have been offered and many of the Negroes have moved to the North which was always more liberal.

All during the hard years when he was a slave, and the years after freedom was granted, when the adjustment to a new life had to be made, the Negro went his way through life, humming his song, whether a spiritual of religious tone or a soft lullaby, and making the best of what life presented to him. A rhythmic individual is the Negro. He personifies his people, works better and faster when he is happy, when he is singing a tune. As the cotton is picked, the picker is usually humming a song. After the day's task is over he may sit upon the bale of finished work, and taking up his banjo, gaily or mournfully, as the mood may suit, strum the strings.

It is surely right to say that the Negro dolls typify the southern picture as much as those dolls which depict the well known and gracious southern ladies, and the white bearded gentlemen who grace the southern scene, famed for their courteous manners and their hospitality. These negro dolls represent the poor, but carefree folk, engaged in their tasks. One doll typifies an aged Negro who is stripping a cotton plant and filling his bag. A ragged old black felt hat protects his white woolly hair from the intensely hot rays of the southern sun. His upward gaze may be towards the sun, or he may be thinking about the chicken, fried southern style, that his wife will have on the stove for him when the work is over. Other dolls represent younger men who, after the days work, forget troubles in music. Both dolls came from Florida.

Doll wearing striped trousers, red and white, and a gay red flowered blouse is a plantation worker from North Carolina. He actually came from Charleston, and always brings to mind the Negro youths who row the boats through the Cyprus Gardens. His black hat is broad-brimmed and boasts a red cord about its crown. His wife probably gathers the lady lilies to sell in the flower market. Mr. Palmetto is a doll one meets in many doll collections. He is made and clothed in the fibre from the southern palm tree and represents the man of the city, the emancipated Negro, who is a business man, and a successful one at that, if the posy in the button hole is at all significant.

Other dolls, of the southern scene, include such well known characters as the mammy with a white baby, the mammy with her own pickaninny; an aged Negro, bent and white-haired, with a knotty cane to guide his tottering steps, a chicken, feathers and all, tucked under his arm; a dignified pastor with prayer book; a prisoner, member of the chain gang, in his stripes; a stout Negress balancing a bundle of wash upon her head and with a wash board under her arm. There are many dolls from this region which might well be titled "Way down south in Dixie."

Many dolls represent these faithful and loyal Americans, revealing the types of work in which they are engaged, and the happy nature that is so characteristic of the colored race, and so enviable. One doll, and not a very modern one, is called "Topsy-Turvey", or "Double-Ender". It has no legs, but two bodies are joined at the extremities. With a twist of the wrist the doll may be turned upside down, and, depending upon how it is turned, either the mammy, or the white maid appears. Usually the Mammy is stout, the lovable type so well portrayed in 'Gone with the Wind', with her billowing skirt, her red bandana and her snow white apron. The white maid often wears a red and white checked dress, with white apron and white cap.

"Southern Darky Dolls" originated in Staunton, Virginia under the skill-ful hand of Helen Siebold Walter. The little Pickaninnies are hand made in brown and black sateen, and the kinks of hair are hand wrapped with cord exactly the way Mammy wraps the hair of her little ones. To perpetuate a phase of the south fast disappearing there are also other colored dolls,—Aunt Peachy and Uncle Hannibal, who were dearly beloved by all the little white 'chillun' they raised in Virginia.

Miss Walter has made her old time "Southern Darkies" as authentic as possible in make-up and costumes and sought to bring to life the characteristics of sweetness and faithfulness. Miss Walter gives the following bit about her southern doll creation 'Aunt Peachy'.

"No tale of Dixie is complete without the story of *Aunt Peachy*. The dolls that model Aunt Peachy are not old but they record a phase of the Old South that is fast disappearing. Peachy was a young slave darky during the War between the States. After 1865 she continued to live her long life in Virginia. She became "Aunt Peachy" to many counties and was a familiar figure and a

Courtesy Helen Siebold Walter

Southern Darky Dolls originated and made by Helen Siebold Walter
"Aunt Peachy"—"Uncle Hannibal"—"Pickaninnies: "Watermelon"—
"Alabaster"—"Peaches"—"Hallelujah"

delightful one as she waddled through the streets of Staunton, a red bandanna knotted around her gray curly head, a spotless apron, her arms akimbo, and balanced on her head a huge wash-basket of immaculate stiff-starched clothes. "Showing off" from the handle would always be a beautifully fluted baby cap for one of her "white chilluns." Therefore with blissful memories stamped indelibly upon our childish minds, of bruised knees, kissed, and countless juicy slices of bread and jam, it was but natural that "Just Folks" Doll House should model Aunt Peachy and Uncle Hannibal, keeping in mind the character-istics of the old-time Southern Darkies with all their sweetness and faithfulness —striving to hear again the echo of Aunt Peachy's voice as she hurried around our kitchen on many frosty mornings crying, "For de Lord's sake, chilluns, aint yuh got no bottoms!—dis is de las skillet of buckwheat cakes!"

A subject to which the average American has paid scant attention is that of the Indian, the first American. Pushed onto reservations, the Indian has been slowly emerging, from his obscurity, in the past few years, and now Indian dolls are coming to the fore, representative of various tribes throughout the land, north to south—east to west, to say nothing of the fascinating dolls from the pueblos of the southwest. A collection of Indian dolls is, in itself, a true picture of Americana and should hold intense interest to any student of the history of this nation.

The actual history of the United States of America began hundreds of years before Christopher Columbus and the other brave explorers who followed him, sailed to these shores. Long before the Spaniards entered the south west, various tribes of Indians were living in pueblo villages, high up on the cliffs or plateau. Because it was not easy to reach their isolated houses, they were not bothered by other wandering Indian tribes, and so were able to develop a high type of culture, in their arts and their dances. Altho ethnologists have devoted a great deal of time to the study of the peoples of the southwest, our knowledge of them, and of their predecessors is far from complete.

Perhaps it will be the doll who serves to introduce the American Indian, his arts, his crafts, his customs and his religion to his fellow Americans.

Collection Janet P. Johl

Authentic dolls representing a Sioux Family

The Hopi Indians whittle their Katchina dolls from the roots of cottonwood trees, ranging in size from two feet down to one inch, and then paint them. The Hopis have resisted the efforts, from out-side, to introduce the white man's civilization into their life. They live in nine villages, the oldest of which is the High Cliff of Walpi. They retired long ago, to escape the raids made by the Apache tribes to rob them of their silver. Today the Hopi Indians continue their peaceful living, content with paintings, with their silver craft,

Navajo Indians

their pottery making and sheep raising. Their Katchina dolls are worthy of study, for the technique and life of these people have changed little since the coming of the first Spaniards, in 1540, and archaeological evidence links their crafts with a pre-historic past. Aloof on their mesas, surrounded by a country side of purple and gold, and with a skyline that touches the pointed peaks of distant mountains, the Hopis have constant inspiration in nature that has undoubtedly served to make them the artists they are.

The Hopis are, of course, only one tribe of many, who inhabit the parched lands of the southwest, living in the pueblo villages, in houses made of native mud and painted, white, and gray or in the brighter colors of yellow or red. Everywhere is the inevitable corn, not white and yellow, only, as the white man knows it, but blue and red and mottled purple. For the corn is the staff of life of the Indian, the source of his prayers for rain, and for the sun, the inspiration for his dances, his music and his art. The corn is symbolic of life itself. The Taos Indians, in white robes, stand like the Arabs upon their roofs, gazing out over the deserts, at the setting sun, and near them stand their women, in colorful red shawls and white buckskin boots. Behind is the lake and the sacred mountain where they carry out their secret ceremonials.

The desert Indians are natural artists for all about them nature has spread her richest, most brilliant colors, and beneath the earth are other riches, silver and copper and turquoise from which they fashion metalwork and jewelry. Their Pottery work is also very beautiful, made possible by the native clay, and weaving seems to be a basic part of the lives of many of the tribal women, the designs going back into the centuries for their inspiration and origin, and their symbolic meanings. Of the many tribes, the Navajos are nationally famous for their exquisite silver craftsmanship and their finely woven blankets. Navajo dolls are splendid examples of the picturesque costumes of the Navajo braves and their squaws. The men wear a velveteen blouse on which jangle silver coins, and loose flapping trousers. Silver conchoes decorate their wide belts. The women are resplendent in a very, very full calico skirt and blouse, and often have a beautiful woven blanket thrown over the shoulders. The squash blossom flower, the motive used in many of the bracelets and necklaces, is sometimes worn in the hair. The Navajos have increased in numbers in the past fifty years. A proud and fearless race, they are like a people apart, true artisans who apply their craftsmanship and ability industriously. A most interesting ceremonial doll is the Navajo Yei-Bei-Cha which represents a spirit, without a face.

In early times the Apache were the dreaded enemies of the Pueblos and later they became the foes of the white man. Now, diminished in numbers, they are a defeated people, living quietly. Dolls from the White Mountain Reservation pictorially portray the Apache. Mrs. Daniel Hampton has in her collection an old White River Apache doll, made of buckskin with real horse hair, reminiscent of the days when Geronimo led his people.

Once a year, a great event takes place at Gallup, New Mexico which no lover of Indian handicrafts wants to miss. It is "The Inter-Tribal Indian Ceremonial" which brings together some twenty or more tribes from the various reservations, all of whom participate in dances, chants, native sports and weird rites. Dress and customs have not changed greatly with the passing of the years and the Indian people journey many miles to take part in the colorful performances. Hopis, Zunis, Apaches, Navajos, Kiowas, Arapahoes, Shoshones, Zias, Taos and others come by horseback or covered wagon, carrying their papooses, their cooking utensils, their blankets, and sacks of food, their woven materials and jewelry, which they hope to sell. White people come, too, to witness the dances and to see the brilliant costumes, the beaded and feathered garments of cotton and buckskin, all reminders of the earliest days of American history.

It is possible for the serious collector of Indian dolls to obtain many authentic specimens, but it is not at all possible to give due consideration to the subject in one small chapter. The merest glimpse into the world of the Indian thru the medium of the doll may be presented, and that by dividing the Indian people into groups, those inhabiting the desert, those living on the great Plains, those of the Everglades, and lastly, those who dwell in the forests. In the culture of many of the Indian tribes in customs and beliefs, there is a similarity, especially among neighboring tribes.

A totally different Indian people live in the southeastern part of this country, in Florida. These are the Seminoles, a tribe that separated from the Creek nation late in the eighteenth century. The name Seminole means 'seceder'. The doll faithfully represents these interesting people, and the unique costumes they wear. A sleeveless cape like blouse of green with bands of orange, blue, pink and white at the neck and at the hemline, is worn loosely over a full skirt made by sewing bands of various colored materials together until a quilt like pattern results. The skirt touches the ground. To this rainbow hue costume, the squaw adds several strings of colorful beads. The braves and little boys wear similar costumes except that their skirts are knee length. The doll is carved from wood but many of the dolls made by the Seminole Indians are cleverly fashioned from the native palm tree fibre.

A bit farther toward the north is the large Cherokee reservation, in Virginia a handful of Indians live on the Pamunkey Reservation and claim relationship to Pocahontas. Considerably farther to the north are the Iroquois who use the eagle feathers for their head dress because the eagle is the symbol of protection and is higher than human beings in its chosen home. The forest Indians were not as migratory as the Plains Indians and among the Iroquois, the Oneida and the Seneca, the corn husk doll seems to have evolved.

The Indian tribes from the Plains, the ones who used the magnificent feather* head dress and were rather war like, received more attention from the world of authors and artists, in earlier times, and so are perhaps better known. Like the forest Indians, they are good hunters and their customs are associated with the buffalo, or bison, which supplied them with food, shelter and clothing, through its meat and skin. The Indian dolls from the reservations of the Plains

_____

* Some ethnologists believe that the Mayans in an early invasion north of their own land, introduced the decorative use of feathers as headdress to the North American Indian.

Indians are very often dressed in soft buckskin beaded in intricate designs. Some of the best known of these tribes include the Shoshone, Crow, Blackfoot, Kiowa, Cheyenne, and Comanche.

The north western part of America is sometimes called "The Land of the Totem Pole", and of the tribes of this area, who live in rectangular wooden houses, dress scantily, and depend upon the sea, and their dug out canoes, for existence, the Tlinget tribe is perhaps the best known. A little doll representing this tribe comes from Ketchican, Alaska and is dressed in buckskin, fur trimmed with a parka, closely resembling the Eskimo fur skin costume. Despite the dolls' clothing it is interesting to note that the climate of the north coast is mild, and warm clothing is therefore not necessary for the native. Leather is neither practical nor sensible where there is considerable dampness. Therefore most of the tribes wear woven fibre garments, and in summer, wear very little, the women dressing in grass skirts like the Polynesian islanders.

Chief Tahan, of Vergennes, Vt. who is known for his talks and writings on Indian Life, legends and customs, contributed this about Indian dolls. "Corn raising Indians of the northern regions make dolls out of corn husks. Prairie dwelling Indians make dolls out of buckskin and stuff them with grass. The boy dolls are dressed precisely like the men, in buck skins, their hair braided on both sides of their heads, and the scalplock on the crown of their heads. This hangs down the back and in it is stuck the eagle feather. The Seminoles of Florida make their dolls out of a piece of an old dress similar to those rag dolls known to white children. The Plains Indians also often put their dolls in toy cradles or on cradle boards."

No short story about these dolls could be complete without a passing mention of the well known Indian Squaw doll and her papoose. This doll represents least of any of the Indian dolls, the real picture of Indian life. She simply shows the way in which an Indian mother carried her tiny red skinned baby. The papoose, in its blanket, peeps over her shoulder, looking out at the 'wide, wide world'.

An Indian friend wrote recently "We Indians have different dress, and all, yet we all have the same belief and traditions, although we talk different languages. A few yards away from me is an old Indian ruins, built before Columbus discovered America. There is several old Indian Missions built by old Spanish and French Missionaries . . . Our American Indians are coming to the front. I believe and prophesied for long time that our people yet will have their right place in the world. Education is fathering this."

From the reservations—from Indians like the woman who wrote this letter, who live in hope, come our Indian dolls.

Mrs. Lulu Kriger writes that when her father was on one of his annual hunting trekking trips to northern Ontario, he asked a Cree Indian guide to carve a doll for him just as he would for one of his own children. Out of a small piece of wood Okoosh, the guide, carved a baby doll. Then he made a carrier and filled it with the moss which is used as a diaper by the Indians. Of course the moss has

Hill Billie Dolls

long since lost its velvety softness, and is now a dry brown straw like substance
. . . but the doll lives on.

Mrs. J. Howard Smith, of Wenachee, Wash., whose Indian dolls of dried
mummified apples are discussed elsewhere, has a fine understanding and love of
Indian life. In one letter she quoted a motto, from an old Indian called
"Kaloola Jim," and gave the Indian symbols, and translation."

| many | Sun God | creed religion | path | winding trail | owl wisdom knowing how | hand kind wishing | world | heart wish want need |

"So many Gods, So many creeds, So many paths that wind and wind, while
just the art of being kind is what this sad world needs."

Indian life is but one phase of America. In fact it is America. Every
bit, and perhaps even more American, than the historical tales of the coming
of the white man and the settling of this land. All this may be studied, and
visioned through Indian dolls.

From the depths of the forest, from the great expanse of the prairies and
the hot deserts, the doll lover looks at the mountain dwellers, the Hill Billie
Dolls. From out of Tennessee come hand carved character dolls of red cedar,
a man and a woman, dressed in authentic handmade clothes, the Hill Billie
dolls, absolutely American types, if there ever were any.

Marie Tracy of Carterville, Mo. has been making representative Hill Billy
dolls of twelve different characters from grandmother down to baby, including
a number of relatives. Some serious, some good looking, some really funny, yet,
all, like the real Hill Billies in their clothes, and the material used for the clothes.

Many an old mountain woman keeps her knotted and gnarled hands busy
making gourd dolls and dressing them in cornchucks, with a hat of braided
chucks, or of corn silk. Old mountain men, too feeble to work have turned to
doll making, turning their 'everlasting whittling' to carving dolls which typify
the characters in the region where the mountaineers dwell. Crude dolls they
all are, perhaps, but patiently made by withered old hands, far in the backwoods of America.

Distinctly American, too, are the dolls carved by the Kentucky mountain people for their children. These peo-p'e live in the back of the Cumberland Mountains, half way between Knoxville and Nashville, Tenn. They have no money to purchase dolls nor are there any near by

Courtesy of Olive O. Jury

A Coal Miner Doll from Shamokin, Pa.

Mennonite mother and daughter.

stores, if they had the money. These dolls are called Poppets. There are no men poppets, only women and girls, and both are well made. Ozark gypsy dolls and clown dolls also belong to the picture of regional America.

There is a cowboy doll made by an old cowboy down in Texas, which is a true replica of a cow-puncher. With felt sombrero, silk shirt and elegant fur chaps, this doll stands with the lariat coiled in his hands ready to go to work on the steer. He is a real American cowboy from the Rio Grande.

Last, but far from the least, come the group of dolls that typify the Pennsylvania Dutch people who live in Lancaster County, Penn.

These people have retained the customs and the costumes of their forefathers. Collectively they are known as Pennsylvania Dutch. Individually they consist of the *Mennonites*, earnest, serious, God fearing upright men and women who like the Puritans sought religious freedom in the new land and believe war to be unchristian. *The Amish*, who broke away from the Mennonites in 1714 because they wished to preserve more severity and simplicity in their form of dress and doctrine. The *Brethren*, sometimes called Dunkers, because they baptize by immersion, who are definitely pacifists, and as a sub-division of the

Amish father and son, Brethren husband and wife.

Mennonites practice thrift, Christian conduct and hospitality. All three sects prospered because they farmed industriously, the land being especially rich and fertile in their locality. The freedom of conscience which all civilized countries practice, was theirs as early as the 1700's.

An article entitled "The Pennsylvania Dutch in Miniature and in Real Life" by Verai de Ferré Fagen, gave a good picture and insight into the lives of this group of people. To quote the entire article is not possible but its points about the differences in dress of the different sects are worth noting for the dolls faithfully follow tradition.

"The Mennonites permit the use of fine rich fabrics of darker colors although Mom, as the Mennonite mothers are called, is dressed in a very fine blue and white check probably her every day dress. The kerchief or shawl fastened at the belt, and the apron tied at the back are made of the same material as the dress proper. A tiny

Collection Janet P. Johl

Amish Dolls from Lancaster County, Penna.

white cap, made of fine material such as organdy or mull is worn by the women at all times. This is the prayer covering and is received about the age of sixteen as one enters the church. The outside bonnet is of different design. The Mennonite women let the two streamers of the prayer bonnet or covering hang down the front and tie the outer bonnet under their chins. The men wear broad brimmed hats and clothes cut in the fashion of other days. The New or Orthodox Mennonites wear beards, the old do not.

"On the other hand the Amish hold to the old traditions. They believe that humility demands the coarser fabrics, and that all must wear sombre colors, clothing cut after their own obsolete patterns and use hooks and eyes for closing garments, as buttons are sinful and worldly. Brown or black are the usual colors but of late years purple, bottle green, certain blue and red are used by the younger folk.

The women dress similar to the Mennonites, but wear no tuck or frill on their outer bonnets, which are let hang loose, while the prayer bonnet is tied under the chin.

The Amish men wear no collar or tie, but instead a shirt of brilliant color, long black coats, heavy beards and broad, black sombrero hats over their long hair.

Collection of Huapala

Hawaiian couple beneath the palm trees.

The Amish children are dressed in the same style as their elders, though the little girls are permitted to wear as gay colors as they desire, over which is the apron of black, with a large bonnet of the same material. The Amish boys seem to favor red shirts and my little boy seems very proud of his as he leaves his coat open in the front to show it off.

The Brethren women wear a fabric of grey or drab cotton made simply with full skirt, fitted bodice over which is pinned to the neckline the kerchief, with apron of the same material, tied at the front. They, too, tie the prayer bonnet beneath their chins and leave the outer bonnet loose. The Brethren men adhere to the conventional garb of long ago, simply cut and dull color. They, too, wear the broad brimmed hat and beard.

Thus we see, that the Pennsylvania Dutch, with all their strange customs, are real people, who combine the simplicity of the past with the times of today and the trends of the future. And the Pennsylvania Dutch dolls are miniature representatives of a very real and interesting people . . .'' The 'Plain People of Pennsylvania.'

Another part of the United States, a territorial part, is Hawaii.

Two Hawaiian dolls exhibited in New York City recently as a part of a collection of Hawaiian doll folk were interesting for their costumes and the use of flowers as decorative touches to the costume.

This collection, assembled by Huapala of Hawaii and New York City portrays the evolutionary costume changes of Hawaii, both before and after the coming of the white men to the islands. They are the result of eight years of study of the Hawaiian native dances, and the feather coats, the helmets and robes in which the dolls are garbed, in miniature, are correct. Tapa cloth, canary feathers and the 'homely though authentic Mother Hubbard of the missionary'', the grass skirt, and even the 'tourist hula skirt' of cellophane, are shown on the dolls.

An article in *The Lutheran Boys and Girls Magazine* tells something of the people the Hawaiian dolls represent. To quote:

The Hawaiians are a brown race with straight or wavy black hair, large dark eyes and fine strong bodies. They resemble the New Zealand Maoris in appearance and in dialect. They excel in athletics, especially in swimming and surf-boarding on the crest of the waves. They are very fond of vocal and instrumental music and the Hawaiian ukulele, although of Portuguese origin, has been developed on the islands.

Because of the soft equable climate, the abundant sunshine and the absence of the usual tropical storms, the native Hawaiian leads an out-of-door life which necessitates a scanty costume. The men usually wear nothing but a girdle, or **malu,** and the women a skirt of paper cloth, called **kapa,** or a skirt of leaves or fiber. Wreaths of flowers, called **leis,** are also worn on the flowing hair, and about the neck. The little dolls truly portray the simple Hawaiian natives, a happy, generous, hospitable and courteous people.

Courtesy Eleanor Bumgardner
Dolls from the Philippines.

In the same magazine, the issue for December 11, 1937 contained an article "Dolls from the Philippines".

"Five hundred miles off the southeast coast of Asia, set in the blue green waters of the Stormy China Sea, the Pacific Ocean, the coastal waters of Borneo and the Sea of Celebes, lies a chain of volcanic coral islands, a mountainous country of lakes and rivers, of forests, ferns and flowers, known to the world as the Philippines.

Long before the Spaniards colonized these islands, the Igorots, a copper-colored tribe of the north, living in the rugged mountains of Luzon, discovered veins of gold and copper which they first mined.

Despite the changes wrought, through conquest and colonization, the brown-skinned Igorots, still wearing their scant gee string costume, their tiny box-like straw hats, gay woven jackets and native beads, inhabit the thickly populated, but deforested, lands of the north where they continue to mine their gold as they have done for centuries. Working hard in the rice fields, weaving cotton, and making baskets, they come to the market to sell their wares in covered wagons. The **Igorot dolls** illustrated are from Baguio, the capital city of the sub-province of Benguet, situated 5,600 feet above sea level. Here the beautiful pine forests grow profusely and cattle graze contentedly in rich grass. The cloud-topped mountains rise majestically above this tropical land, where 1,000 species of flowers bloom abundantly, and more than 600 varieties of trees are to be found.

Zamboanga is an alluring tropical town bright with sunshine. Here the banana trees, growing close to the tiny houses, bend low beneath the weight of the heavy fruit. The houses themselves are shacks built on posts about ten feet above the ground, with notched logs for stairs leading to the doorway. The roads in front of the houses are made from broken bits of shell and coral, and are bordered with palm trees and papaya plants.

The two **Moros dolls** come from Zamboanga, and they represent a class of people who are descended directly from the native pagans of the Philippine Islands. The Moros are of darker skin than the Igorots, and they work out in the rice or pineapple fields, ploughing behind the faithful water buffalo, or **carabao.** They make their clothes from the leaf of the pineapple, called **pina,** weaving it into a silken material that is most attractive, and wearing bright colored turbans which shine in the sunlight.

The name "Moros" was given to these people by the Spaniards, who thought the dark-skinned natives were moors, or "moros." Many of the Moros men are fishermen, going out to sea in quaint boats known as **vintas,** with broad-striped sails and wide riggers of bamboo. Once the home of famous Moro pirates, this part of the islands is now safe and prosperous, and its inhabitants are famous for their weaving, fine metal work and wood carving.

The Philipino people proper are descendants of the Malays, and divided into eight different peoples. They are very hospitable and charming, eager to be educated, and great lovers of music. Filipino man and his wife, both in doll form reveal the typical Malayan features, the soft, mild brown eyes, the broad nose and slightly thick lips. The man wears a thin, muslin, outside shirt, called a **camisadentro.** The woman, whose coal black hair is combed neatly back from the forehead into a knot at the back of her neck, has on a loose, thin, graceful gown, or **kamisa,** woven from the fiber of the banana leaf. The dress is cut low at the neck, with straight, short sleeves gathered high and full on the shoulders. Flowers are appliqued on the sleeves. Drawn over one shoulder and worn like an overskirt, is a **tagalano** apron, of silk plaid. A large jewel in the center of a simple necklace completes the costume.

Doll Talk notes that Igorots, Moros, Baltinta-waks and Mestiza are interpreted in highly individualized native dolls.

To pass so very lightly and briefly over the dolls that typify the many interesting localities of America and the people who characterize them, seems unfair. This is indeed a topic that, given a really concentrated effort, would prove a fascinating one, and would take the student afar into many and varied fields in this country, and its territories, some of which have not been mentioned here.

An Arab and a Philippine Couple

Kimport Dolls, of Independence, Mo. have a printed list of foreign dolls, and the collector who possesses most of these has indeed something of intrinsic worth.

Africa	Denmark	Indians	Moro Land
Alaska	Ecuador	Indo China	Negro Dolls
Albania	Egypt	Ireland	Norway
American	England	Italy	Peru
Armenia	Estonia	Japan	Philippines
Arabia	Finland	Jerusalem	Poland
Argentina	France	Korea	Portugal
Azores	Germany	Lapland	Russia
Bahamas	Greece	Latvia	Scotland
Brazil	Guatemala	Lithuania	Serbia
British Guiana	Haiti	Macedonia	Sweden
Bulgaria	Hawaii	Martinique	Switzerland
Ceylon	Holland	Mexican	Turkey
China	Hungary	Mexico	Virgin Islands
Colombia	Igorot Land	Montenegro	Wales
Cuba	India	Morocco	

This is not a complete list, either. Bermuda and a few South American countries are omitted, so are Iceland, Greenland, Labrador, the Dutch East Indies and the West Indies. This is simply a more or less comprehensive list showing the possibilities open to the doll lover. It is extremely doubtful if any one individual could ever hope to possess all the dolls, of all the countries of the world. Miss Ariel Bissell Cutler of Petersborough, New Hampshire, has a good start with some two thousand dolls. There are, of course, many others who have equally large collections. The Doll League of Nations is found in many a private home!

Mrs. Virginia Woodin, of Arlington, Va., has a collection of one thousand dolls which represent all races if not all places—Caucasian, Ethiopian, Mongolian, Malay, and Indian, Mrs. Woodin writes that her dolls reveal 'all stages of development in the art of doll making.'

THE LATEST MOST POPULAR DOLLS

(Composition   Types—Patsy—Dy-Dee—Magic   Skin   Baby—
Parachute   Dolls)

NOTE: This final chapter is cut short from the original edition, since it is given more complete and up-to-date coverage elsewhere. Pictures called for here appear on forward pages.

Modern American Doll Manufacture

IN the year 1925, the doll business was estimated at $12,000,000 in the United States. In 1940 it had risen to the sum of $30,000,000, with 99% of the dolls made in America, and Japanese and German imports totaling less than 1%. Toymakers claim that today twice as many dolls are being produced as there are human beings, and that if the birth rate of the American doll numbers more than twenty million dollars a year then it is more than twelve times the human birth rate. The baby doll is still the most popular of the dolls offered to the public, totaling 70% of all the sales.

There is a similarity in the manufacture of this type of doll, here and in England. These modern composition doll heads do not break so easily as the older types,   THE END.